Fr Daniel Brandenburg

The New Fundamentalists

by Br Daniel Brandenburg, LC

CIRCLE
PRESS

Cover photograph of Michelangelo's statue of Moses by Alessia Giuliani
Cover & book design by Joseph Hilliman

Circle Press
PO Box 5425
Hamden, CT 06518-0425
www.circlepress.org

Printed in the United States of America
ISBN: 1-933271-15-9

Contents

Foreword

This book is for seriously open-minded people.

If you don't fit into that category, toss this book out the window or use it to roast marshmallows, but don't waste my time and yours.

This is not a book about liberal or conservative positions, Democrat or Republican, left or right. This is a book for those who worry about the current situation of our world, see the need for changes, and want to do something about it. The problems that confront our society run deeper than just conservative/liberal discussions; they are complex, just as the solutions are.

Yet a fundamental danger is threatening this entire process of discussing our problems and applying solutions. What we are seeing more and more of – and this is the topic we shall soon pick apart – is a brutalizing tendency to latch on to one's position, ignoring all evidence to the contrary, come hell or high water. This ideological trench-digging, expressed in mindless name-calling, inability to articulate one's own position, and stubborn close-mindedness, cuts off all possibility of a rational debate on the issues we face, thus impoverishing all attempts at finding lasting solutions.

As a nation, we need open debate, diversity of opinions, and free speech; democracy cannot exist without them. Yet we also need intellectual honesty and reason based on reality. Yet sadly both are often lacking nowadays.

For many, feelings count more than reasons, tolerance more than truth. This present scourge of irrational debate is plaguing society with a corrosive relativism that threatens to dissolve the very fabric of our democracy.

This book is an attempt at an antidote.

> "A dictatorship of relativism is growing that doesn't recognize anything as absolute, leaving our own ego and its whims as the only standard."[1]

— JOSEPH CARDINAL RATZINGER, APRIL 18, 2005

The Operating System

A GLITCH IN THE SYSTEM

Jeff Runyan could be a model for a university brochure. He's your typical good 'ole American boy, complete with earthy brown hair neatly combed to the side of a handsome face, a light polo shirt tucked into khaki pants, and a pair of glasses to give a slight intellectual air. He's an easygoing guy, well-liked on campus, and at the top of many girls' wish lists. Originally from Greeley, Colorado, he decided to major in Political Science and Spanish with a certificate in Latin American studies at nearby Colorado State University in Fort Collins.

In his freshman year, Jeff jumped right into extracurricular activities. Besides some intramural sports, he flirted a bit with student government, got involved with several Christian groups, and was soon elected to the leadership team of the Catholic youth group. Yet the more Jeff got into these social activities on campus, the more he realized that some strange things were going on. The values and outlook on life he had grown up with in small town Greeley were frowned upon, sometimes even ridiculed.

But Jeff was a nice guy, a tolerant American, and he wasn't about to ruffle feathers or stir up dust. Maybe he was just overreacting to a few isolated incidents. So at the drum beating sessions to get the students "in rhythm with themselves," during the bawdy sex education session in freshman orientation complete with condom and contraceptive distribution, and throughout the constant slurs by professors to Christian values he simply kept silent. When the college newspaper published articles such as "Sex Toys 101," "The Lost Art of a Quickie" (describing the dorms as a full house of fresh virgins waiting to be taken), and a host of others slamming Christianity and basic values, Jeff shrugged his shoulders. Sometimes he just wished the conflicts would disappear, sometimes he wondered, "Doesn't anybody else see what's going on here?"

He expressed his doubts in a discussion with the Catholic campus minister, suggesting that if the Catholics on campus got together they could make some improvements. He expressed that perhaps the group could discuss current events using official Catholic teaching and reach out to other students. The minister balked at the suggestion. A bit taken aback, Jeff assured her, "Our religion is not politically correct." Her response was, "That is only a statement," basically contending that his assertion had no validity.

Lacking support even from Catholic quarters, Jeff withdrew for a few months from any potentially controversial positions. He had already been labeled as a "reactionary" for hinting on two or three occasions that something might be wrong with the campus situation. The support he depended on through church, retreats and friends began to dwindle and all but disappeared; no one wanted to risk their own reputation by associating with a "fundamentalist."

In the spring semester of his sophomore year, Jeff broke the silence. In the midst of a media frenzy on sexual abuse by clergy, the *Rocky Mountain Collegian* ran a cartoon depicting a Catholic cardinal with the pope in the Vatican and the caption *"Pedophilia, huh? Well, he better NOT have used a condom!"*

This was going a bit too far. Using an unfortunate situation to attack his church's position on a totally unrelated topic was downright dirty…and distasteful. Jeff, sat down to his computer, typed up a heated – yet balanced – letter to the editor, and sent it off to the paper.

His letter appeared in the April 8, 2002 edition of the *Rocky Mountain Collegian* with the title "Cartoon Offensive."

I am writing to express my shock, disappointment, and outrage over the political cartoon that the Collegian *chose to print in the March 26th issue. The cartoon depicted the pope and a Catholic cardinal in the Vatican with the pope stating "Pedophilia, huh? Well, he better NOT have used a condom!"*

This cartoon was a blatant affront toward my religion that slandered the Catholic Church in a reckless manner. The cartoon sent subliminal messages that this event was in some way approved by our Church and furthermore taunted the hardline moral issues stance that the Church embodies. Placing these words in the mouth of our pope is a defilement of our religion.

I also am outraged at the Collegian's *blatant discrimination against our minority. This is a state institution, and the day that racial or sexual discrimination is promoted by our school newspaper is the day that riots and lawsuits break out. Why is discrimination against Catholics the only accepted form of discrimination that remains at this school and in this society? I know that many people don't agree with the hard-line issues that the Church stands for but it seems as though the media are acting as vultures, taking advantage of the negative press in order to express their own biases. Perhaps this stems from the intimidation that basic morality evokes in this society. When I speak of my culture, I always include my Catholic faith. It is a piece of me that transcends almost every aspect of my life.*

As a student representative at John XXIII Catholic Student Center, I must express my profound disappointment in the Collegian's *discriminatory choice to print this defiling cartoon. In the future perhaps the* Collegian *may avoid the hypocrisy of selective discrimination.*

— Jeff Runyan, Sophomore Political Science

Admittedly, Jeff was a bit heated, throwing into the letter his pent up passions and frustrations of the past months. Yet he stated himself intelligently and gave legitimate arguments worthy of either an apology or an explanation.

He got none. Instead, he was ridiculed.

In the subsequent days, the *Collegian* published several responses to his letter. In the April 9th issue, the editor included a letter with the disclaimer, "The following letter is intended as a parody of a letter in Monday's *Collegian*. Any use of exact phrasing is for satire and not intended as plagiarism of the original letter written by Jeff Runyan." This may have freed the editor of any denunciation of plagiarism, but certainly not from an accusation of avoiding the issue at hand.

I am writing to express my shock, disappointment, and outrage over the political cartoon that the Collegian *chose to print in the April 8th issue. The cartoon depicted a couple being robbed by a man with a five-o-clock shadow stating "They made it harder for people like you to buy them (guns)."*

This cartoon was a blatant affront toward my personal choice not to shave that slandered the shaveless in a reckless manner. I am outraged at the Collegian's *blatant discrimination against our minority.*

This is a state institution, and the day that racial or sexual discrimination is promoted by our school newspaper is the day that riots break out. Why is discrimination against the nighbearded an accepted form of discrimination that remains at this school and in this society? I know that many people don't agree with the issues that we razorless people stand for, but is seems as though the media are acting as vultures taking advantage of us to express their own biases. Perhaps this stems from the intimidation that basic morality evokes in society. When I speak of my culture, I always include my moustache. It is a piece of me, literally, that transcends almost every aspect of my life.

As a student representative of CSU, I must express my profound disappointment in the Collegian's *discriminatory choice to print this defiling cartoon. After all, Jeff Runyan, it was only a cartoon.*

— Rick Grotzky, Senior Music Education

The following day, the paper ran another letter with the title "Spiritual Offense." The issue of Jeff's letter is again ignored, the arguments overlooked, and the author goes so far as to charge him with wanting to be another Hitler.

This letter is in response to the letter by Jeff Runyan. On March 26th, the Collegian printed a cartoon that contained the Pope and a Cardinal having a conversation about condom use. This poor young man found the cartoon quite offensive.

The only thing that I have to say is now you know what it's like to have one view crammed into your face. Recently, the Collegian has sold full page and other large ads to church organizations that have rhetorically spewed "images" of Jesus and propaganda preaching to students that without going to church you will have no chance of being considered an up standing [sic] citizen. I am offended every time I see these ads because my perception of what many would call "God."

My view is not the normal Catholic/Jewish/Agnostic/Islamic view of "God." It encompasses much more than just one document and one right and wrong. It actually encompasses the spiritual mediums' mind, something that most organized religions frown upon. Everyday, from the moment I wake up, I am bombarded by "images" and "teachings" of the organized religions, and I just laugh inside. This is because I know that my views of spirituality are right for me and your view of spirituality is right for you. No living, rational human has the right to tell people what they are allowed and are not allowed to believe, unless of course you would like to be remembered with the likes of Hitler. That seems to be the way that this whole issue is going.

So please, I ask this of all the spiritual (not just the religious) people: Let us all be. Don't fret over political cartoons, and don't be in everyone's face. It disrupts the flow of energy. Open your heart and mind to the world and spread love and knowledge, not hatred and lies.

— Jason Adams, Sophomore Liberal Arts

The confusion of this student in his religious views is no justification for confusing the issues of the argument. There is a substantial difference between paid publicity in a newspaper and the editorial direction of stories and photographs that are printed. A newspaper that claims objectivity and neutrality should be ready to justify itself when it starts taking sides. And why should Jeff's views be labeled as "hatred and lies"? That seems to be a rather "in your face" assertion, and certainly would "disrupt the flow of energy." Why does Jason Adams find the need to speak out? Why doesn't he just "let Jeff be"?

Jeff's letter to the editor even came under fire from fellow Catholics. Entitled "Catholic Counter-Argument," the following letter encourages us to "limit our comments to what we feel, not what we think." And the issues at hand? Intelligent debate? Justification for one view over another?

As a Catholic, I was utterly disgusted by the letter to the editor entitled, "Cartoon Offensive," in Monday's Collegian. *Despite Mr. Runyan's obvious passion for his faith, his words are in no way representative of all Catholics. I respect the offense taken by Mr. Runyan, as he is certainly entitled. The* Collegian *was obviously attempting to make light of a particularly nasty situation currently tearing up the Roman Catholic Church, not to blatantly offend Catholics.*

Mr. Runyan's statement that "discrimination against Catholics is the only accepted form of discrimination that remains at this school and in this society," is not only ignorant but is completely misrepresentative of the diversity the church [sic] strives for.

Please open your eyes, Mr. Runyan. We, as Catholics, have

it easy. I wonder if you have any idea what it is like to be a person of color in Fort Collins? I wonder if you have any idea what it is like to be a Muslim in Fort Collins? My guess is that you have absolutely no clue. Until you are able to truly walk in someone else's shoes, please be sure and limit your comments to what you feel, not what you think may or may not be patently offensive to an entire group of people. You have misrepresented Catholicism and John XXIII Catholic Church [sic], not to mention coming across as a provincial citizen with no grasp on the reality of discrimination here in the Front Range.

— Joseph J. Lanter, Graduate Student,
Student Affairs in Higher Education

Mr. Runyan's "ignorant" statement is certainly a generalization, but Mr. Lanter provided no evidence or arguments that his generalization was false. Indeed, much evidence exists that anti-Catholicism is much more widely accepted and prevalent than discrimination against blacks, Muslims, or Hispanics[a] and often overlooked – even by many Catholics. Perhaps Lanter "has it easy" because he is not as Catholic as he thinks he is. He would do better to walk in his own shoes a bit before attempting to "walk in someone else's" and if we all limited our comments "to what we feel" the only result would be irrational anarchy.

The most amazing chapter of this flurry of letters is the lack of positive support for Jeff. Aside from a few private words of encouragement, whispered in dark corners or written in furtive emails, there was no support. He had stepped out on a limb and challenged the prevailing opinions and it seemed no one wanted to step out there with him. Discouraged but not deflated, he later commented, "I am disgusted how people twisted what I was trying to say but I would do it again in a heartbeat to defend our faith."

He received just two personal responses to the letter. On a student retreat the weekend following the letters one girl introduced him to her boyfriend as "the one that wrote the letter." He congratulated Jeff and said, "We need more people with the guts to speak out as you did."

However, during a discussion group later in the retreat with about forty fellow students present, Jeff mentioned the cartoon, his letter, and the responses. He followed it up by saying that, "Catholics shouldn't just sit back while our religion is defiled and ridiculed. We should defend our faith."

An immediate response came from another student at the discussion. "I actually agreed with the editorials in response to Jeff's letter. We need to start acting more like Jesus and turn the other cheek and I found his letter very offensive." He continued on, railing against "fundamentalist" tendencies, advocating the need for "tolerance," and ridiculing Jeff's letter and idea of sticking up for the faith.

As Jeff sat through the tirade, he was shaking inside. Not a word of support from other students, priest, or campus minister. All silently admitted that, yes, Jeff had probably overreacted, a bit like a "bull in a china closet." After all, there is no sense in making more enemies on campus or stirring things up. Tolerance is more important than truth. In this "discussion" debate was useless and Jeff hung his head in silent acquiescence.

Jeff was outdated software running in the new operating system of society.

RUNNING IN RELATIVISM

Jeff's case – and thousands more like his – reveals that our society is running two conflicting operating systems: *realism* and *relativism*. Various versions of each are in use, but they all work in pretty much the same way:

- □ *realism* builds upon our knowledge of the world as it presents itself to discover truth and goodness (not make them) and affirms that absolutes exist.
- □ *relativism* doubts human capacity for knowledge or truth, leading to each person creating their own "truth" and a rejection of any absolutes... or at least those that curtail the relativist's appetite.

Some people would explain the opposed systems as the difference between childish naïveté and adult sophistication. Children – and realists – are naturally dogmatic about what they know. Everything is black or white, right or wrong, with a clear-cut answer for everything. Adults, on the contrary, are more refined. Dogmatism is frowned upon and we no longer ask "why" about many things. Grown-ups are wiser, discerning grey areas and difficult cases where it is not clear what is right or wrong. This "adult," sophisticated, relativistic view of the world discovers that we can interpret things differently depending on our point of view.

From this comparison of children and adults, it would seem that dogmatism and relativism are on opposite ends of the spectrum of knowledge. If this were true, then skepticism would be the epitome of maturity. If we extend this growth in "maturity" to society, we would find simplistic absolutism represented by poor uneducated peasants of the "dark ages" and a "repressive" Christianity, or by the fascist and Nazi regimes that explained all of reality by race and the State, or by a Stalinism that imposed by force its economic and political views on millions of people. As an alternative, we are presented with a relativistic modern democracy: equality and freedom for all. No imposed ideas or structures, no Inquisition or purges, no concentration camps or gulags, no Ayatollah or terrorist training camps. No black or white, no right or wrong.

Is this really our choice: totalitarianism or relativism? Childish naïveté or sophisticated skepticism?

This simple theory of knowledge in the end falls victim to its own critique, because it is – simply put – too simplistic. Knowledge is *not* either/or, all or nothing; it is a process of gradual growth. A small child knows more than a baby, but the knowledge of a teenager greatly surpasses that of a first grader. The experience of someone in the work force for many years gives them understanding beyond a fresh college grad, yet the wisdom of the elderly exceeds them both. We never stop learning. New experiences constantly enrich our view of life and reality until the day of our death.

Mature knowledge is neither dogmatic nor relativistic. In fact, dogmatism and relativism are merely the first two of *three* stages for growth in knowledge. If absolutism comes with childhood, relativism comes with adolescence and teenagers. True maturity – realism – comes *after* relativism.

Alexis de Tocqueville described well this maturing process: "Perhaps it would have been more correct to have said, that absolute convictions are to be met with at the two extremities, and that doubt lies in the middle; for the human intellect may be considered in three distinct states, which frequently succeed one another. A man believes implicitly, because he adopts a proposition without inquiry. He doubts as soon as he is assailed by the objections which his inquiries may have aroused. But he frequently succeeds in satisfying these doubts, and then he begins to believe afresh: he no longer lays hold on a truth in its most shadowy and uncertain form, but he sees it clearly before him, and he advances onwards by the light it gives him."[2]

Naïve and sophisticated caricatures aside, there is no doubt that there is a legitimate complexity of many things in life and answers are not easy to find. Yet this will never legitimate the lack of absolute answers to anything. Maturity means moving from doubt to renewed conviction about what is good and true. Yet our modern society is stuck in puberty. Relativism has become the dominant operating system in a culture that scoffs at what we once knew, too rebellious to respect the wisdom of our forefathers, too self-sufficient to seek the truth, and worst of all, many times just too lazy to bother.

Despite is shaky theoretical base, relativism maintains its practical attraction and as a theory it has had a perennial following. In fact, the Sophists that Plato argued against so fiercely four centuries before the birth of Christ were already spreading it, and their intellectual children have proliferated over time, all the way down to our current day. The two modern children of relativism have different daddies: one from laziness, the other from willfulness.

When we encounter the grey areas in life and the difficulty of applying principles to concrete situations, *laziness* often kicks in. "Why bother?" It takes effort and serious reflection to figure out what is true or false, right or wrong. Many people just avoid the effort. We fall victim to the experience of our limitations, falling into the pragmatic realization that "I'm never really going to change" and a cynicism that asks "why even bother?" For the lazy relativist, "tolerance" seems to imply that the older you get the more you will accept anything... just as long as they don't take away their nightly beer or La-Z-Boy®. Seeking out the truth, justifying your actions, or converting when you find that you were wrong – these are all difficult. They require study, discipline, and change. In a culture that considers the remote control for the TV a vital necessity, the breed of lazy relativists will always abound.

Willful relativism is of a different stripe. All of us want to be happy, and our first experiences of pleasure or power indicate that we'll be happy when everything is pleasant or going our way. However, this oversimplification of human reality ignores the fulfillment that comes from overcoming obstacles or in sacrificing ourselves out of love for another person.

This second species of relativism is hatched from a strong desire to ignore any universal values, solid truths, or objective good and evil... not usually because one has solid intellectual reasons, but simply because the truth is inconvenient for holding onto some pleasure or power. The reality of things continues to call out to conscience, but when you are running from guilt, it is often easier to wish things were not as they are rather than actually change. These relativists seek to convince themselves – and others if they can – that what they are doing is not really wrong and that society, authority, or an antiquated morality is really at fault. Willful relativism will exist as long as people sin.

In the sexual revolution – perhaps the single most defining movement of modern society – we find a mix of both strands of relativism. Sexual pleasure is real and the natural sex drive leads to experiences and personal choices to optimize that pleasure. The "old school" frowns upon that, but the 'liberated' youth forced to choose between moral norms he doesn't understand and pleasure that he experiences naturally chooses pleasure. To justify his choices against truth claims, he oftentimes rebels against the "antiquated" sexual mores and traditional morality by denying any absolute truths, any clear-cut good and bad.

The old saying is proven true: if you don't practice what you preach, you'll end up preaching what you practice. That's why the "sexually liberated" preach relativism and tolerance – it lets them keep practicing what they are not willing to give up. It may not be intellectually honest, but it is practically convenient. As Benjamin Franklin once said, "The brain is a wonderful mechanism, and it's most awesome ability is its capacity to deceive itself."

If our society is so progressive, why is it that we are still stuck in the same old problems? Why is our society running in relativism, unable to recognize what is true and good? Why is modern man stuck in rebellious puberty? On closer analysis, there seem to be three key factors in this stagnation of our maturing process:

1. philosophical ideas rooted in the Enlightenment
2. a shift from pluralism to relativism
3. a corruption of the democratic process itself

A closer look at each of these developmental factors will

allow us to peer into the internal circuitry of the relativist operating system.

Enlightened Roots

In 1641, with his publication of *Meditations,* René Descartes opened up a new way of looking at things that would revolutionize Western thought. Before him, most of the great philosophers had taken the route of Aristotle, Augustine, and Aquinas: we reflect on things around us and come to a surer and more certain knowledge by a gradual process. Aristotle recognized that different objects of study can permit varying degrees of certainty (i.e., a sociologist knows that his "scientific" results always depend on the accuracy of his data, which by its nature is unstable; a geometrician can arrive at absolutely certain conclusions because his data is unchanging and based on an ideal world). Reality was the solid foundation for knowledge before Descartes.

But Descartes wasn't satisfied with this foundation of knowledge. There seemed to be too much uncertainty in reality, too many unknowns and incalculables. He wanted clarity and certainty in *all* knowledge, so he set out to find a new foundation for knowledge. Instead of starting from things, he decided to start from his own mind. By reflecting on his own ideas, he thought he could arrive to this complete clarity and certainty. Descartes found certainty in his own thinking, or in the midst of his thinking, he found certain knowledge of himself as a "thinking-thing." *I think therefore I am.*

The next question was how he could attain certain knowledge of the world outside of himself. He based this on the innate idea of God, who would guarantee knowledge beyond the thinking subject. Yet when subsequent philosophers negated the existence of innate ideas, Cartesian thought could never escape solipsism; the whole system rests on sand. Descartes began the disconnect from reality, but other philosophers were not far behind.

In 1784 Immanuel Kant published a short tract entitled "What is the Enlightenment?" which provided the rallying call for the current of thoughts sweeping across Europe: *Sapere aude!* (Dare to think!). Influenced by Descartes and the empiricists, Kant wanted to come to scientific knowledge in which everything was universal, certain, and necessary. The transcendental idealism that he proposed in his 1787 work, *Critique of Pure Reason,* established a system in which his own mind organized reality, providing the certainty he sought. It was not reality that showed itself to him as already organized, but his mind that structured reality. He claimed that we could never know things in themselves, but only the impressions they leave on us. The end result is that reality as it exists in itself is unknowable, according to Kant.

It takes a lot of study to knock the common sense out of people. That's why these philosophical ideas and the revolution they began took root slowly. Common people tied to the tilling of the soil and the everyday realities of life are incorrigibly down to earth. But intellectuals will often think themselves into circles and justify the most ridiculous ideas. The bricks of the foundation for modern society were changed one by one.

Over the years, professional philosophers based much of their own reflection on this subjective foundation of Descartes and Kant. John Stuart Mill, Hegel, Karl Marx, Herbert Spencer, William James, John Dewey, Martin Heidegger and countless other intellectuals who influenced the course of American thought were grounded in part upon this shifty base. They never stopped to examine the foundations they were building on, so it is no wonder that house started to crumble.

When the torrent of modern philosophers like Quine and Rorty came along, denying that truth exists, the foundation started to give way. We were in no position to refute their ideas. If I can refer only to my own mind, to my own ideas, then there is only *my* "truth" against *your* "truth." And whoever is stronger wins. Might becomes right, because we have lost the foundation of a reality bigger than us that judges us and makes rational discussion possible. In this scenario, no one wins – we all lose!

The philosophical distinctions are complicated, yet a simple (and therefore limited) example can give us an idea of the radical change involved in this shift. If we saw a man jump off the Sears Tower to commit suicide, Aristotle would say that the man fell to the ground and died; subjectivists might say that the ground rushed up toward the man and struck him, causing his death. Many modern philosophers scoff at Aristotle's realist explanation and exercise an impressive dexterity with words that deflects evidence and evades common sense. This does not mean to say that all modern philosophy is defective. On the contrary, profound insights and a deeper understanding of our world come through philosophical research; yet as in any science, conclusions need to be sifted through, accepting what is true, refuting what is false. The smokescreen of words and scientific jargon makes this task daunting, but not impossible.

The bloody French Revolution was the crowning achievement of the Enlightenment – the goddess of Reason was enthroned upon the altar in Notre Dame Cathedral in Paris as a completely secular government hostile to Christianity took the reigns of power. The "Dark Ages" of religion were left behind for the glory of Reason. Religion was rationalized (Kant's 1793 work *Religion Within the Limits of Reason Alone* is but one example), reduced to its capacity to create ethical citizens, and relegated to the private sphere alone. And all this was hailed as progress, civilization, and the true advancement of humankind.

The Enlightenment did bring some points of light, but its mature fruits show just how much of that "light" was actually darkness. The goddess of Reason has turned out to be an irrational dictator, and the modern defenders of reason tend to be, ironically, men of faith

Two revolutions in European history followed upon the heels of the philosophical revolution: the *scientific* and the *industrial*.

Philosophy and science were one until the dawn of the *scientific* revolution, and in fact Isaac Newton's main work was entitled *The Mathematical Principles of Natural Philosophy,* though after his findings philosophy and "science" parted ways. The new sciences that were born quantified all of reality, rejecting as unscientific anything that was not measurable. Spiritual realities, morality, feelings, and whatever couldn't be counted, weighed, or measured was set aside, leaving us with an increasingly inhuman world: mechanistic, materialist, and positivist.

If reality were a birthday cake, modern science has handed us the pan – perfectly square, measured, and hard – while we were forbidden to eat the cake inside. Science gives us the quantity but not the quality. But authentic science does not have to reject qualities and spiritual realities. That is where the flavor and sustenance of life is. Real science should be able to present to us the whole: both cake and pan. In part, the rise of "soft sciences" such as psychology, history and sociology are due to this human need to recover values.

The *industrial* revolution soon followed upon the philosophical and scientific revolutions. New discoveries, inventions, and systems of organization provided fresh sources of wealth, and the use of capital and labor for wages were not far behind. Some unscrupulous individuals took advantage of these new tools to build their own wealth while ignoring the condition of their workers. They committed serious injustices through unjust wages, long hours, unsanitary working conditions, and job insecurity. At times workers were treated as machines and were disposed of when they no longer "worked."

At the culminating point of these three revolutions, Karl Marx proposed a theory that united these social realities and pointed out the path to salvation in communism. Class struggle and the change of structures would overcome the alienation of the proletariat, oust the corrupt bourgeois capitalists, and create heaven on earth. This pseudoscientific theory of socialism/communism spread like wildfire. It took root in Europe because it addressed real problems; Marx and Engels appeared as saviors upon the horizon of history. They offered a solution to real problems and many progressive intellectuals and disillusioned workers embraced the theory and took up the red banner. Socialism conquered minds long before subduing nations.

Though "real socialism" never took root on American soil, many leading intellectuals were caught up with its basic tenets; labor unions and workers were often deeply influenced by socialist thought. However, as capitalism lost its harsh edges in America and work injustices decreased, it was hard to justify a worker's revolution. Fat, well-paid workers don't strike, much less rebel. The intellectuals had to search out a new battlefield for their Marxist model of reality.

The civil rights movement presented just the right combination – unjust conditions, a repressed class, and bourgeois white rulers – and it was adopted as the new crusade of many socialists. Instead of a class struggle, there was a racial struggle where the structures and super-structures were to be replaced and equality established for all. Though the battle changed, the Marxist model of class struggle and power did not. Ground was gained, rights established, and as injustices between races declined and equality increased, the call for civil disobedience quietly died down. After all, minorities with equal or preferential treatment aren't likely to drop those privileges for nothing. A new struggle was needed.

Equality of the sexes took the fore during the subsequent years and feminists reigned supreme. Yet the underlying Marxist interpretation of power, alienation, and class struggle did not fade away.

Environmental issues came to the forefront next, always within the Marxist reading of reality. Man was the evil bourgeois alienating the power of Nature and abusing it. Trees, bees, and monkeys should have equal rights. Environmental Marxism was always an intellectual stretch, so when society and businesses started recognizing the common sense in taking better care of the environment, the cause for revolution evaporated and the socialist intelligentsia had to look for a new cause.

The cause would soon present itself, but let's not jump ahead of the story.

From Pluralism to Relativism

Having analyzed briefly the three revolutions of the Enlightenment era, we discover a second historical factor that has played a pivotal role in the spread of the relativist operating system in society: the corruption of the authentic meaning of pluralism

The United States of America was the firstborn child of the Enlightenment. Great figures of the period, authors and statesmen such as Baron de Montesquieu, Benjamin Franklin, and Thomas Jefferson, all contributed directly or indirectly to the establishment of the governing principles of our nation: division of powers, private property, capitalism, and religious tolerance. And as the national motto, the founding fathers chose *"E pluribus unum"* (out of many, one) to exemplify the spirit of the New World: open arms to immigrants of any nation.

In the first decade of the 1900s, 8.8 million immigrants passed through Ellis Island and other ports of entry. The waves of foreigners continued to sweep in through the twentieth century and in the decade of the 1980s, 8.5 million immigrants arrived to the United States through the main national airports alone. The new arrivals were invited to civics classes, English courses, and they learned the Pledge of Allegiance and the National Anthem. The children quickly picked up the new language and moved ahead in society. There was a common spirit, the American *ethos* that the immigrants absorbed, despite various bumps and occasional outbreaks of xenophobia along the way. The United States was a true melting pot. From their many backgrounds, languages, and cultural heritage the immigrants became Americans. *E pluribus unum*. Out of many, one.

There were core values that a "good American" was supposed to adopt, certain characteristics that made us one. In America, you respected people and everyone had the chance to get ahead. No favoritisms or special classes. You could pull yourself up by your own bootstraps.

Yet the situation has changed today.

The common threads that once united us are frayed and worn thinner with every passing day. According to education analyst Diane Ravitch, "Modern America lacks a common, shared culture worth speaking of, much less preserving." Perhaps the affirmation is a bit too broad, but certainly our values have been increasingly dumped into the trash bin of antiquated ideas. The idea of absolute values, or of truth – something that is stable and unchanging – meets with derision and scorn. One opinion better than another? Forget it. One point of view truer than another? How narrow-minded!

Instead of a *pluralism* of different people, cultures, and ideas sharing common principles, we have shifted to *relativism*. Diversity is affirmed in both systems, but relativism denies any common values besides "tolerance" and eliminates the possibility of forming a cohesive unity as *one* nation, even if on the surface the civic framework seems to hold together. Pluralism respects principles and common values based on truth; relativism scoffs at them.

Relativism – the idea that one opinion is as good as another, that any ideas or actions **must** be respected by everyone else, that "no one can tell me what is right or wrong"

– has become the operating system of western society. All the "programs" are written to run in it. Yet while everyone seems to worry about the programs – Democrat, Republican, socialism, democracy, liberal, conservative, fundamentalist, etc. – no one seems to be noticing crucial flaws in the system in which all these programs are trying to operate.

The Democratic Process

For many years this change from pluralism to relativism was not evident. The house looked strong from the outside: society was in order, people more or less fulfilled their duties and life went on. Christianity provided the guiding ideas for moral life and illuminated political discourse. It seemed that any normal person could tell right from wrong. While the rest of the world agonized through repressive monarchies, religious violence, dictatorships, totalitarian regimes, and genocide, the United States of America enjoyed peaceful co-existence, stable democracy and religious tolerance.

However, throughout these years of peace, three major changes were taking place. It was part of the transition of operating systems, a revolution nobody seemed to notice.

Firstly, Americans began to associate morality with legality. If something is legal, it must be good; if it is illegal, it must be bad. In almost all cases, this was true. If you killed someone you went to jail because it was illegal *and* it was bad. People forgot the concept of an unjust law, the possibility that government could legislate something bad. It never occurred to people that the government might possibly legalize killing babies with birth defects or enact laws making it dangerous for parents to discipline their children. Law became the measure of morality and many Americans lost the sense that morality is bigger than legality, just like a tree is bigger than one of its branches. People lost a sense of the difference between *natural law* (written on the hearts of man) and *positive law* (written as the law of the land).

Religion, especially the brand of Protestantism that guided the nation's founding, played right into this conception by focusing on the Ten Commandments as the basis of morality. People knew the law of religion – the Commandments – though this "what" did not always have the "why" to back it up. As Enlightenment thought evolved into new forms of liberality, oftentimes rejecting revealed religion and natural law, that missing "why" left civil law increasingly alone on the pedestal of moral authority. Society maintained the external trappings of religion and continued to follow the Commandments, but the foundation was being stripped away brick by brick. Only a metaphysical[3] base or religion can provide the ultimate answers to the "why."

A second change, no less important, was to associate morality with majority: if the majority agrees on something, then that must be the right thing to do. Again, in most cases this was true because the majority in America was down-to-earth people rooted in Judeo-Christian values. People's faith influenced their decisions and their outlook on life, and that influenced their voting and involvement in political life. Religion was the great stabilizer of America.

We forgot quickly the lesson of Nazi Germany, where a majority had been hoodwinked into support of a genocidal system. The majority does not make morality, but we trusted that our majority was moral. "That could never happen to us…"

The third change, however, has created the greatest upheaval. The cultural revolution of the 60s and 70s brought a progressive disintegration of the positive influence of religion in public life. As mainline Protestant churches faltered in their faith and moral demands, Americans began to falter with them. Beginning with the Lambeth Conference in 1930,[4] the mainline churches began to change their teaching on moral issues, adopting standards consistent with the society around them... and at times much more progressive than the general public. They ceased to be leaven in society, and became increasingly just one more social group.

As pastors preached a social gospel and neglected the truth of Christianity, Christians themselves became more secularized. The American "majority" – Christians – began to change their ideas, customs, and outlook on life. This in turn created or permitted a revolution in morality. Contraception, adultery, divorce, premarital sex, and abortion – all once universally condemned by the Christian churches – became subjects of contention, insecurity, and open debate. And once the debate was open, permissive laws came not far behind.

This third change was so blatant and alarming that most people didn't notice the first two. Modern culture became entrapped in its own confusion. The change in customs and ideas led to a shift in morality in the majority that was subsequently enshrined in law. Now that very same law only serves to confuse many who had come to associate morality and majority, morality and legality. The relativist system, though not yet fully dominant, was gaining more and more users.

AN INCREASINGLY UNSTABLE SYSTEM

In the growing confusion of the twentieth century, the relativist operating system continued to gain market share, and the 1968 generation took a leading role in that expansion. Four new concepts stormed to the foreground – even among the baby boomers who didn't grow long hair, smoke pot, or camp out at Woodstock: peace, equality, freedom, and tolerance.

These seem like real American values. In fact, democracy itself seems to depend upon these core principles. Our nation was founded on the basis of equal rights for all; "Give me liberty or give me death," was the key cry of the War of Independence that marked us as a nation; tolerance seems crucial to peaceful coexistence, the greatest good that we strive for in the modern world. Could there be anything wrong with these values?

In themselves, no; yet when separated from the truth, yes. For example, hard work is a laudable value – unless used in the service of evil. Many of Hitler's henchmen were undoubtedly dedicated and hardworking, but that doesn't make their work good. In fact, they carried out very well their evil work; "good" values can be employed in the service of "bad" objectives. Only the truly good is really good.

Peace

Take peace for example. This concept underwent an unprecedented paradigm shift with the hippie generation. Antiwar sentiments galvanized the political and cultural force of thousands, uniting them in a common cause against the evils of war... which were very real. The peace sign became the mark of rebellion and unity. Yet many of the peaceniks would have had trouble answering a fundamental question: what is peace?

A first approach to the question gives us a simple reply: tranquility, peace and quiet. It evokes images of a cold beer in hand while soaking up the sun on the back porch, a morning without changing diapers or email and voice messages, or the week your boss is out of town. This is peace on the personal level. On the global front, peace means the end of war and cessation of all hostilities. Dismantle the missiles, send home the soldiers, tear up the battle plans. This is the peace that pacifists seek.

Peace is good, a great good, and should be sought and maintained whenever possible. Yet this is only a preliminary level. To make this partial peace the absolute aim is to forget that authentic peace comes only as a fruit of justice. True peace is, as the Roman and medieval scholars loved to say, *tranquilitas ordinis*; it is not merely tranquility, but the tranquility of order. It goes beyond mere cessation of hostilities; it is based on the order of justice where each receives his due and the common good triumphs over egotism and violence.

A father who ignores his baby daughter's crying so he can enjoy Monday night football might have his moment of relaxation and peace, but he has left aside his responsibility and his love for something less important. A serial killer could be at peace after strangling another victim because it satisfies his sadistic tendency, but that tranquility he feels is detached from the correct order of things. A dictator could establish "peace" in his country by controlling education, stifling the free press, and imposing military rule over all the citizens, but he would do so at the cost of just order, respect for freedom and truth.

The preliminary level of peace – tranquility – is not enough. Peace is tied to order, an order that begins with justice and is crowned with charity. This order is not relative or subject to anyone's opinion, but is discovered in the truth that frees us from subjectivity. "There is no peace without justice. There is no justice without forgiveness."[5] This is the order of true and lasting peace.

Equality

The Woodstock generation championed the spread of a better world, a just world, where peace and equality would be the norm. The dream was good, but the idea of equality – like that of peace – was often a bit too naïve.

Imagine a society of perfect equality: everyone gets the same paycheck regardless of what job they do or how they do it; everyone lives in the same type of house, goes to the same quality of school regardless of merit, shops at the same stores. Sound a bit boring? Not only that, it is terribly unjust. This type of equality fails to take into account the reality of inequality in human existence. Not everyone has the same qualities. Not everyone can do a job just as well as another. Not everyone shares the same interests. People are different, not all cookies out of the same cookie cutter.

There are two basic approaches to equality: mathematical or ontological. Whenever someone says equality, we usually think "="; two = two and AB = AB. We learn this in our first math lessons. This type of equality looks for completely identical realities, no differences allowed. Although this type of equality is very useful in the *ideal* world of mathematics, it does not apply well to the *real* world of everyday life. Mathematical equality can't comprehend differences, nuances, motivations, and values. This equality can never fully explain love, sacrifice, friendship, or any of the most important realities of life. Equality of opportunity does not mean equality of outcome.

Ontological equality is different. It is not based on what we see and feel, but on the underlying reality. This type of equality can recognize that I am still me, even though nearly every cell in my body has been replaced in the past few years. Despite the biological changes I am still (ontologically) who I was. Ontological equality can also recognize that men and women are equal, not because they are biologically equal or because they can do the same type of work, but because at their core both men and women are human. They share equal human dignity, even though their functions in society and the family are different.

Any mathematical approach to equality – whether in economics, race, or sex – would end up committing injustices greater than those it might remedy. This is why communism failed. This is why affirmative action taken to the extreme will fail and why radical feminism that tries to make women into men and men into women will fail.

As black columnist Thomas Sowell stated so succinctly, "Trying to explain inequality is like trying to explain why people don't flap their arms and fly. There was never any reason to expect people to fly and there was never any reason to expect people's performances to be equal, when there are innumerable influences at work differently for each individual and group."[6]

Mathematical equality must cede its rightful role to ontological equality. It is necessary to recognize the differences between people while at the same time acknowledging their equal dignity in the eyes of God. This is the real equality. It is based on reality and our relationship to God, not on a social program or simplistic leveling of the playing field. Truth is the measuring stick for true equality.

Freedom

Perhaps an even more dramatic shift than that of equality came in our idea of freedom. "I can do what I want" is the prevalent attitude today. For much of the English speaking world, John Stuart Mill summed up our idea of freedom in his 1869 work *On Liberty* when he wrote, "In the part which merely concerns himself, his independence is, of right, absolute. Over himself, over his own body and mind, the individual is sovereign." Basically, I can do what I want and no one can tell me what to do.

He goes on, describing the limit of this freedom. "The only freedom which deserves the name, is that of pursuing our own good in our own way, so long as we do not attempt to deprive others of theirs, or impede their efforts to obtain it." Basically, my freedom can only be restricted if it starts to infringe on others' freedoms.

This radical individualism advanced in our society until the United States Supreme Court enshrined it legally with the 1992 *Planned Parenthood vs. Casey* ruling, declaring that individuals are free to organize "intimate relationships and make choices that define their views of themselves and their places in society." No reference to any reality – you make your own reality. "At the heart of liberty is the right to define one's own concept of existence, of meaning, of the universe, and of the mystery of human life. Beliefs about these matters could not define the attributes of personhood were they formed under compulsion of the State."

The Supreme Court – fully in line with the development of Enlightenment thought – agress with Friedrich Nietzsche that modern man is free to create his own world, his own reality, his own values as if there were no standard and no reality outside himself. But is this possible? Is this the freedom we want?

That's the "freedom" we are getting, whether we want it or not. In the 2003 Supreme Court case *Lawrence v. Texas* striking down sodomy statutes, the court flip-flopped on its 1986 decision in *Bowers v. Hardwick*. Justice Stevens' dissenting opinion in the 1986 case became the majority opinion in 2003. "Freedom" now means, in principle, freedom from any enforceable moral standard. You can hold your personal views, but neither you nor the government can impose those views on others. As Stevens phrased it in judicial jargon, "The fact that the governing majority in a State has traditionally viewed a particular practice as immoral is not a sufficient reason for upholding a law prohibiting the practice." This has now become the law of the land. This new style of freedom liberates us *from* outside pressures and the opinions of others, allowing us to act and be as we please. It seems like a fairly reasonable principle, espousing respect and tolerance of others. But does it really?

This is the freedom that brought us the sexual revolution. Each person was freed from the prudish morality of their parents, free from the outdated ideas of the past, free to follow their impulses and natural drives to the maximum. The result was skyrocketing drug use, proliferation of sexual disorders, venereal diseases, teen pregnancies, and suicide rates that continue to climb. Is there perhaps something wrong with this idea of freedom?

Animals have a nature programmed by instinct that leads them to migrate, mate, and feed. They are free when they are not impeded from following this nature by being tied to the fence post, locked in a corral, or attached to a leash. Their freedom is always a freedom *from* restriction. It is a negative freedom and there is no responsibility tied to it.

Human freedom is decidedly different. Our freedom begins with animal freedom, but our nature opens to us the capacity of a higher freedom, a freedom *for*. We are not determined by instincts and impulses. We can think, reason, judge, innovate, and act in ways other animals never can. We are open to higher realities of truth and goodness, realities outside of us that transcend us. Our human freedom is positive, a freedom for these higher things, a freedom that gives meaning and purpose not because we arbitrarily give it meaning, but because we discover in reality and in our higher vocation this purpose to our life on earth. This is authentic freedom, a freedom that continually transcends the here and now to strive toward the truth and goodness of God.

This authentic freedom is clearest in our choices. As human beings, we are free to choose between Kellogg's Corn Flakes or Wheaties. We can choose to watch the White Sox play on TV or take a ride down to the stadium for the game… or not bother with the game at all. Life is full of choices. And we are free to choose.

How I use my freedom is not indifferent. I am free to do whatever I want, but if I choose the wrong things I can sell myself into slavery. Bad choices automatically begin limiting my freedom because they strip my capacity to choose the greater goods. I am free to take cocaine, but that choice brings consequences and limits my chances to land a decent job or even to think coherently; my freedom to refuse cocaine in the future is hampered with chemical addiction.

A man is free to check out pornographic websites, but that choice can become an addiction that enslaves him and strips him of the capacity to think of and relate to women[7] in a normal relationship. He also becomes less capable of refusing to look again at these websites. It is addictive, and anything addictive erodes my personal liberty and thereby my dignity as a human person.

My freedom brings with it responsibility. If a dog chews the couch to pieces, I will punish it so it doesn't repeat the offense, but I certainly wouldn't say it is responsible. However, if a college student decides to rip up the couch, we would hold him responsible. Why? Because he is free, he knows better, and he made a poor decision. He could have acted otherwise and he did not. For that he is held responsible, and he will pay the consequences.

Choices are not unlimited either. A hundred years ago I could not choose to fly, but with new instruments now I can fly with United Airlines or in a private Cessna plane or even with a hang glider. But I still cannot just flap my arms and fly. If I jump off a building flapping my arms and choosing to fly, I will soon have a hard knock with reality.

I can choose to have an abortion, but I cannot choose to make abortion right or a good thing. My choices are limited by reality, by truth, by morality. Reality judges my choices and says, "That was wrong." I can choose to backstab a rival, give alms to a beggar on the street corner, or disobey my parents. I am free to choose within certain parameters, but I also freely assume the consequences.

Human freedom is not absolute. We can choose many things…but not everything. We can decide what good thing we want to do today…but not what is good. We can use scientific discoveries, calculations, and truths to make human life better, longer, and more comfortable…but we cannot *make* scientific truths according to our whims. Reality shows us our limits. With our intellect we can transcend many of these limits, but not all. True freedom recognizes what it can and cannot do.

Authentic freedom is tied to responsibility. When we know what we are doing and have a choice, that choice brings responsibility. It is an unavoidable reality for humans. To shirk responsibility only leads us back to a negative animal freedom; but when a man sinks to that level, he is lower than an animal. In real life practice, the animal freedom of Mill and of relativists is a dismal failure. It leads to serious abuses, rejection of our spiritual nature, and deep unhappiness. Authentic human freedom is tied to truth and responsibility; this is what elevates our freedom to its real grandeur.

Tolerance

Even though it is clear that equality is not mathematical, and freedom is tied to responsibility, it would seem that tolerance could still make a claim for itself. After all, what could be more un-American than shoving your beliefs and opinions down someone else's throat? Shouldn't we respect everyone's opinion on equal footing? Isn't tolerance the basis for peace, stability, and democracy?

In our minds, tolerance is a good thing and intolerance is bad, but we struggle to define what it is. Ancient philosophers thought of tolerance as "putting up with an evil," though its more modern definition came into common use in the years of the Enlightenment when John Locke and Voltaire wrote influential papers about it, urging Europeans to set aside the bloody religious wars of the Reformation period and learn to live in peace. Tolerance meant to set aside the divisive beliefs – get along with each other as civilized human beings. Tolerance in a negative manner means "not imposing opinions on others." Taken in a positive way, it means respect for others.

The meaning of this seemingly innocuous term has amplified and mutated over the years, becoming the modern mantra that no one really seems to understand anymore. Is tolerance about personal opinions, actions that affect others, personal thoughts, religious beliefs, science, grammar? Does tolerance extend to everything, or just to certain aspects of life? Locke and Voltaire never gave clear answers to these questions. In fact, this has led to some serious confusion, because tolerance is a very ambiguous term. We are told to tolerate pain, to show tolerance with the religious beliefs of others, to avoid intolerance with homosexual activists, and to show tolerance and flexibility in our moral judgments.

But the idea of tolerance cut off from truth is a house without a foundation, a tree without roots, or a computer without a hard drive. That tolerance won't work. According to Bernard Lewis, "Tolerance is, of course, an extremely intolerant idea, because it means 'I am the boss: I will allow you some, though not all, of the rights I enjoy as long as you behave yourself according to standards that I shall determine.'"[8] True tolerance can never be attained by ignoring truth. That would be like kicking out the ladder beneath our feet while changing a light bulb.

Many people now prefer the warm fuzzies of "compassion" and flexibility to the *seemingly* cold and uncaring appeal to truth. We shouldn't offend anyone – that might bring a lawsuit – and avoid anything that makes someone feel guilty. After all, who are we to judge?

Yet, if I see a friend ready to jump off a bridge, would I just let him jump? Not if I'm a real friend. Would I warn a friend if he were about to eat a poisoned apple? Of course, because I care about what is best for him. So why should we sit by in silence when our friend is doing something that endangers his integral good?

True compassion for others is not to sit by and watch – or even less applaud – when they do what will hurt themselves. True love seeks what is best for the person loved, even when they might perceive those actions as hurtful and intolerant. No parent enjoys punishing their child – and the child certainly doesn't appreciate it – but they discipline because they love him and want the best for him. In the real world, compassion does not always mean doing what seems simple and kind on the surface. For example, a doctor might feel sorry for a sick child. He doesn't want to cause the child pain by giving him a shot, but failure to give the shot might result in the child staying sick or even dying. He makes the truly "compassionate" decision to cause a little pain now to prevent greater pain later.

In the real world, we have to judge. It is impossible to go through life without making some judgment about what is true or false, good or bad. What if I witness a friend shoplift a candy bar? What should my reaction be? Obviously, knowing that the candy belongs to the store and that he did not pay for it, I will naturally conclude that he stole it and that that was wrong. His action was bad. That does not mean necessarily that he, as a person, is completely bad, but that action was bad. Withholding judgment of his action would be false tolerance.

Judging actions is different than judging persons. Every one of us has to judge actions; God alone is the judge of persons. We can judge what actions are right or wrong, which answers are true or false, but it is up to God to judge the moral value of a person and their final destiny.

Jacques Maritain, the French philosopher who helped draft the *Universal Declaration of Human Rights* for the United Nations, made some distinctions that could help clear up the confusion about tolerance. He speaks of the three main areas of life where tolerance is typically applied: religion, philosophy, and politics.

In the area of religion, he argues that "tolerance" is not an appropriate word choice. It would be better to speak of *charity*. Respect for the religious beliefs of others is positive, not merely a negative "I won't impose my views on you." It is respect based upon the dignity of the person who believes, not upon the validity or non-validity of their beliefs. Charity restrains us from any coercion and allows us to respect the person. But it does not take away the possibility that the person's religion might be false or be mixed with elements of truth and falsehood. Though I recognize their beliefs might be wrong, in charity I can respect the person who believes.

In the area of philosophy and science, "tolerance" still does not really fit the occasion. Some thinkers explain reality better than others. Others are simply wacky. A scientist should not "tolerate" a man who affirms that the moon is made of cheese. Not all ideas are equally true because not all correspond in the same degree to reality. Rather than tolerance, we should speak of *intellectual honesty*. We should make a sincere effort to understand the ideas of others, see where they are coming from, get inside their thought, and present it accurately. This intellectual honesty will prevent us from academic laziness, straw-man arguments, labeling, name-calling, or dishonest neglect to tell the whole story.

In the area of politics, "tolerance" could be accurately applied, though "compromise" would be a better term. Politics are concerned with very concrete applications of true human and social good in particular historical, geographic, economic, technological and cultural contexts. Though the principles are the same, the variety of circumstances makes possible many acceptable policies and solutions. Tolerance, both in a positive and negative sense, plays a key role in politics. But this tolerance is not based on a lack of truth – as if politics could cancel out truth – but on the application of truth and unchanging principles to many varied circumstances.

Over the past forty years, tolerance has become increasingly the most important virtue in all public and private relations, but an idea of tolerance cut off from truth leads us into very dangerous waters, as we shall soon see.

The rise of relativism in Western society – sown in philosophical ideas of the Enlightenment, sprouting from changes in pluralism and the democratic system, full grown in twisted concepts of peace, equality, freedom and tolerance – give us good reason to worry for the future, since the rejection of truth was at the core of every totalitarian regime of the past century.

RESET

Confused by these rapid shifts in the contents of public discourse, and faced with the instabilities of an increasingly relativistic operating system, many people look for a reset.

In our society's new relativist operating system, anyone running in realism is scorned by the advocates of tolerance and political correctness. Jeff's case – like so many others in similar situations – is eloquent witness to that. Standing up for principles is out of style. In fact, it seems like the *only* acceptable principle is that there are no unchanging principles. And you are free to think what you want… as long as it's what everyone else thinks.

This is an erosion of our authentic freedom. We cannot speak our mind freely anymore, and increasingly it seems that we live under the tyranny of laws designed to protect special interests. The real danger that faces our society is not that of terrorist attacks or the imposition of a fundamentalist Islamic theocracy, but rather what the British scholar G.K. Chesterton once wrote, "Our chief peril is not attack; it is decay."

What we ought to fear – whether we consider ourselves liberal or conservative – is a parody and perversion of democracy, far from the ideal of our founders and from the authentic basis of freedom and equality. While it keeps the external trappings of democracy – elections, polling, public debates, law-making, and free market – the heart has been ripped out. What is *true*, what is best for the country, what is good for each citizen according to human nature is subordinated to the selfish interests of those squabbling to be king of the hill.

We ought to fear what John Stuart Mill called the

"tyranny of democracy" where "the body is left free, and the soul is enslaved" [9] to public opinion. We ought to fear a society in which our citizens are not capable of sound reasoning and can be manipulated by slogans and craftily orchestrated propaganda campaigns. We ought to fear losing our internal freedom to a "what everyone thinks" that shuts down rational thought, closes off discussion, and demands a total obedience beyond the external coercion of the totalitarian regimes. When power is separated from truth, we should indeed begin to tremble. We ought to fear a "dictatorship of relativism"[10] that doesn't recognize anything as absolute, and leaves personal whims or greater power as the only arbiters of right and wrong.

Yet, aren't we still free?

You are still free to express your opinion... as long as it fits the mold of society's accepted orthodoxy: relativism. One opinion is as good as another; after all, according to the dogma of relativism all ideas are equally true, even when contradictory. If you have a new idea – no matter how wacky it might be – go ahead and throw it into the pluralistic pot. Newcomers always welcome.

But if you pretend to have an idea that is better than all the others, or perhaps a "truth" that excludes other's ideas, then *anathema sit*. In the tyranny of political correctness, tolerance is the first principle, the only fundamental truth. To claim any other universal truth, any idea that is better than others... that is the only sin left. "Repressive," "narrow-minded," "outdated," or "racist/sexist/homophobic" you might be called; or if someone wanted to be really nasty, "fundamentalist."

Fundamentalist. With this one word we can string together Islamic suicide bombers and right wing religious fanatics, moral absolutists and Bible thumpers. Since 9/11 the word "fundamentalist" has become even more a part of our everyday vocabulary.

You could get away with calling someone a dogmatist or a fascist or a marxist or even a disestablishmentarian (no one seems to know what these old insults mean anymore), but to call someone a "fundamentalist" is the modern epithet at which politicians cringe and businessmen call their lawyers: no one wants to hear *that* attached to them. Who wants to be associated with narrow-minded bigots?

But even though we use a word, it isn't always clear what we mean by it. Try defining "fundamentalism." Set the book down for a second and explain to someone what it is. Not as easy as you thought? A bit confused? Having a hard time putting into words your thoughts?

Our natural reaction to "fundamentalism" is negative. It conjures up pictures of frenzied preaching, Arab mobs, and dictatorial repressions. If I label someone a "fundamentalist," you will judge them negatively. You'll have associated them with radical actions and ideas. And the reality? Maybe the person isn't like that at all? What if that "fundamentalist" I introduced you to is your own grandma, the same one who loves to bake cookies and bottle jam and couldn't hurt a fly.

So what exactly is fundamentalism?

As a first attempt to respond to this question, let's take a look at how the popular press would perhaps define a fundamentalist Christian:

- ☐ Goes to church every Sunday
- ☐ Tithes 10 percent
- ☐ Waits until marriage to have sex and remains faithful

to his/her spouse
- Prays three times a day
- Sends children to private school that teaches full observance of the Ten Commandments
- Believes that truth is more important than tolerance

These are considered "radical," unacceptable actions. Turning the tables, let's say a critic of the above-mentioned fundamentalist exhibits the following characteristics:

- Visits the herbal health food store every Saturday
- Writes regular checks to Greenpeace and Save the Whales
- Believes it is important to have sexual relations with a wide range of diverse partners to fully experience life
- Attends aerobics class five days a week
- Sends children to inner city school where they will be exposed to wide range of moral dilemmas and will have to learn how to make decisions
- Believes that tolerance is more important than truth

Is this any less a collection of fundamental doctrines? Try telling a Greenpeacer – just for laughs – that you think mass clearing of old-growth forests for paper is fine, and see what happens. Every person lives with fundamental principles, whether they are a convinced Christian or an atheist anarchist. They may not agree on those principles, but there is no doubt that they hold them. Even those who claim to have none – the pure relativists – are implicitly asserting the principle that there are no principles. In this sense, every person is a "fundamentalist."

But this is getting us nowhere. "Fundamentalist" in modern language is really no more than a nasty insult. The tag is slapped on precisely because the name-caller wants to provoke the negative reaction evoked by the name. What use is such an ambiguous label?

Yet before we give up on the term, let's make a second attempt to clarify our ideas on fundamentalism. A brief look at its historical origins can shed light upon this modern phenomenon.

The Birth of Fundamentalism

In the 1890s, in response to secularization and critical scholarship of the Bible, many Christians felt the need to affirm and defend the basics of their faith. Acting on this need, several prominent Protestant theologians gathered at the Princeton Theological Seminary to formulate the "Princeton theology." Between 1909 and 1915, Milton and Lyman Stewart underwrote the printing of a twelve-book series on *The Fundamentals*. Three million copies were disseminated to pastors, theology students, and the faithful from many different Protestant denominations that quickly identified themselves with the new formulations.

The name "fundamentalism" was born on July 1, 1920. On that day, Curtis Lee Law wrote an editorial in the *Watchman-Examiner* of New York on the new religious movement arising within Protestant Christianity. Law coined the term "fundamentalists" for these Christians "who mean to do battle for the fundamentals."

Though these "fundamentals" were not strictly uniform, most within the movement agreed on five basics: 1) the inspiration and infallibility of Scripture, 2) the deity of Jesus

Christ, 3) the substitutionary atonement of his death, 4) his literal resurrection from the dead, 5) and his literal return at the Second Coming.[11]

Since the 1920s, the fundamentalist movement has continued to grow and attract new adherents. No organized church structure or denomination exists; fundamentalism is just a loose association of Christians who adhere to these fundamentals. They share other common elements, especially their commitment to evangelism (the conviction that they hold the truth and must spread it), Puritanism (adherence to a strict moral code), and literal interpretation of the Bible as God's revealed word to man.

Displays of emotion and dramatic conversions are encouraged in some fundamentalist congregations, leading many of their detractors to label fundamentalists as feeble-minded, low class, or irrational. But such is not necessarily the case. Fundamentalist congregations draw their followers from all social classes, and although their reasons are not always well founded, they do have firm convictions and doctrinal sources to back up their theological positions.

The fundamentalists were nonetheless branded as backwards, religious fanatics by more progressive religious and cultural leaders who oftentimes secretly – to put it bluntly – considered themselves culturally superior to these fellow Christians. Though they cloaked their arguments in intellectual jargon, their own naked orthodoxy – beneath all the layers – was oftentimes just another "fundamentalist" position.

Despite this ambiguity, the fundamentalist label stuck because it explained well the reality of these Christians who insisted on the fundamentals of their faith. It was not considered an insult, but a legitimate title for the theological position they held.

Language, however, is alive and the meaning of words changes with time. The original meaning of "fundamentalist" mutated quickly: the first twist used it as a derogatory label to indicate doctrinal rigidity, then expanded with time to include any religiously minded person who practiced what they preached. What began as a term for a movement within American Protestantism was then applied to other Christians, Catholics, Jews, and even Muslims. During the decade of the 1990s, with the upsurge of radicalized forms of Islam and then into the new millennium with the tragedy of 9/11, the term has been increasingly used for radical elements within Islam.

With this evolution in meaning, what does fundamentalism really mean anymore? And what possible use is a term indiscriminately applied to label Islamic suicide bombers, Bible thumpers, and today's relativists? The fundamentals each type advocates are mutually exclusive, with the relativist even insisting, incredibly, that he has *no* fundamentals – with one exception: that there are no fundamentals.

Though our common notion – that fundamentalists are religious fanatics – seems clear-cut, in reality it is misleading. Due to the evolution of language, a fundamentalist today is no longer confined just to the traditional religious sphere. In fact, the newest forms of fundamentalism are really quite far from any classical religion, and branch into fields previously occupied by ideology. Our historical review and common notions have stirred around our ideas, and now it is time for a definition.

A Definition and an Explanation

Ideology could be defined as rigid adherence to narrow concepts linked to the desire to reshape reality, often by force, to fit a preconceived worldview without regard for the humanity of the persons being coerced. Fundamentalism – in its modern sense – adds only one simple notion to this definition: the religious motive.

The more complex our society becomes, the more people look for simple answers to life's questions. The more hectic daily life is, the more we seek a release from the rat race. Both ideology and fundamentalism offer just such an escape hatch. One radical act of faith – whether in the Book, the Guru, or the Prophet – solves all the woes of life. Have a problem? Just consult the Book. Not sure what to make of this contradiction? Find out what the Guru has to say and believe. Wondering what to make of the dynamics of world history? Ask Stalin or consult Mao's little red book. Is the planet an awful mess of questions and no satisfying answers? Just assert there are no answers and indulge yourself.

Simplicity is beautiful. This is what makes fundamentalism so attractive. There are no complicated dogmas to learn, no sophisticated reasoning, just plain black and white answers to everything. God or Big Brother speaks; man obeys. The Qur'an declares non-Islams to be infidels, so I treat them as such. The Bible says, "Call no man your father," so I scrupulously avoid using that word for my "dad" or any religious leader. Truth does not exist, so I debauch myself and my acquaintances. Ideology of whatever stripe brings a certain feeling of peace, because it is so *clear* and has a ready reply to even the most complex problems.

However, this simplicity often fails to satisfy fully our

human desires. The responses of the fundamentalist to many of the deeper questions about life leave us wondering if they have really understood them. The answers are, consequently, so very superficial; sometimes just a string of Bible verses or Maoist or Nietzschean aphorisms. These kinds of answers tell us the "what," but not the "why." And when they answer the "why," the foundations often seem shaky at best.

But just try to tell an ideologue this. In order to affirm his beliefs, he must resort to some proof, some confirmation. But oftentimes the first proof – and the second and the third – are not so clear to the fundamentalist's interlocutors—to us, in other words. Reality and the facts suggest to us that the ideologue might be mistaken. So what is his reaction, when we call him on possibly getting the real really wrong?

Here we encounter the ugly tail of ideologies: irrationality and abuse in several forms – and, as often as not in this relativistic age, from those who profess "reason" and "reasonableness" as gods. Confronted with facts that contradict their beliefs, the ideologue rejects the facts outright and turns to attack the questioner – often with considerable violence. Or he applies tortuous cleverness in order to twist the data to his present purpose.

Rejecting Reality

Reasons can be found for believing in anything. Take the most ridiculous example you want and you will find someone believing it or finding reasons for it. Societies for the advancement of trade treaties with extraterrestrials, foundations to save the fire ants of lower Bohemia, and collectors clubs of the cigarette butts of Elvis Presley will all find some followers

who discover meaning for their lives in such odd activities
– and can give you many "reasons" for their beliefs.

Erich von Daniken, author of *Chariot of the Gods* and
more than two-dozen "true-life" accounts of alien visitation,
has written books that have sold nearly 60 million copies. He
also served three years in jail for tax evasion and spent the
past thirty years trying to convince the world that famous ancient structures were built by creatures from another world.

Scientists have heaped contempt on the Swiss author and
repudiated virtually every claim he has made. Historian Brian Fagan described von Daniken's book *Arrival of the Gods*
as "a grotesque parody" of scientific inquiry devoid of intellectual credibility or literary merit. "This is not science; Erich
von Daniken has raised his astronaut theories to the status of
a cult, with himself as the Great Prophet."[12]

But the criticism hasn't bothered von Daniken much.
In fact, the free publicity has raised enough interest that
major companies like Coca-Cola and Swatch have funded
the construction of the 55 million dollar "extraterrestrial"
theme park in Switzerland. Von Daniken's Mystery Park
– containing recreations of major "extraterrestrial works"
that include Stonehenge, the Pyramids of Egypt, the Ma-
yan temples, and others – opened to visitors in the spring
of 2003 at a cost of twenty dollars a head.

Reasons can be found for the silliest ideas, which the
above certainly are, and these are pretty harmless. But
some ideologues are not so harmless, even though in their
logic they can remind one of silly children. Deaf to reason, closed off to rational argument, they prefer the simplicity of absolute statements and the sense of comfort
and stability they provide. They reject complicating evi-

dence at hand in favor of a satisfying system of myopic interpretation.

Take a modern reductionism of traditional religion, for example. Sigmund Freud, the father of modern psychology, used a new form of ideological cogitation to demonstrate that anyone who believes in any religion at all suffers from neurosis. As he recorded in his 1907 work *Obsessive Behavior and Religious Practices,* he had observed in a mental hospital that many of the patients suffered from what we now call obsessive-compulsive disorders: they would often repeat actions over and over, without knowing why they did so or sometimes even what they were doing. One woman felt she had to wash her hands every five minutes. When asked why she offered no reason, just a blank stare as if it were the most bizarre question she had ever heard. For her it was obvious; for those around her it was lunacy. She continued with her rite of hand washing.

Freud took this fact and compared it to religious acts. Since religion seems to be made up of rites, and most of those involved do not really know what they are doing in those rites, and, furthermore, these are repeated over and over, Freud concluded that religion is a type of universal neurosis.

He later compared religion to illusion. For Freud, an illusion is a belief that is motivated by a strong desire disconnected from reality. This desire can become so strong that it even creates its own reality – like children at play who create dragons that they slash with their sword from their mounted steed. Freud claimed to show that the existence of God is so strong a desire that we create for ourselves this reality of God. Religion is, therefore, for Freud, just a flight of fancy, a fiction of our own imagination.

Freud's pseudoscientific conclusions about religion tell us a lot more about his own psychological condition than about the nonexistence of God. To focus on a narrow external aspect of religion as Freud does, and then proceed to a universal judgement, is no different from the logical fallacy that leads to the conclusion that cars are mammals. All mammals release carbon dioxide when they exhale; cars release carbon dioxide; therefore, cars are mammals. Neither conclusion is valid.

That said, we should do justice to Freud's study of religion by pointing out that he did manage to highlight the fact that religious believers can often fall into very irrational behavior. As in the case of the Scopes Monkey Trial (evolution versus creation), or that of Galileo (sun at the center of the universe), believers are often unwilling to adapt their present understanding of biblical truth to scientific facts. Conversely, scientists who automatically write off any reality that cannot be measured or counted are no less irrational.

What we like to call Islamic "fundamentalists" often exhibit this kind of irrational behavior – a barefaced rejection of the facts. During the period of Ramadan in Egypt at the close of 2002, state-run television ran a series, *Horseman Without a Horse*, drawn from the *Protocols of the Elders of Zion*, a book in which Jews plot to take over the world. The book is a nineteenth century forgery created by anti-Semites to discredit the Jews, but the material was used by Nazi Germany and other European governments in the propaganda campaigns that culminated with the extermination of six million Jews during World War II.

When a spokesman from the U.S. State Department complained about the series, noting the false basis and distorted facts, Egyptian authorities reacted angrily. An editorial in the government's daily newspaper, *Al-Akhbar*, said Egypt was the victim of "intellectual terrorism" perpetrated by Israel and its supporters. It accused the United States of infringing on Egypt's freedom of expression, which, it pointed out, is one of the pillars of democracy.

Twisting Reality

To the human mind that naturally seeks the truth, the mere rejection of reality is rarely satisfying. It is much more appealing to "interpret" the facts, even when that means going against the facts. By finding rational justification for their irrational decisions, they can ease their conscience and even feel good about their brilliant intelligence. Twisting or reinterpreting facts is often a defense mechanism, but it can also be a deliberate deception either for oneself or for others.

Dispensationalism[13] is a clear example. As a system of theology within fundamentalist Protestantism, dispensationalism has had many proponents and followers since the 1830s, but it really gained in popularity with Hal Lindsey's book *The Late Great Planet Earth* which has sold 40 million copies since the 1970s. Throughout the 1990s and into the first years of the new millennium, the immensely popular *Left Behind* series of books has sold many more millions, thrilling readers with stories of end-of-the-world scenarios. The proponents of these ideas interpret the Bible, and especially the book of Revelation, in light of current events, claiming to have the *true* knowledge about when the world will end and how to prepare for it. They have gone so far as to predict the precise date of that end...repeatedly. And when one date passes and the world continues on, they find a way to reinterpret the facts. They propose a new date, claiming confidently that *this* time they will be right.

It does not seem to cross their minds that maybe their system is wrong; that perhaps their calculations are off because there are some fundamental problems with their fundamentalism. Yet here lies the problem. As long as they remain firmly convinced of their system, no arguments or facts can contradict them. They can always reject the evidence or interpret it some other way.

That seems to be the case in present-day Russia also. "If you repeat a lie enough times, it becomes true," was a favorite adage of the communist propaganda leaders in the former Soviet Union, and though the Soviet system may be gone, Russia still bears a heavy legacy of fact twisting, false history, and turning a deaf ear to the voice of reality.[14]

In the early 1990s, a movement began gathering momentum within the Russian Orthodox Church to canonize Rasputin and Ivan the Terrible, two of the most brutal figures in Russia's history. It began with a series of pamphlets and books, and then several newspapers and Internet sites began backing up the campaign. The movement attracted a growing number of adherents, particularly in the Russian countryside.

The campaign, repeatedly condemned by Orthodox officials as contrary to historical facts and as a distortion of the faith, is spearheaded by a growing revisionist movement in the church that shows more interest in new ideas than in actual history. It believes that "Grigori Rasputin, a notoriously dissolute Siberian monk who was murdered by two royalists in 1916 because of his growing influence over Empress Alexandra, was the victim of a Jewish conspiracy."[15]

The movement also defends Ivan the Terrible, who murdered hundreds of priests and even his own son, claiming that he was a "deeply religious and humble man who showed great mercy to his enemies."[16]

In an official statement issued in 2001, Patriarch Alexy II, head of the Russian Orthodox Church stated: "This is madness. What believer would want to stay in a Church that equally venerates murderers and martyrs, lechers and saints?"

Konstantin Dushenov, the editor of *Rus Pravoslavnaya*, a St. Petersburg newspaper backing the campaign, said: "Rasputin was a good man whose reputation was destroyed by his political opponents. We want to discuss this with the heads of the Church, but all they will ever say is that Rasputin was a womanizer and Ivan the Terrible a murderer. There are already many icons of them and there is even an icon of Ivan the Terrible in the Kremlin. The Church is furious only because we belong to a movement that is outside its control."[17]

If you repeat a lie enough times, it becomes "true." It seems some Russians, ignoring their church leaders and historical facts, would rather believe the lie than the truth.

Though neither Russians nor communists, leaders of the Church of Jesus Christ of Latter Day Saints – more generally known as the Mormons – have often used similar twists of the facts and creative additions to history to justify their religion.

In September of 2002, Thomas Murphy, a Mormon college professor in suburban Seattle, WA, discovered some facts. Using genetic science he proved that American Indians did not come from ancient Israel, contrary to a basic part of

the history laid out in the Book of Mormon. When he published his findings in an essay, local Mormon elders ordered
him to recant the academic article.

He refused, and a disciplinary hearing was set for that
weekend at which he says he expected them to order him
excommunicated from Mormonism. At the last moment,
however, the elders postponed the hearing. Negative publicity and pressure from many of Mr. Murphy's supporters
counseled against raising any more dust.

The Murphy case is not by any means isolated. Excommunication is a threat leveled – and carried out – against
many scholars who "don't believe the way they want [them]
to believe." In another recent Mormon expulsion, an Egyp-
tologist in California faced excommunication proceedings for
posting an essay online saying Joseph Smith committed an
error in translating the Book of Mormon. The scholar wrote
that in Smith's nineteenth century translation of an "ancient
Egyptian text," he wrote incorrectly that a certain character
stood for the Jewish patriarch Abraham, when it was really
just the equivalent of the letter "w."[18]

Joseph Smith, the founder of Mormonism, based his new
religion on the claim that God appeared to him and then
later sent the angel Moroni with the scriptures. He "said that
he received the record, written on gold plates in 'reformed
Egyptian' a language that no one but he could understand.
He was also told not to show these gold plates to anyone, but
that some time later a few selected people would be given the
privilege to view them."

Unfortunately for posterity – and for anyone who might
want to check that translation – Joseph "translated the plates,
published the material as the *Book of Mormon* and then gave

the gold plates back to the angel Moroni."[19]

Telling a story is easy; keeping track of your story afterwards is the hard part. It seems Joseph Smith's memory was not quite as strong as his imagination. In 1842, he claimed for the first time that twenty-two years earlier, in 1820, he had a visit from God the Father and his Son, Jesus Christ. He said that they told him that all churches were wrong and were an abomination to God and that he should not join any of them.

But, already showing signs of a weak memory, Joseph disobeyed God's command and sought membership in the Methodist Church, where his wife was a member. He was expelled in 1828, as historical records show, because of his belief in magic and also because of his "money-digging activities."[20]

Joseph couldn't quite keep his story straight, and three official versions of his vision experience exist. Though the stories contradict each other on several points, this did not seem to slow down Joseph Smith, nor the continued growth of Mormonism to this day. Mormon leaders have shown amazing flexibility in adapting history and facts to their beliefs, or of excommunicating those who "falter in their faith."

When the facts don't fit the faith, religious ideologues opt for the faith, even if they have to twist or hide the facts. Such was the case with members of a Japanese cult – the Panawave Laboratory – who were busy draping trees and buildings in white sheets in May of 2003, awaiting Armageddon. They believed that white would deflect the electromagnetic waves that were supposedly destroying the world and the health of their leader Yuko Chino. According to her, the approach of a tenth planet would trigger the destruction of the earth on

May 15, though as the deadline passed by without the planet's appearance, a spokesman for the cult said the apocalypse had been postponed until the next Thursday.[21]

Interest in Panawave rose dramatically when it emerged the cult had planned to capture a bearded seal, which became the darling of the nation after it began appearing in rivers around Tokyo during 2002. The cult has argued that Tama-chan, or Dear Little Tama, as the seal was known, was led thousands of miles from her natural habitat by electromagnetic waves to save the world.

Off the wall cults are not the exclusive property of the Japanese; the United States has had its fair share of outlandish religious groups. Images of David Koresh and the flames roasting him and his followers alive in Waco, Texas in 1993 are firmly etched in the American mind. The history of this religious cult is a prime example of tendency toward radical behavior in fundamentalism. Koresh and his followers traced their history back to the Protestant Reformation, claiming Martin Luther as the initiator of a journey toward the fullness of truth. Luther was succeeded by Knox, Wesley, Campbell, Miller, then the Seventh-day Adventists, then the Davidian Adventists, and finally the Branch Davidians. The particular cult of the Branch Davidians, of which David Koresh was the prophet, believed they were God's chosen people, especially set aside for the last days before the end of the world. An offshoot of the Seventh-day Adventists, they believed God sent messages to them through five prophets: Ellen White, Victor Houteff, Ben Roden, Lois Roden, and finally David Koresh.[22]

The Branch Davidian view of doctrine is dynamic and evolutionary - they are constantly expecting "New Light" to be shown by God to his people. The prophets are the means by which God reveals New Light, but this is always by drawing out the "real" meaning of texts from the Bible. Hence a prophet does not simply announce a new teaching, it always has to be shown to be what the Bible has taught all along, but people have been "blinded" to.

"True Believers" are not those who are morally good - Branch Davidians claim that the Bible teaches that no one can be perfect - but those who believe "Present Truth" (the latest teachings from God). It is by constantly following the new teachings from God that the believer will be saved.

This flexibility in doctrine and a selective interpretation of history are fertile ground for radical measures... after all, something has to firm up the flimsy foundations. Koresh's personal charisma provided that solid ground, attracting followers who gradually developed dependence on him, undermining their critical facilities and creating a blind acceptance of everything he taught and claimed. Individuals didn't change overnight, but slowly evolved from individuals seeking a healthy and charitable Christian life to those capable of overlooking child abuse, sexual exploitation, and violence to please a leader and adhere to his doctrine.

Koresh claimed an adolescent girl as a wife. He then – like religious leaders Joseph Smith and Jim Jones – moved on to bigamy, polygamy, ultimately declaring the marriages of his followers a sin and all women as his. One cannot but be struck by the almost cookie-cutter mold from which the most destructive cult leaders tend to come and the similar power-hungry, unethical, immoral choices they make, unleashing their perversions on their followers and *creating doctrines to justify their own abusive behavior.*

What about other religious movements like Islam, so

readily associated with fundamentalist terrorism? To be a Muslim is to accept the revelation about God – Allah – received and passed down to man through his last and greatest prophet, Mohammed, a merchant from Mecca in what is now Saudi Arabia.

According to revelations from the angel Gabriel – which Mohammed claimed to receive for about twenty years until his death by poisoning in 632 – God is one (not Triune, thus rejecting the Christian belief in the Trinity). Mohammed was purportedly God's chosen messenger to bring the true religion to mankind and he began that mission by writing the Qur'an and unleashing a campaign of military conquest that, within 100 years of his death had subdued much of the civilized world.

You know a man by his actions, and Mohammed is no exception. On one occasion, the prophet and his companions conquered a neighboring Jewish village and began searching for the hidden treasure which the villagers had buried. The prophet took one of the captives and threatened him with torture and mutilation if he did not reveal the treasure's location. Upon his refusal, "The apostle gave orders to al-Zubayr b. al-Awwam, 'Torture him until you extract what he has,' so he kindled a fire with flint and steel on his chest until he was nearly dead. Then the apostle delivered him to Mohammed b. Maslama and he struck off his head."[23]

Perhaps this was just one isolated event? It seems not. Even the most superficial reading of an authentic biography of Mohammed – such as that written by Ibn Ishaq around 773 A.D. – reveal a man who could be "both compassionate and cruel," vindictive, ordering assassinations, orchestrating massacres, and utilizing torture.

This violent nature was not limited to actions or to the personal life of the prophet; it is just as prevalent in the *doctrine*. There are five basic tenets, or "pillars," in Islam that taken in themselves are quite positive:

1. Affirming there is only one God and Mohammed as his prophet
2. Praying five times a day
3. Giving alms
4. Fasting from dawn to dusk during Ramadan (the lunar month during which the Qur'an was allegedly revealed to Mohammed)
5. Performing the "hajj," the pilgrimage to Mecca

To these positive religious practices, some believers add a sixth, that of *jihad,* the holy war to spread the true faith. The concept of *jihad* is tied to another concept – *Shari'a* (Islamic law). Many of the world's more than forty majority-Muslim countries have embraced Shari'a, and those that have not are under pressure to do so. For example, over the past decade in Algeria, some 100,000 Muslims have been killed directly or indirectly by militant Muslims. Why? These fundamentalist Muslims want political control of the nation. This is a growing trend in the Islamic world – even though it is certainly not shared by all Muslims.

In peace-loving societies such violent doctrine doesn't go down well, so it is no wonder that there are new interpretations of Islam in the western world. These revisionists highlight the religious tolerance passages in the Qur'an and assure the world that Islam is a "peace-loving" religion.

However, revisionist efforts cannot change the actual text

of the Qur'an. Over 100 passages in the Muslim scriptures speak of using violence to propagate the faith, vengeance, and brutality with unbelievers. Take for example the following passages:

- (Qur'an 47:4) "Therefore, when ye meet the unbelievers, smite at their necks, at length when ye have thoroughly subdued them, bind a bond firmly (on them) ... but if it had been God's will, he could certainly have exacted retribution from them (himself), but (he lets you fight) in order to test you, some with others. But those who are slain in the way of God, he will never let their deeds be lost."
- (Qur'an 98:6) "The People of the Book [Jews and Christians] and the Pagans will burn forever in the Fire of Hell. They are the vilest of all creatures."
- (Qur'an 48:29) "Those who follow Mohammed are merciless for the unbelievers but kind to each other."
- Qur'an (60:4) "Enmity and hatred will reign between us until ye believe in Allah alone."
- Qur'an (8:39) (2:193) "Make war on them until idolatry does not exist any longer and Allah's religion reigns universally."
- Qur'an (9:123) "Fight the unbelievers in your surroundings, and let them find harshness in you."
- Qur'an (9:5) "Kill the unbelievers wherever you find them, capture and besiege them and prepare for them every kind of ambush."

Fireworks erupt when fundamentalists have the gumption to stick to the letter of the Qur'an. On June 6, 2003, the imam of Rome's Great Mosque, Abdel-Samie Mahmoud Ibrahim Moussa, urged the faithful to mobilize to "ensure the victory of the nation of Islam everywhere in the world" and urging the faithful to "destroy the enemies of Islam."[24] Other Islamic leaders throughout Italy and Europe reacted immediately, distancing themselves from the Egyptian preacher, and the Islamic Cultural Center of Rome quickly ousted the imam.

While a great many Muslims would not approve of the violence perpetrated in the name of their religion, and westernized mollifications of doctrine strive to make Islam more tolerant and open to the world, literal readings of Islamic scripture continue to foster attitudes of violence and oppression. "Violence in Islam, whether in the form of terrorism, or the persecution of Christians and other minorities in the Muslim world, or capital punishment for an individual who turns away from Islam or death threats on Salman Rushdie for allegedly insulting the prophet Mohammed, are not simply some isolated incidents or aberrations from the true and peaceful religion of Islam. Such violence in fact goes to the very roots of Islam as found in the Qur'an and the actions and teachings of the prophet of Islam himself."[25]

A balanced study of the prophet and doctrine of Islam reveal that when preaching and reasoning fail to convert, violence, coercion, and imposition of the "truth" are not only justified but even *mandated*.

Does history perhaps reveal another story or a kinder face of Islam? On the contrary.

"The remarkable speed of [Islam's] religious expansion can be attributed to the fact that it was accomplished primarily through military conquest. Mohammed drew Arabs of the Arabian Peninsula to Islam by his forceful personality, the promise of salvation for those who died fighting for Islam, and the lure of fortune for those who succeeded in conquest. The caravan raids of the early years of Islam soon became full-scale wars, and empires and nations bowed to the power of this new religious, military, political, economic, and social phenomenon."[26]

The Islamic Cultural Center in Tempe, Arizona, would beg to differ. In a pamphlet entitled *The Basics of Islam at a Glance*, we read: "There is no historical proof that Islam was 'spread by the sword.' Even non-Muslim scholars now admit that this is nothing more than a vicious myth which cannot be substantiated by historical fact."

If you don't examine the facts you won't find anything; if you are ignorant of history you can pretend that Islam did not spread primarily through military force. But if one examines the facts without prejudice, he'll find what an honest Muslim would say: "Islam was spread by proof and evidence, in the case of those who listened to the message and responded to it. And it was spread by *strength and the sword* [emphasis added] in the case of those who stubbornly resisted, until they had no choice and had to submit to the new reality."[27]

We are not engaging in polemics when we point out the prevalence of violence throughout the foundations and the subsequent history of Islam. We are only pointing out the teachings in the original and authoritative sources of Islam. It is essential for people to know that underneath all the political, social and cultural causes for the rise of violence among Muslims, there is a *religious* foundation for violence deeply embedded within the very worldview of Islam.

"There are millions of peace-loving Muslims in the world today, but Islam is unique among the world's religions in having a broad and highly developed theology, law, and tradition mandating violence against nonbelievers. This is a fact that is borne out by all the schools of Islamic jurisprudence."[28]

Islam is more than a religion. It is a political ideology with the answer to every aspect of personal, family, and social life. While peaceful interpretations of Islam exist, they are often a result of adaptation to western society, not of fidelity to the Islamic scripture and historical precedent. Islam is a totalitarian ideology providing the whole package of truth: religion, culture, and government. And is it "truth" not only for the Muslim, but for all; he who does not accept it by argument must accept it by force and imposition.

That is precisely why the facts must often be doctored. In Yemen, for example, Sheikh Abdul Majeed al-Zindani – mentor of Osama bin Laden – has molded many of the facts of current events to fit the goals of Islamicist ideology. He leads the Iman University in Sanaa, a powder keg of radical ideology and activity. There, he sermonizes to some 5,000 students, convinces them to hate the West, and justifies terrorist attacks. Zindani has released cassette tapes of his rhetoric, in which he maintains that President Bush and Jews conspired together to create September 11. Ridiculous as it may sound and as contrary to the facts as it may be, Zindani continues to affirm that the September 11 attacks were a CIA plot.

In an article in the *National Review,* Josh Devon comments that "Saudi Arabia has further legitimized Zindani, treating him as a respected scholar. The Al-Haramain Foundation, a large Saudi charity whose assets have been frozen in two countries for terrorist activities, chose Zindani to spearhead its 'It-Is-Truth' Internet campaign. The campaign seeks to prove that the Qur'an presaged all of mankind's scientific knowledge, from the Big Bang to gestation."[29]

That will be a challenging intellectual task, but given Zindani's success in explaining September 11 we can be confident in the success of his "truth" campaign.

An Antidote to Ideology?

Yet all these examples of religious nuttiness leave us a problem, indeed a very serious problem. We want securities in life; that is why the rise of varied forms of fundamentalism – life systems based on clear and unwavering concepts – and their rapid diffusion in modern society should come as no great surprise. Men and women want to know the *why* of life, the meaning of existence, the purpose of our life; we seek a knowledge that is sure and certain and that will not be deceived. All men seek to know, and not just *"know-how,"* but the real thing, the *"know-why."*

In other words, all men and women are religious. We seek to know, and the natural object of this desire is truth. "I have met many people who wanted to deceive, but never anyone who wanted to let themselves be deceived," affirmed Augustine of Hippo. This search for truth, for ultimate meaning, springs up naturally from what we are as human beings. We are naturally religious. That is why every authentic religion has recognized that "God has placed in the human heart a desire to know the truth – in a word, to know himself – so that, by knowing and loving God, men and women may also come to the fullness of truth about themselves."[30] Man is, without a doubt, a religious creature.

In our search for the *know-why*, "faith and reason are like two wings on which the human spirit rises to the contemplation of truth."[31] Faith is not contrary to reason, but *blind* faith is. True faith is not blind; it is not darkness or a "leap into the unknown." True faith is light, certainty, security. It is not contrary to reason and it is not equal to reason – it is above reason. Faith is super-rational, but also fully in accord with reason. It doesn't close the mind, but rather opens it to its highest and best use.

Blind faith, absolute trust in someone or something that does not merit such totality or that contradicts reason– though often comforting or comfortable – cannot fully satisfy our natural desire for truth. We can make an act of blind faith, but our reason keeps whispering in the background, "Are you sure it is true?"

Religious and cult leaders like those cited above are not alone in the irrational and radical measures employed to get their way. The human heart is the same everywhere. The same manipulative tactics are followed by politicians and rulers whose power is not checked by morality or external force.

Take for example the greed of King Philip the Fair with the Knights Templar in medieval France. The Knights Templar was a religious order that had grown rich during the crusades through an early form of international banking. Philip, involved in expensive military campaigns, had despoiled the Jews and Lombards of France to finance his schemes and already owed money to the order. Financing had to be found somewhere, and the Templars were the only source of wealth left open to his greed. In 1307 Philip arrested all the Templars in France and seized the Order's goods and possessions, claiming that members had confessed to crimes of heresy and homosexuality. Through imprisonment, public executions, and the harshest of medieval tortures he was able to extract "confessions" of guilt. Although these were later renounced when the torturer's knife was withdrawn from the throat, Philip ignored the recantations, relied on circumstantial evidence, bullied through the legal process, executed the chief members of the order, and appropriated to himself all their lands and wealth.

Without a doubt the radical measures of Philip the Fair have "some relevance to the world of the late twentieth century [where] so many of whose people have been, and continue to be, oppressed by regimes which use terror and torture to enforce conformity of thought and action."[32] The tens of millions lying in common graves across the Russian steppe, into the Chinese heartland, and down through the Vietnam peninsula bear silent witness to the enormous barbarity of secular ideologues.

Though the unfounded rationalizations of ideologues and fundamentalists can never fully satiate our desire to know, they certainly have succeeded in causing unprecedented havoc in the twentieth century. Any thinking person would stop to ask themselves the question: Is man's search for truth the cause of our problems? Many modern thinkers would argue that this religious tendency – or at the very least the fundamentalist versions – is indeed the problem.

As the Bangladeshi writer and secular humanist Taslima Nasrin wrote, "I don't find any difference between Islam and Islamic fundamentalists. I believe religion is the root, and from the root fundamentalism grows as a poisonous stem. If we remove fundamentalism and keep religion, then one day or another fundamentalism will grow again."[33] For her, religion itself is the problem, not fundamentalism. "Religion is now the first obstacle... Religion pulls human beings backwards; it goes against science and progressiveness. Religion engulfs people with a fear of the supernatural. It bars people from laughing and never allows people to exercise their choice."[34]

Taslima may be on to something here and her comments perhaps could apply to Islam, the religion she knows best. Her conclusion, however, is not necessarily valid for other religions either historically or logically. In fact, when we survey recent history, we find that the most radical and coercive measures had nothing to do with religious belief, but rather with "religious" atheism.

Alexander Solzhenitsyn – well versed in the communist ideology that devoured his Russian nation – warned, "to the human being who has faith in some force that holds dominion over all of us, and who is therefore conscious of his own limitations, power is not necessarily fatal. For those, however, who are unaware of any higher sphere, it is a deadly poison. For them there is no antidote."[35] In fact, fundamentalism is always rooted in some kind of religious belief, whether it is a belief in God, *or a belief that there is no God*.

Indeed, atheism seems more prone to fundamentalism than theism. "A widespread prejudice…is that secular creeds depend on reason while religions depend on faith. Both halves of the prejudice are mistaken. Many of the creeds conventionally called 'religions' give a very high place to reason indeed. Likewise, many of the creeds conventionally called 'secular' expect blind acceptance of dogma. It begins to look as though so-called secular creeds are nothing other than incomplete religions – when not, indeed, complete."[36]

It is easy enough to recognize religious fundamentalists, but how can we call "fundamentalist" those who most clearly dissociate themselves from any religion? The answer is simple if we consider the revelation, trinity, prophets, and Ten Commandments of this newest type of secular fundamentalism.

For the New Fundamentalists, relativism has been *revealed* as the ultimate truth about human reality (never mind the internal contradiction there). Nothing is right or wrong. Everyone is entitled to their opinion of things and let's all learn to be tolerant and respect whatever anyone else decides is best for them. Tolerance is the first, last, and only virtue that we need to practice. (And God help those who don't.)

The evil *trinity* of racism, sexism and homophobism must be eliminated as the last vestiges of judgmentalism before a truly "democratic" (read "relativist") society can be established. Since this is the one thing that will bring us to the ideal society, any means can be justified (just make sure to make it sound nice).

The *prophets* of this new orthodoxy are "forward thinking" politicians, "compassionate" religious leaders who preach the feel-good culture, and activist groups who "struggle" courageously for the recognition of their "rights."

These prophets of relativism have their own *Ten Commandments* (perhaps it would be better to say "suggestions" so that we don't sound too judgmental):

1. Thou art the Lord, thy God yourself. There shall be no other god besides you yourself.
2. Be nice.
3. Keep the weekend entertaining.
4. Honor your mother and mother (or father and father) by ensuring homosexual "rights."
5. Do not kill animals. (Unless it is a defenseless human

in the womb, a vegetable in a hospital bed, an elderly person, or anyone else lacking "quality of life")

6. If it feels good, do it. It must be natural.
7. Do not judge the actions of others or you shall be judged (that is, sued for every penny you have).
8. Take what you can get.
9. Broaden your sexual horizons. Experience it all.
10. (Fill in the blank with whatever you feel like justifying today)

This new relativism is actually a type of secular religion. If religiously minded people can be labeled "fundamentalists," this contrary group deserves that name as well – maybe even more so. More often than not, the *real* fundamentalists are those labeling others as fundamentalists. Who, in the end, is who?

While ordinary religious fundamentalism can be dangerous, atheistic fundamentalism that rejects any truth beyond itself has proven to be far more oppressive, intolerant, and bloody than any religion. Radical fundamentalism in religion that leads to violence and coercion should be deplored, rejected and halted. Yet the "secular religions" showed in Auschwitz and the Gulag that they hold much more danger for our freedom and safety than any religion. They are not held back by Jesus' teaching. They are not afraid to impose their "virtuous" terror.

This has been true since the dawn of that first infamous Reign of Terror in revolutionary France, when Maximilien de Robespierre rationalized his brutal actions in executing thousands of innocent French citizens and nobles in the name of virtue and justice. "Terror is naught but prompt, severe, inflexible justice; it is therefore an emanation of virtue," he claimed. The communist regimes of China, southeast Asia, and the Soviet Union agreed with Robespierre, and these totalitarian systems of the twentieth century brought their tactics of "persuasion" to unheard of brutality and effectiveness. Whether in the form of imperialism, fascism or communism, the past century witnessed the greatest atrocities committed in the name of ideology in the entire history of the world. Doesn't such blind faith merit the name of "fundamentalism"?

"When people think they possess the secret of a perfect social organization which makes evil impossible, they also think that they can use any means, including violence and deceit, in order to bring that organization into being. Politics then becomes a "secular religion" which operates under the illusion of creating paradise in this world."[37] When we deny any power outside of ourselves, rejecting God, or man's search for God (religion), the end result is arbitrary and tyrannical power. This atheism can become the worst kind of fundamentalism, the kind that is rooted in religious belief in Class, State, diversity or other abstract principles.

Modern society needs to avoid the extremes of fundamentalism, both in its believing and unbelieving forms. What is the best antidote? How can we counteract the new fundamentalism of our age? Before we can offer a solution, we need to recognize just how far ideology has infected key issues that affect our society. The extent of our sickness will be clear once we have examined the symptoms of this new fundamentalism: the tactics of manipulation.

"We know that the persecutor does not always assume the violent and macabre countenance of the oppressor, but often is pleased to isolate the righteous with mockery and irony."[1]

— JOHN PAUL II

Symptoms of a New Fundamentalism

Ideologies and fundamentalisms are systems of religious adherence to narrow concepts, linked to the desire to reshape reality. By definition, their intellectual foundation is shaky, because they are based on principles that do not correspond to the complexity of reality. And because they put principles before persons, the dignity and freedom of the individual can be trampled on whenever necessary for the advancement of those narrow concepts.

In this context, it is no wonder that ideologues resort to manipulation – in one form or another – in order to impose their "brave new world." But before their utopia is born, many persons will suffer from their manipulative techniques and meretricious rhetoric. Though the symptoms of this new fundamentalism are many, they fall into two basic categories: the manipulation of words and the manipulation of facts.

THE MANIPULATION OF WORDS

The simplest level of manipulation begins with our words... or lack thereof. We are capable of expressing neutral information, but generally our words are directed towards some goal, and to achieve it we naturally highlight certain facts and filter out others, or resort to elements of rhetorical persuasion. When the ideologue's interlocutor does not reach the desired conclusion on his own, verbal pressure is the next step: gentle chiding, name-calling, an appeal to be "more reasonable" and not get stuck up on minor points. When that fails, the pressure increases: thinly veiled threats, reference to difficulties that could arise "if we don't see some cooperation", coercion. When this 'persuasion' fails, the most dedicated fundamentalists resort to force – whether it be physical, legal, terrorist, or military – in order to make their ideology triumph.

This is the path of religious cults that "overemphasize subjective religious experience, spiritualize issues to justify their actions, make confusing and inflated promises of fellowship, manipulate through emotion rather than substance, and encourage others to 'just believe' rather than think critically."[2]

This is also the path of political ideologies that demand unwavering loyalty to the State, absorbing individuals into the totalitarian power wielded by an absolute leader and his cronies, and suppressing human rights by propaganda and force.

Both these branches of ideological fundamentalism share the same methods in their efforts to convince catechumens and disciples of their doctrine: smooth talking, trash talking, and false talking. Let's examine each in turn. By setting down these parameters now, our later probing into the entrails of culture will help us to distinguish more clearly the cancerous growths of fundamentalism.

Smooth Talking

Language is a power. The ability to communicate, to express oneself clearly, to transmit your ideas and feelings is a capacity fundamental to human life.

On a purely natural level, we use words to communicate. Toddlers taking their first steps learn that certain sounds (words) indicate things, and that by repeating those noises, they can get a desired reaction from those around them. Labeling things is just a part of this natural human process of development, and "name-calling" in this sense is a necessary component of life and communication. Signifying, naming, name-calling, or labeling on this natural level means simple relation of a word to a thing as it is in reality. It means putting a jersey on the things of life, sticking a label onto the cans in the grocery store. We could even call this "profiling," though there is nothing pejorative in this type of "name-calling" that is purely natural and corresponds to reality. Words are natural to real life.

Yet our words can go beyond this rudimentary level of signifying single objects. Children can create fantasy worlds full of knights in shining armor and damsels in distress, and divert themselves for hours on end with a rock, tin can, and lively imagination. Their creativity builds an ideal world.

Adults channel this creative capacity by bringing the ideal world into the real world. Art, literature, inventions, science, and history are all things first envisioned in the mind and then brought to life in the real world. They are based on physical reality, yet from man's spiritual reality they bring something new into physical reality. The genius of literature, poetry, and oratory is not in merely writing words or communicating ideas; it is in using verbal artistry to make those ideas attractive. Man is meant to be moved, and moved powerfully, by words.

Yet there always exists "the possibility that something could well be superbly crafted – that it could be perfectly worded; brilliantly formulated; strikingly written, performed, staged, or put on screen – and at the same time, in its entire thrust and essence, be false; and not only false, but outright bad, inferior, contemptible, shameful, destructive, wretched – and still marvelously put together!"[3]

Words have the power to communicate reality as it is; but they also have the power to communicate reality as it is *not*. That is what we call in old-fashioned terms a lie. A lie is the opposite of communication: it corrupts reference to reality and our relationship with another person. Words can express things as they are or as I want them to be. And if they are used in the latter fashion, words, instead of having a salutary effect, can be abused and inflict harm on our fellows. This is where smooth talking begins.

We all know what a smooth talker is. It's the greasy haired, sport-jacket-and-tie, used car salesman out to make a quick buck. It's the Marine officer who proposed to fifteen different women by email – all at the same time – while on assignment in Iraq (defending himself with the argument that he had to make sure he had some women lined up for him when he got home). It's the insidious character of Grima Wormtongue, whose sly and crafty counsel is typified in *The Lord of the Rings*.

Smooth talkers are those who skillfully weave their words to get what they want.

Skillful speech in and of itself is not bad, but when that skill is turned to a selfish or twisted end, it can become quite sinister, especially if the orator is not averse to lying. Of course, he very rarely admits to be lying and he hides his true intention – which if exposed would be shameful – beneath the cloak of words. George Orwell once stated that, "The great enemy of clear language is insincerity. When there is a gap between one's real and one's declared aims, one turns as it were instinctively to long words and exhausted idioms, like a cuttlefish squirting out ink."[4] Just like the United Airlines annual report listing the loss of a plane in a terrible crash as "an involuntary conversion of assets."

History has known plenty of people who abused words by twisting them to their advantage. The sophists that the philosopher Socrates argued against in fourth century BC Greece were highly paid and popularly applauded experts in the art of twisting words. They could sweet-talk something bad into something good and turn white into black. They would argue one side of an issue, and when the entire audience was convinced, they would switch to argue the opposite side of the problem. They were smooth talkers ready to argue for whatever position was to their personal advantage.

The sophists were experts at making convincing arguments. Truth mattered not at all to them. Words were no longer concerned with reality, but with flattery and *power* over others. All their words were designed to *get* something from someone else. Others became an object to be manipulated, sometimes even to be dominated, to be handled and controlled. Words were nothing more than an instrument of power.

Here lies the danger of smooth talking. When words are disconnected from reality and truth, they become corrupted, and when you corrupt the word, you corrupt the language. When language is corrupted human existence itself cannot remain unaffected and untainted. The German philosopher Josef Pieper – who spoke out against the Nazi regime and lived to tell about it – had firsthand knowledge of this corruption of language. In his work, *Abuse of Language, Abuse of Power,* he sets the stakes out clearly:

> "This much remains true: wherever the main purpose of speech is flattery, there the word becomes corrupted, and necessarily so. And instead of genuine communication, there will exist something for which domination is too benign a term; more appropriately we should speak of tyranny, of despotism... Public discourse itself, separated from the standard of truth, creates...vulnerability to the reign of the tyrant. Serving the tyranny, the corruption and abuse of language becomes better known as propaganda."

All this is not outside our own experience. Yet propaganda in this sense by no means flows only from the official power structure of a dictatorship. It can be found wherever a powerful organization, an ideological clique, a special interest, or a pressure group uses the word as their "weapon". And a threat, of course, can mean many things besides political persecution, especially all the forms and levels of defamation, or public ridicule, or reducing someone to a nonperson – all of which are accomplished by means of the word, even the word not spoken."[5]

When rhetoric is twisted to suit selfish ends or is unrestrained by moral principles, smooth talking can soon turn into outright deception and lies in order to get my way, or even trash talking.

Trash Talking

Trash talking is the older brother of smooth talking; their parents are selfishness and power. When smooth talking does not succeed in getting its way, trash talking steps in to beat up the opponent and squash all resistance. Trash talking is simply name-calling grown up... or grown more immature, depending on how you look at it.

If you really want to sound childish, just call someone a name. In my family, I learned them all. With five brothers, I soon became very adept at finding just the right name to get someone's goat. "Idiot," "brat," and "jerk" were some of my favorite epithets, though others I commonly used are not fit to be reprinted here.

There were ejaculations for moments of anger, patronizing phrases to mock mistakes, and words for baiting. When I was steaming mad or boiling over with revenge and couldn't express my feelings or reasons coherently, insults and profanities came tumbling out.

Like the time I was shot. Well, sort of. My little brother Jonathan and I were taking turns pinking away at tin cans with dad's antique one-pump Crossman BB gun. We were six and four at the time, but dad wasn't too worried letting us use the gun; the BB left the barrel so slowly that we could watch it on its trajectory to the target and we were never able to kill birds because the BBs just bounced off them.

Dad left me in charge of the gun while he went off to do

some work in the shop. A six-year-old mind likes to work things to its advantage, and I figured I deserved a little more shooting time. After all, Jonathan was two years younger than me, so he should get two shots less each turn.

"Jonathan, you're only four and I'm six. That means you get four shots and I get six shots. It's my turn now," I said with matter-of-fact logic as I reached for the gun.

"Nuh-huh! That ain't fair," he protested.

"Stop whining or I won't let you shoot at all," I replied as I yanked at the stock.

He pulled back and his face turned defiant, "No, you jerk! I get two more shots."

"Don't be a brat! It's my turn."

"No it ain't, idiot!"

"C'mon you baby! Let go!" and as I pulled with one last yank my little brother kicked me in the... well, he kicked me and my hands fell off the gun to attend to more important matters. With a howl of pain, I roared at him, "You brat! I'm gonna kill you!" and reached for his throat.

At that, his survival instinct kicked in and slipped the trigger, releasing a puff of air and one little copper BB. The barrel of the gun guided the BB directly to my right palm, and as it bounced off and hit my left hand, my brother realized that it was time to run.

I cried out in pain and screamed, "#$"$#! I'm gonna..." My words died off as tears of pain rolled down my face, and I just bellowed and chased after him. Fortunately, my dad was close by and heard the commotion in time to arrive on the scene to save my brother from certain death.

There's nothing new about name-calling. Our earliest childhood experiences testify to that. Adults, of course, are much more sophisticated in their name-calling. Take for example Winston Churchill, the former prime minister of England, well known for his cutting wit. Once while at a dinner party, he downed a few too many cocktails. His wobbly walk and flushed cheeks betrayed the facts, and a self-righteous chairwoman of a temperance society decided to set him straight.

"Mr Churchill," she exclaimed impertinently, "You are drunk!"

Churchill responded with an inebriated sarcasm, "Yes, but you are ugly, and tomorrow I'll be sober."

To understand trash talking – why we use it and how it works – it will be helpful to analyze more carefully the process by which we meet, form judgements, and associate with other persons.

There are three basic stages to the process of getting to know people, beginning with *preconceptions*. For example, let's say that from past experiences, from various articles I've read in the newspaper, and from my studies, I've picked up the idea that Italians are vain and self-centered. When I happen to meet an Italian exchange student for the first time, I measure him up, thinking back to all the things I have heard about Italians. At this point, there is always a danger that my preconception will be too rigid, and that instead of seeing the person as he is, I fit the person to my prejudice.

Here I move into the second stage. I make my own *judgment* based on what I see and hear for myself. We need to be flexible, open to changing our ideas by looking at the facts. I have to move beyond the preconception and begin to pick up on the hundreds of details that make up the real person: his tone of voice, how he twitches his nose, somber eyes, meticulous dress, and hesitancy to start the conversation. From these nuances I form my own judgment, naturally classifying the type of person he is, oftentimes changing my preconception completely. We recognize that this person is friendly, sincere but shy, and attentive to details. We could even go so far as to say that this *judgment* is a "stereotype," but only in the broadest sense of the term. We are "profiling" the person, but in a completely natural way that corresponds to my knowledge of reality.

Yet our knowledge is not static. We are constantly learning new things, taking in fresh data, and our conception of a person and things must be open to change. Knowledge passes through the stage of *refinement:* the more time we spend with someone, the more we get to know them. On a trip with the exchange student I might discover that he likes 60's rock and is a great fan of the Beatles. He shakes off the shyness and turns out to be quite garrulous; what I first took for refined taste in clothes I discover was actually just due to an over-protective mother. He actually could care less about his attire, but his mom bought him all the latest designer clothes for his trip.

Our knowledge of the person changes because we get to know them better, as they really are. We have to be flexible and open to the person so that we can get over all the prejudices and stereotypes.

But people also change, and the way a person was two years ago might be completely different from the way they are now. Leonardo da Vinci, the great Renaissance artist and scientist who painted *The Last Supper* sought live models for the figures in his painting. After searching the streets of Florence, he found an energetic young man with pious countenance and innocent eyes, the perfect model for the apostle John.

After painting that segment, he sought out models for each of the other apostles, hiring as model for Peter a burly fisherman visiting from Ostia, then a mercenary soldier for Simon the Zealot, and so on. However, he could not seem to find a suitable model for Judas Iscariot. The months passed by and the patrons grew anxious for da Vinci to finish his work, but he still had not found someone vile enough to represent the traitor.

Desperate after a long day's search, he headed to a tavern in the roughest part of the city where the brigands and lowlifes hung out. He searched the faces blackened with evil deeds, thefts, and murders until his eyes lighted upon the perfect subject: a man whose cynical sneer and blackened, shifty eyes veiled a sin-stained soul. Da Vinci approached him, offering a rich reward if he would accept to model for his painting. The criminal's glare softened and a tear formed at the corner of his eye. "I was your model one year ago for the apostle John."

People are not like other objects. They change, not just from place to place or in secondary things, but *morally*, in their goodness or badness. They are persons who think, judge, love, and suffer just like me. To treat them like objects, lock them into a certain category forever, or fail to recognize their freedom would be wrong. That is why the third stage of our knowledge is always expanding and growing, never locking a person into a stereotype of class, race, color... or political orientation. I should recognize how these naturally affect the person, but at the same time I must allow the person to change, develop, and grow.

Name-calling and trash talking lock people into a stereo-type: instead of a person they become an object, a category, an abstract type. That is why name-calling never does full justice to the person. A person transcends categories, devel-ops, and can change – yet always within the parameters of reality.

When someone resorts to name-calling, it is a sign of the will to power and lack of respect for someone. I want to con-trol the person, like an object. There is no dialogue. I want things my way, so forget rational arguments: It's my way or no way.

Our educated and sophisticated adulthood may have taken us past "idiot" and "jerk" and disguised our selfishness beneath a slick veneer, but we still call names, get in our jabs, and insult others in order to get our way. But what is new to this name-calling process – and what distinguishes mature adults from little kids – is that we have the capacity to con-trol our tongue and speak civilly; we can carry on a rational debate even with someone we do not agree with.

At least, we used to be able to.

But rational debate seems to be disappearing from mod-ern society. We rely increasingly on trash talking, name-call-ing, sentimental appeals, or underhanded tactics to get our way. The arts of conversation, of dialogue, of debate are being lost. Perhaps we do not see words like "idiot" and "jerk" in the newspapers or on the evening news, but sophisticated and mature name-calling is more prevalent than ever. You only have to listen to a few minutes of talk radio, pick up an edito-rial of the *New York Times*, or tune into the network news to discover the epidemic of infantile name-calling and character assassination.

Trash talking becomes particularly bitter when the name-caller recognizes that they really are weaker than the person they attack, either because they lack physical strength to defend themselves or because they lack reasons to defend their position. That is why pipsqueaks at school develop such sharp tongues and why minority parties tend to be so strident.

In the 2002 best seller by Ann Coulter, *Slander: Liberal Lies About the American Right,* there is a clear portrayal of name-calling and trash talking. Coulter highlights how liberals often distort the language in which social questions are framed. Republicans are branded as "dumb" and even invincibly stupid; Democrats are "compassionate" and "fresh thinking." When these personal attacks are exhausted, they pull out the bulldozers of intelligent discourse, accusing conservatives of cruelty, intolerance, racism, and narrow-mindedness. Though Coulter's insights are valid, at the end she, too, falls into name-calling by belittling liberal thinkers and using the same *ad hominem* attacks she decries.

Labeling can come from any side of the political spectrum; it is not a sickness exclusive to the "liberal left," even though an examination of public discourse might give that impression. Take for example radio host and *USA Today* columnist Julianne Malveaux, who caught no flak when she prayed aloud for the death of Supreme Court Justice Clarence Thomas on PBS. "I hope his wife feeds him lots of eggs and butter and he dies early like many black men do, of heart disease."

Not exactly a pleasant way to speak about another person, especially when you claim to be an unbiased journalist. "Such venom should be beyond the political and social pale.

But too many liberals would still rather dismiss conservative ideas with an ugly slur than actually grapple with them on the merits. Debating the pros and cons of racial preferences or US foreign policy can be difficult; much easier to simply hiss 'Racist!' or 'Nazi!' or some equally poisonous insult."[6]

All the same, within politics there is room for diversity of opinion about what is best for the *polis;* freedom of thought and expression is essential to democratic government. There will always be differing opinions in politics, and there should be. There will always be labels to identify political positions, and as long as the terms describe the *reality* of a person's thought and action, there is no problem. They correspond to reality; they are true.

But what happens when these labels are twisted? What if I use them to mock an opponent, undermine his position, or undercut his moral authority? What if I call peaceful protestors "racketeers," opponents of homosexual leaders of boys in Scout troops "bigoted gay bashers," or someone who attends church on Sunday a "religious fanatic"? Do these names correspond to reality? Are they true? Or is there a twist in language and reality going on here?

When the Catholic Church issued a document on June 3, 2003 clarifying issues regarding homosexual unions, activist groups were quick to denounce it as "intolerant," "homophobic," and "religiously close-minded babble." Yet an examination of the document finds nothing intolerant or homophobic. On the contrary, the document clearly reaffirms that persons with homosexual tendencies "must be accepted with respect, compassion and sensitivity. Every sign of unjust discrimination in their regard should be avoided." Those words are backed up with actions. The Catholic Church provides 25 percent of HIV/AIDS care worldwide and no state, government, or individual comes even close to matching this commitment.

Had the document stopped there, no uproar or name-calling would have occurred. However, the reasonable arguments that followed (not based on religious arguments at all) stated that the homosexual inclination is "objectively disordered" and homosexual practices are "sins gravely contrary to chastity." What enraged critics even more was the level-headed statement that "The principles of respect and nondiscrimination cannot be invoked to support legal recognition of homosexual unions. Differentiating between persons or refusing social recognition or benefits is unacceptable only when it is contrary to justice. The denial of the social and legal status of marriage to forms of cohabitation that are not and cannot be marital is not opposed to justice; on the contrary, justice requires it."[7]

The document affirms – and this is what activists could not stand – that there is no injustice in "discrimination" as such, but in unjust discrimination. That means people can in all justice "discriminate" against homosexual acts and unions as being disordered and bad for society.

Discrimination implies making a judgment call or making a selection based on certain criteria. In this sense, there is acceptable and unacceptable discrimination. For example, the hiring policies of a business should not discriminate according to sex or race, but it *must* discriminate when judging the capacities of the applicants for getting the job done unless it wants to take the fast track to bankruptcy. This second type of discrimination is not unjust in the least; it is necessary for human life.

These distinctions are lost in the climate of name-calling and advocacy that reigns over society today, even in the sports world. Rush Limbaugh was branded a "racist pig" for a comment in 2003 on ESPN regarding Philadelphia Eagles' quarterback Donovan McNabb. The president of NAACP, Kweisi Mfume, criticized Limbaugh's remarks as bigoted, ignorant, and racist. Eagles' owner Jeffrey Lurie went so far as to call Limbaugh's comments "despicable." Democrat presidential hopefuls were quick to cash in on the political opportunity, condemning the "racist" comment and standing shoulder to shoulder with their black constituency.

So what did Limbaugh say that drew so much ire? His exact words were, "I don't think he's been that good from the get-go. I think what we've had here is a little of social concern from the NFL. The media has been desirous that a black quarterback do well."

Black columnist Walter E. Williams was a bit bewildered by the whole incident. "Being sixty-seven years old, I've personally experienced racist language as well as racist acts, not only in my hometown of Philadelphia but during my 1959 to 1961 stint in the Army while in South Carolina, Georgia, Korea and California. I'd like someone to tell me precisely what it is that Limbaugh said that can rightfully be characterized as racist. For the life of me, I can't find it. Limbaugh's statement is opinion that can be characterized as correct or incorrect – but racist, no. The true tragedy of the flap over Limbaugh's remarks is that it's reflective of an ongoing process in our increasingly politically correct world where people are losing the freedom to say what they think lest they be subject to intimidation, extortion and other costs by our well-established grievance industry."[8]

Herein lies the great problem of our age: not all labels correspond to reality. Not everyone is telling the truth. Manipulation and little white lies have become standard tools not only of politics, but also business, personal life, and education. Belittling someone with names or nasty labels is a way to assert my power over them, to get my own way or advance my personal or party agenda.

Simple name-calling isn't the only way to bolster weak positions, though. We can distinguish three more sophisticated methods for attacking opponents with words: *ad hominem,* strawman, and voodoo.

Ad Hominem Attacks

An *ad hominem* attack heads straight for the person. It comes from the Latin words for "to the man." Let's take an example. If a politician proposes a new government investment for developing oil resources in Texas, I could argue for or against the proposal based on reasons, or I could attack the personal integrity of the politician. If I note that he is from Texas, has friends that own a private development company, and suggest that perhaps he proposes the program only for his own profit, that would be a light *ad hominem* attack. Instead of addressing the idea itself, I bring in personal issues and motivations which can be more or less relevant to the issue at hand.

Ad hominem tactics are most effective when they stretch the truth. If it is believable, many people will believe it. Take one possible motive and turn it into the *only* motive. By framing the argument and attributing base motives you suppress debate without ever having to counter the actual arguments of the other side.

These *ad hominem* attacks are especially useful when someone is lacking good arguments. Attacks against the character and convictions of another sidetrack attention from the real issues at hand. Single out one defect of a person and put it under the microscope of media attention. Tarnish their reputation with personal assaults and they lose all moral force.

A key example of *ad hominem* attacks took place during the impeachment proceedings for former president Bill Clinton. Public opinion was distracted from the real issues at hand – perjury and obstruction of justice on the part of the president – by shifting attention to Kenneth Starr and the prosecution. He was personally vilified, labeled a "peeping tom," and every aspect of his investigation subjected to vocal criticism. *Ad hominem* attacks changed the frame of the entire issue, allowing Clinton to be the second president ever to be impeached, and yet still remain in office.[9]

Strawman Attacks

The strawman argument is similar and politicians use it frequently. When they recognize that the opposition's arguments are sound, the research clear, and intentions are morally impeccable, they have to find some way to justify their own weaker position.

As the American army planned to leave the Philippines after the Spanish American War of 1898, soldiers of the new government were so afraid of tribal rebels that they would literally run away at their appearance. Years of failure and defeat had sapped their courage. They knew they were weaker and knew what those savage tribesmen would do when they captured a government soldier.

The American military advisors came up with a plan. They set up special training exercises for the soldiers, stuffing the captured uniforms of the tribal rebels with straw and sticking them on a pole with wooden rifle in hand. One by one, they made each soldier run up, thrust his bayonet through the straw soldier, and dash back to the lines. Using this method, the soldiers gradually lost their fear of the rebels.

The strawman argument is similar. Instead of attacking the opponent's real arguments and actual position on an issue, a "straw man" is set up. I define the opponent's position in the weakest terms possible. The "position" of the opponent is clearly explained... and then mercilessly attacked. Because it has been set up in a way easy to tear down, the speaker comes away looking like a hero, a brave soldier, a brilliant spokesman.

Like the *ad hominem* argument, it doesn't really address the issues at hand. It only pretends to face the arguments of the opposition. It is a charade, but it works to fool plenty of people. But as Abraham Lincoln wisely said, "You can fool some of the people all of the time, and all of the people some of the time, but you can't fool all of the people all of the time."

The problem is that in modern democracy you don't need to fool everyone, just enough to swing public opinion polls in your favor.

Voodoo Attacks

The voodoo argument falls into the same category of pulling the wool over people's eyes. Voodoo, or vodou, is an ancestral religion mixed into the culture and national identity of Haiti and its 8.3 million people. It is a hodgepodge of West Africa animist religions mixed with Indian traditions and a veneer of Catholic practices. Voodoo rites invoke spirits who link the human with the divine, summoning them with offerings that include everything from rum to roosters. Following the advice of witch doctors – and with a small fee – you stick pins in dolls, tear up pictures, and send curses to hurt your enemy. Instead of facing that person you cannot stand, you get back at them through the spirit world.

Voodoo arguments use the same underhanded tactics. They avoid direct confrontation with the person or the issue at hand. Instead, third persons or objects are targeted that can discredit, shame, or dishonor the enemy. You don't have to prove the person to be guilty or corrupt; they can be tainted by association.

Phyllis Schafly is an attorney and political activist who frequently speaks out against feminist ideology and homosexual activities. Her impeccable law career and savvy argumentation made her a tough target, so opponents took the voodoo route. Gay activists set their sites on John Schlafly, her wayward son, "ousting" him and pushing a public declaration of his homosexual lifestyle. When his mother declared, "I love my son," the press chortled over the exposure of Phyllis Schlafly's "hypocrisy." Presumably, if she were really sincere in her criticism of homosexuality, she would hate her son.

President Bush was subjected to voodoo attacks after his wildly popular Thanksgiving Day meal with the troops in Iraq in the fall of 2003. His critics and political enemies, unable to find any good reason for criticizing the move, combed through the video shots and photos until they discovered that one of the turkeys on display was a plastic make-up. By harping on the fake turkey – which had absolutely nothing to do with the trip – they attempted to associate Bush with artificiality, thereby popping the balloon of his popularity.

Common to these three tactics of *ad hominem,* strawman, and voodoo is the tearing down of your enemy. They are all based on some aspect of reality that gets twisted, distorted, and convoluted to suit the goals of the attacker. Ignore the real issues; assault the integrity, motives, and professionalism of the opponent. Dehumanize and stereotype him until he's been ostracized from good society.

When language is detached from the search for truth, it becomes a not so subtle attempt to control others and impose a new reality. It's all about power: power to do what I want, when I want, and how I want.

When words and language become mere tools of power, without any reference to reality or truth, the path lies wide open to abuse. We think we can create our own "truth" using the power of words. This is otherwise known as "lying."

False Talking

Simply put, false talking is the use of smooth talking and trash talking for propaganda campaigns. Instead of merely twisting reality, false talking denies or ignores the facts and instead works to invent a new "reality."

Words have a marvelous power to enlighten, enliven, and entertain, inviting us to a fresh experience of reality. However, they can also obscure or even truncate reality. Words are not indifferent and they are never neutral. If I see a dog before me, I can communicate it to others by saying "four-legged canine," "cuddly basset hound," "animal," or "it." Each of those word combinations could stand for the dog before me and the concept in my mind, but they all certainly don't carry the same image to others. The core reality is the same; the words are different.

Words can be tools for construction or destruction. We can direct or twist reality to suit our goals. Of course, this is not always negative. In the film *La Vita è Bella* by the Italian actor-producer Roberto Bernigni a Jewish father shields his son from the dark horror of their concentration camp by translating and twisting everything into a grand game of hide-and-seek. He convinces his son to win points by not complaining, hiding from the soldiers, and feigning to be a little German boy. The father hides the full reality from his son to the last, concealing his own death on the eve of their liberation from the camp.

Though hiding reality can be sometimes positive – or even necessary – manipulation of language to create a 'reality' or to attain a goal is always dangerous. When this false talking begins, truth is abandoned to *invent* a "reality" contrary to the truth. There is nothing real about it (even though it may be plausible): we create a fact that has never existed. Simply stated, it is a lie.

The basic principle of every liar was well summed up by Humpty Dumpty. "When I use a word," Humpty Dumpty said, in rather a scornful tone, "it means just what I choose it to mean: neither more nor less."[10] The problem with Humpty Dumpty (and with his idea) is that he's hollow, so when he impacts with reality, not even all the king's horse and all the king's men can put Humpty Dumpty back together again.

Despite knowing the fate of Humpty Dumpty, many from his fan club are driven by ideals that take them to the edge of a "brave new world," a grand new scheme of reality. They vaunt their audacity, their "free-thinking," their activism and counter-cultural individuality. And language is their "tool of power," Little "adaptations" in definitions and subtle twists in the usage of words generate chaos, making it possible for the confusion-makers to move ahead with their utopian vision.

Imagine if everyone applied Humpty Dumpty's grand principle, and people started changing everyday language to suit their fancy. Try to carry on a conversation with someone who calls a *dog* "tree" simply because he wants to. If he tells you about the trees in the park, all would be fine, but if he starts complaining about the noise the trees make barking at night, the mess they leave on street corners, and how they terrorize his cat, we might begin to think he is either paranoid, mentally unbalanced, or just a bit strange.

What's a person to do? If someone just starts changing the language arbitrarily, confusion is the natural result. Who's to blame? Arbitrarily changing words and manipulating definitions creates confusion… and undoubtedly many people are trying to create confusion in society today to advance their agenda.

If you stick a frog in boiling water it jumps out immediately. Stick it in room temperature water and slowly turn up the heat and you'll get a boiled frog. The principle works exactly the same in society. Don't make the changes too quickly because you'll stir up those "reactionaries" and create opposition. Lull people to sleep, talk about the good economy, entertain them to death, and then little by little you can transform society towards the "ideal."

Lying – whether subtly or outright in the manipulation of words – is not the only form of false talking. There exists a yet more sinister type: slander. This is the lie, surpassing mere trash talking, that is aimed at destroying a person's moral standing.

The famed Italian priest of the Renaissance, St. Philip Neri, once gave a strange penance to a person guilty of spreading malicious gossip. He instructed him to take a feather pillow to the top of a church tower on a windy day, rip open the fabric, and release the feathers to the whims of the winds. After that he was to come down from the tower, collect the feathers dispersed over the countryside, and put them back into the pillow. Of course the poor fellow couldn't do it, and that was precisely the point. Slander and calumny have a way of spreading to the four winds and, once released, can never be completely recalled. Even when accusations are firmly nailed as false, the reputations of those falsely accused bear a lingering taint. "Oh yes," it is vaguely said, "wasn't he once accused of..."

Slanderous name-calling is worse than trash talking or even a simple lie because it destroys a man; it is moral murder. The words of Shakespeare ring true:

"Good name in man and woman, dear my lord, Is the immediate jewel of their souls: Who steals my purse, steals trash; 'tis something, nothing; 'Twas mine, 'tis his, and has been slave to thousands: But he that filches from me my good name Robs me of that which not enriches him and makes me poor indeed."[11]

Applied Manipulation: Word Wars

At the outbreak of World War I in 1914, American public opinion was evenly divided between the causes of Germany and of the Allied Forces. Numerous immigrant groups from Germany, Switzerland, and Austria had flocked to the United States in the decades before the war and many German-speaking communities still existed throughout the country. Americans in general were averse to entering into this "European conflict," especially since neither side had a clear moral advantage. The nation remained decidedly neutral.

Well aware of this fact, yet in dire need of a new force to break through the gridlock on the front lines, the British government launched a propaganda campaign aimed at destroying the moral credibility of the German cause and winning over the Americans. The British propaganda office circulated stories about the injustice of the German blockade and the destruction of peaceable trade, all the while ignoring the English blockade of Germany. British agents prepared and distributed shocking news stories to American newspapers about the brutalities of German soldiers in Holland. These stories of the "horrible Huns" who cannibalized children and committed unheard of atrocities soon swung American opinion – and eventually American armed forces – into the war on the side of the Allies.

It was all an invention. The atrocities never happened or were grossly exaggerated. It was a vicious lie formulated for a political purpose. Unfortunately, the Germans learned their lesson from the British propaganda effort, and when the Nazi regime arose from the ashes of World War I they used political and social propaganda to create the bloodbath of World War II.

Twisting language is a tool of confusion and behind orchestrated confusion lies an agenda. But propaganda is really nothing new. Plato warned us of the sophists several thousand years ago, and Nietzsche prophesied well before the Nazi regime, "The era of the sophists? Our time!"

We live in the age of new sophists and the very idea of truth is considered a mirage, a pipedream, or an outdated concept that simply doesn't fit with our "modern" ideas. Words and language are detached from the search for truth, and the consequent verbal manipulations are merely tools to control others and impose an agenda. It's all about power: power to do what I want, when I want, and how I want. It's all about power and it's all about me... even though this radical egotism is often brushed beneath the curtain of altruism.

The mixed motives of smooth talking, trash talking, and false talking often culminate in our modern word wars. A cursory glance at the recent history of bellicose conflicts reveals a curious pattern: a war of words always precedes and accompanies armed aggression. Before the Civil War, white slave owners justified their domination of blacks by labeling them "animals," "lustful demons," and "dregs of humanity." They went so far as to consider them "exactly intermediate between the superior order of beasts such as dog or orangutan and the European White man." Other slave owners referred to the slave's "ignorance," "brutality," "obscenity," "animal appetite," "viciousness," and "illegitimacy," and called them "ignorant," "perverse," "wicked," "the pest of the White man," and "agents of Satan."

If you can strip away someone's humanity, you can take away their freedom. Name-calling did the stripping, slave owners and legislation stole the freedom.

The Nazis were no less experts at vilifying their enemies. Germany historically had been much more open to Jews than nearby Russia; Christian and Jewish communities lived in peaceful coexistence and even friendship before the advent of Hitler to power. Since it was difficult to see the Jews

– often your friendly banker or next-door neighbor – as an enemy worthy of death, a vigorous slander campaign was necessary.

Capitalizing on fear of Bolshevik socialism in Germany and resentment to unjust compensations for the first war – both often directly or indirectly tied to Jewish personalities – Adolf Hitler created a new current of anti-Semitism. In his book *Mein Kampf,* he referred to Jews as "maggots in a rotting corpse"; "a plague worse than the Black Death," "mankind's eternal germ of disunion," "drones in the human hive," "spiders sucking blood out of the people's pores," "a pack of rats eating one another," "the eternal bloodsucker," "the vampire of peoples," and "a harmful bacillus that spreads," among many other degrading terms.

Nazi propaganda took up Hitler's personal invectives and added "human ballast," "garbage," "human weeds," "empty shells," and "infections." Jews and others not of Aryan ancestry or quality "had to be treated like tuberculosis bacilli, with which a healthy body may become infested." This was not cruel, since "even innocent creatures of nature such as rabbits and deer have to be killed so that no harm is caused by them." Destroying the Jews in words made their bodily destruction a possibility.

During World War II, Americans fell into the same pattern of verbal aggression. Once hostilities had commenced, soldiers began referring to the enemy as "krauts," "Japs," "greasers," "slants," "wops," and "gooks." The Nazis engaged in name-calling in order to build a case for their actions while the name-calling for the American soldiers came to add some psychological justification on a personal level for the individual soldier. Slapping a nasty nametag on your enemy made it easier to shoot him. In both cases, the word wars killed the humanity of the enemy before a shot was ever fired.

THE MANIPULATION OF FACTS

When the exchange of words escalates into verbal battle, the desire to win over or coerce the opponent often opens the floodgate to a deliberate manipulation of the facts themselves. We examined amply this tendency previously in several examples of fundamentalist religions and ideologies that reject reality or twist it to suite their purposes. However, there are other tactics of manipulation that we have yet to expose. These fall into the realm of actions aiming to *create* reality. How can someone create something that does not exist?

In 1998, a controversial movie hit the big screens across the United States. *Wag the Dog* brings alive the fictional recreation (with clear historical insinuations) of a sex scandal that threatens to cripple the president's bid for a second term, less than two weeks before election day. Before the incident can cause irreparable damage, the ultimate spin doctor is called to the White House to anticipate the reaction of a frenzied press corps, and deflect attention from the president by creating a bigger and better story – a war. With the help of a Hollywood producer and his irreverent entourage, he assembles a crisis team and orchestrates a global conflict unlike any ever seen on CNN. Though the war was nonexistent, the press, politicians and public are all duped by the skillful manipulations of news leaks, false footage, and deceptive data.

Creating reality is really not quite so far-fetched, and of the many tactics used today we will examine two of the most common: polls and scientific studies.

Numbers and Polling

Numbers would seem to be the basis for the most objective science, with no room for manipulation. After all, two plus two equals four, whether I have a prejudice against the number four or not. There's no room for manipulation here.

Yet it's not quite so simple. Numbers still have to be interpreted, and any accountant can tell you that figures can hide reality quite well. The Enron scandal is only one high profile example of slick accounting putting up a screen for illegal activity.

Statistics, averages, and polls can give impressive support for an argument, but "when statistics are not based upon computations which are strictly accurate, they mislead instead of guiding aright. The mind is easily imposed upon by the false affectation of exactness, which prevails even in the misstatements of science, and it adopts with confidence errors which are dressed in the forms of mathematical truth."[12]

Surveys and polling base their claim for scientific certainty on numbers, but even in the best of cases those numbers are subject to a 3 percent margin of error. That's with a near perfect poll. But when there is a bad survey – either by sampling errors, a flawed way of asking a question, or a query order that pollutes the results – then polls often become a tool for asserting what you want to assert…and swinging public opinion in your direction.

In the case of sampling errors, let's say that I find a survey telling me that 76 percent of Americans polled agreed that there should be more stringent guidelines placed upon buying and owning guns. The final data is there, clear for all to see. But where did that 76 percent come from? If I poll people from an inner-city neighborhood infested with violent crime and reeling from a recent wave of shootings, the results will differ from that of asking residents of an elk-hunting village in Idaho. These people have different concerns and see the issue from opposite angles. The sample of population that is polled should be as representative as possible of the public. Otherwise, that 76 percent doesn't tell me anything.

Yet the way you ask the question is crucial, too. A basic tactic used in bad surveys is "bait and switch." Imagine that I form my question for the previous survey like this: "Given the current wave of violent crimes committed with firearms, recent school shootings, and the threat of terrorism, would you agree that the government should do more to protect the people by regulation of buying and owning guns?" Detect any bias in that question? Is there any baiting in order to elicit a certain response?

Let's phrase the same question a bit differently. "Since America is a country of freedom and responsibility and the Second Amendment speaks clearly of the 'right of the people to keep and bear arms,' would you agree that the government should responsibly enforce current legislation and respect the rights of citizens by avoiding new regulation on the buying and owning of arms?"

The issue is the same; the question is totally different. People will obviously respond differently to each of the questions because it highlights different concerns. So what is the moral of the story? Never believe a poll if you haven't seen the actual questions asked. It makes all the difference in the world.

A poll can be critically flawed by lack of objectivity in the questions or the order in which they are asked. The book *It Ain't Necessarily So: How the Media Make and Unmake the*

Scientific Picture of Reality analyzes a case involving conflicting reports of public support for school vouchers.

> "A 1996 poll of Republicans commissioned by the National Education Association (NEA) asked respondents, 'Do you think that tax dollars should be used to assist parents who send their children to private, parochial, or religious schools, or should tax dollars be spent to improve public schools?' Forced to choose between school vouchers and improving public schools, 61 percent of respondents sided with aiding public schools. But when the Christian Science Monitor cited the poll results, it omitted any mention of the contrived question.
>
> "The pro voucher *Center for Education Reform* countered the NEA finding by commissioning a poll that asked, 'How much do you support providing parents with the option of sending their children to the school of their choice – either public, private, or parochial – rather than only to the school to which they are assigned?' By framing the question in a way more favorable to vouchers ("how much do you support"), the poll elicited a positive response from nearly 60 percent of the respondents."[13]

The lesson is clear: Don't trust a poll's answers unless you can examine the poll's questions. "In particular ... don't trust a poll commissioned by an organization that uses the poll to support its own predetermined position, since the questions may well have been rigged to reach the organization's desired conclusion." [14]

Scientific Studies

Science builds upon words and facts, not just experimental data and objective results. Every science is subject to theory, communication of discoveries, interpretation, and application – these all depend on words. In the end, science itself is subject to possible manipulation because of the necessary "translation" of data into everyday language.

The history of science is eloquent witness to the dangers of exploitation when preconceptions are put before the full facts. For example, Aristotle determined that the perfect motion is circular; since his cosmology put celestial bodies in the perfect realm, planets and stars must necessarily have perfect circular orbits around the earth. Scientists struggled for nearly 2000 years to fit their measurements into this preconception before Johannes Kepler discovered that planets have elliptical, not circular, paths. Galileo Galilei, famous for challenging the prevailing opinion that the earth was center of the universe, wasn't free from error. Though meticulous in his observations, he came to conclusions about tides that modern scientists laugh at.

Science can discover the truth about reality or it can be wrong, even when practiced by a distinguished researcher. In his book *Fads and Fallacies in the Name of Science*,[15] Martin Gardner highlights dozens of hoaxes and pseudo-scientific theories that have attracted gullible followers in recent centuries.

Modern scientists are subject to the same limitations. Frank J. Tipler, a distinguished mathematician and physicist who teaches at Tulane University, developed the Omega Theory, claiming that the most recent discoveries in cosmology and particle physics establish the basis for a new scientific religion that corroborates the basic intuitions of Christianity... but without any need for Christ or indeed any divinity. Using scientific calculations, he "proves" that physics – not God – will grant resurrection and eternal life to us all.[16]

Government and corporations are often hoodwinked into funding outlandish and expensive research projects which often prove only one thing: that gullibility is not overcome with time, power, or money. "Major power companies have sunk tens of millions of dollars into a scheme to produce energy by putting hydrogen atoms into a state below their ground state, a feat equivalent to mounting an expedition to explore the region south of the South Pole. There is, alas, no scientific claim so preposterous that a scientist cannot be found to vouch for it."[17]

Yet despite the limitations of science and clear cases of "scientific" swindlers, modern society continues to place extraordinary confidence in any "scientific study." Label your product with "scientifically tested" or "clinically proven" and it is bound to sell. Just ask the producers of "Vitamin O," the dietary supplement that turned out to be saltwater.

Agents of social change have capitalized on this naïveté. And wherever ideology trumps truth, errors, misapplications, and even outright manipulations of data run rampant. Using shoddy studies or gently manipulating the results of authentic studies, they twist "science" to their cause.

Peter Berger, a key player in the development of sociology in the 20th century, observed recently that "sociology has fallen victim to two severe deformations. The first began in the 1950s; I would label it as *methodological fetishism*. The second was part of the cultural revolution that started in the late 1960s; it sought to transform sociology from a science into an instrument of *ideological advocacy.*"[18]

As Berger himself states, "The ideologues who have been in the ascendancy for the last thirty years have deformed science into an instrument of agitation and propaganda (the Communists used to call this "agitprop"), invariably for causes on the left of the ideological spectrum. The core scientific principle of objectivity has been ignored in practice and denied validity in theory. Thus a large number of sociologists have become active combatants in the 'culture wars,' almost always on one side of the battle lines. And this, of course, has alienated everyone who does not share the beliefs and values of this ideological camp."[19] Sociology is no longer a science for studying society as it is, but a weapon for making society what certain people want it to be. It no longer faces the facts and uncovers the truth; it seeks to create the facts and formulate the "truth" that will allow them to attain their goals.

It doesn't really matter if this is a backwards approach. After all, logical inconsistency has only rarely been an obstacle to ideological dominance.

A good dose of truth is what our society needs. But can we expect much of that in the fields of sexual ethics, education, media, and government?

> "Be careful not to be so open-minded that your brains fall out."

> — G.K. CHESTERTON

The Pathology Exposed

SEX AND CONSEQUENCES

The symptoms of a new fundamentalism are nowhere more clearly seen than in the modern culture war. The relativistic mindset and manipulations of word and fact are signs of an obvious pathology. Though many commentators began noticing the symptoms in society only recently, the indicators can be traced back much further... and much of it has to do with sex.

Sex is one of the most intimate of human activities. This extremely personal act involves love, communion with another person, and the gift of oneself. Woven into the tapestry of this expression of love are the physical and psychological pleasures of the sexual act.

The sexual revolution riveted all attention on the pleasure aspect of sex, pushing to the sidelines the characteristic of love, communion, and self-giving. Sex became the supreme act of "getting something," of self-indulgence. Teens began speaking of their "conquests" and open talk about sex became increasingly commonplace. Old taboos were removed and the intimacy of the bedroom was opened up for the whole world to peep in.

This "openness" brought its consequences: skyrocketing teen pregnancy rates, the alarming spread of venereal diseases, abortions, sexual addictions, single parent families, increased contraception use with its side effects of infertility and disruption of stable family life.

A generation ago, the five most bothersome problems complained about in polled American high schools were:

a. disrespect for property
b. laziness; not doing homework
c. talking and not paying attention in class
d. throwing spitballs
e. leaving doors and windows open

Does this sound like another world? It is. The same poll was retaken a few years ago. The five leading problems in those same high schools now are: [1]

a. fear of violent death; guns and knives in school
b. rape
c. drugs
d. abortion
e. getting pregnant

Is this merely collateral damage for the great good of the sexual revolution? If we drop an egg from the second story, we shouldn't blame the ground for breaking the egg. Nature has its rules: eggs are fragile, gravity is always at work, and the ground is hard. Only the most dedicated revisionist could blame the ground for breaking the egg. In the same way, the disastrous consequences of the sexual revolution are not merely bad side effects; they are direct effects of a tough encounter with reality. When we go against nature, we are bound to run into problems. Rebelling against the authentic nature of sex is no exception.

Yet instead of recognizing reality, many Humpty Dumpty's are working hard to change the terminology of sex, thinking that will resolve our society's new problems. Negative words like "fornication," "masturbation," and "adultery" have been substituted for the more pleasant-sounding "serial monogamy," "self-gratification," and "love." Consider a few other shifts in terminology:

contraception ➡	responsible family planning
euthanasia ➡	death with dignity
pornography ➡	sexually explicit material
sexual perversions ➡	alternative lifestyles
partner in fornication ➡	significant other
bestiality ➡	interspecies love
sadomasochism ➡	exchange of power
child molestation ➡	intergenerational love
modesty, chastity ➡	sexual hang-ups
self-discipline ➡	unhealthy repression
moral irresponsibility ➡	"freed up"
abortion ➡	women's right

Terminology has changed. About that there can be no doubt. The real question at hand is whether this change is part of the normal evolution of language or if it is not rather a masterful orchestration and manipulation. In reality, as we shall soon see, both forces have been at work.

This shift in language is due at least in part to normal human psychology: no one wants to be bad. If you catch a four-year-old coloring the wall with his crayon red-handed, he usually reacts in one of two ways: either he confesses his crime and cries for forgiveness, or he proceeds to deny his actions. "It was that other little boy," he might cry, even though there are no other little boys around. He'll claim innocence, blame it on others, or try to hide the evidence.

Adults may be sophisticated, but they are not much different. When our conscience or our neighbor points out our faults, we either recognize and repent, or start looking for some explanation or scapegoat. Twisting words and lying are just two of those possible escape tactics... and "twisting" is a mild word for the verbal transformations of the past decades.

"As the rigid [sexual] code relaxed, new concepts evolved. At the same time vocabulary was altered: Perversions became abnormalities, abnormalities became deviancies, deviancies became variations, variations became options, options became preferences, preferences became choices, and choices became life-enhancing experiences."[2] Now no one is a pervert, they just have a different "sexual orientation."

The Hidden Epidemic

The verbal manipulation regarding sex has given way to willful ignorance of some basic facts. Take for example what the Centers for Disease Control and Prevention has called the "hidden epidemic" of venereal diseases. In the 1950s there were only five known sexually transmitted diseases (STDs), but medical advances discovered − and three decades of "free love" and sexual degeneracy unleashed – new strains of STDs, bringing today's total to more than twenty-five. According to the Centers for Disease Control and Prevention, five of the top ten reportable infectious diseases reported in 1996 were STDs. That news is bad enough, but it gets worse. There was a sharp rise from the previous 12 million new STD cases per year to an estimated 15.3 million new cases per year in 1996.

In its report for the year 2000, the Centers for Disease Control (more likely to underrate than exaggerate) outlined the gravity of this outbreak in which already 25 percent of the population is infected. "In the United States, more than 65 million people are currently living with an *incurable* [emphasis added] sexually transmitted disease (STD). An additional 15 million people become infected with one or more STDs each year, roughly half of whom contract lifelong infections. Approximately one-fourth of these new infections are in teenagers. And while some STDs, such as syphilis, have been brought to all time lows, others, like genital herpes, gonorrhea, and chlamydia, continue to resurge and spread through the population. Because there is no single STD epidemic, but rather multiple epidemics, discussions about trends over time and populations affected must focus on each specific STD. More is known about the frequency and trends of some STDs than others, since many of the diseases are difficult to track. Not including HIV, the most common STDs in the U.S. are chlamydia, gonorrhea, syphilis, genital herpes, human papillomavirus, hepatitis B, trichomoniasis and bacterial vaginosis. The latest estimates of incidence and prevalence are provided below."

STD	Incidence (Estimated number of new cases every year)	Prevalence (Estimated number of people currently infected)
Chlamydia	3 million	2 million
Gonorrhea	650,000	Not Available
Syphilis	70,000	Not Available
Herpes	1 million	45 million
Human Papillomavirus (hpv)	5.5 million	20 million
Hepatitis B	120,000	417,000
Trichomoniasis	5 million	Not Available

*No recent surveys on national prevalence for gonorrhea, syphilis, trichomoniasis or bacterial vaginosis have been conducted.

Source: Centers for Disease Control and Prevention[3]

The conclusion of the report goes on to affirm, "STDs are one of the most under-recognized health problems in the country today. Despite the fact that STDs are extremely widespread, have severe and sometimes deadly consequences, and add billions of dollars to the nation's healthcare costs each year, most people in the United States remain unaware of the risks and consequences of all but the most prominent STD—the human immunodeficiency virus or HIV."[4]

According to a 2003 report released by the United Nations Population Fund, every fourteen seconds a young person is infected with HIV, the forerunner of AIDS. *Yet the new infection rate is even higher for other STDs.* And while everyone knows that AIDS is a deadly killer, not everyone knows that each one of the other STDs brings serious health consequences and if untreated, can lead in some cases to infertility, cancer, and death just as surely as AIDS.

Are you wondering why you've never heard of this epidemic before? Perhaps that is why the Centers for Disease Control and Prevention calls it the "hidden epidemic." It has been generally ignored by the media, even while passing threats like Mad Cow Disease or SARS or West Nile are hyped to the extreme.

Why the silent treatment? Perhaps because no one likes to talk about such intimate diseases. After all, if you've got the disease everyone knows what you've been up to and that can be rather embarrassing.

But there is more at work here. The scientific facts condemn as extremely unhealthy – and often life-threatening – a key component to the relativist ideology of our day. All that scientific evidence, if spread around too much, might scare people away from "free love," thereby "repressing our sexual drive" and "throwing us back into the Dark Ages." Perhaps that is why even while the root causes of the public health crisis brought on by the sexual revolution have been hushed up, voices ring out loud and clear in promoting their proposed *solution*: "safe sex." Use a condom and everything will be just fine.

Encouraging condom use to prevent STDs is current standard medical advice from the U.S. Department of Health and Human Services, the Centers for Disease Control and Prevention, institutes of medicine, public health organizations, and other health care providers including school health centers. Everyone seems to be on the bandwagon promoting "safe sex." But do condoms really guarantee "safe sex"?

The first objective of condoms is to prevent pregnancy. However, studies of condom effectiveness for this "safe sex" reveal a failure rate of anywhere from 5-15% in preventing pregnancy, depending upon conditions such as slippage, anal/vaginal sex, experience and age of users, age and type of condom, and defects in workmanship. Considering that a woman is fertile only a few days a month, this failure rate is worrisome. It translates into a one in six or one in seven chance in pregnancy in a year for a woman whose partner uses a male condom in every sexual act throughout the entire period. But that failure rate is much higher when it comes to the transmission of STDs.

In June 2000, the United States National Institutes of Health sponsored a workshop to survey the scientific evidence on condom effectiveness in safeguarding users from STDs. The final report, released on July 2001, concluded that the consistent and correct use of male condoms provides an 85 percent reduction in HIV/AIDS transmission between women and men. However, according to the Centers for Disease Control and Prevention, only latex or polyurethane condoms provide a barrier against HIV, but there are many other types of condom currently in use around the world. In an earlier study conducted by the Food and Drug Administration, scientists found "that normal intact condoms are able to leak enough HIV-sized particles to cause concern."[5] This means that even assuming a best-case scenario, there is absolutely no guarantee that condoms are in fact effective against HIV infection. Would you buy – let alone drive – a car that had a 15 percent chance of a fatal crash every time you drove it? Would you be reassured if that percentage dropped down to 5 percent?

The same 2001 report of the NIH revealed a lack of adequate data to confirm that condoms protect against other sexually transmitted diseases. Many of the most contagious STDs are regional – the infectious agent is not just located

at one place on the body – and many infect the entire genital area. That means that oftentimes the condom does not
cover enough of the body to prevent infection. "CDC and
NIH data confirm that condoms offer little or no protection
against human papilloma virus, which has been linked to
cervical cancer in women. In the U.S., 75% of the population
of reproductive age is estimated to be infected with HPV and
more women die from cervical cancer than from AIDS."[6]

Despite these facts, "safe sex" experts continue to tout
the effectiveness of condom use and criticize programs that
promote abstinence. Yet even here, scientific evidence begs to
differ. The African nations of Botswana and Zimbabwe are
ranked among the top countries worldwide for HIV prevalence, even though both countries are condom-friendly and
make condoms readily available. Their infection rate has remained stable or increased over the past decade, despite the
active promotion of condom use for "safe sex."

In 1991, the African nation of Uganda also had an HIV
infection rate of more than 20 percent. "By 2001, however,
the rate was only 6 percent. A 2002 Harvard study conducted by anthropologist Edward C. Green and Vinand Nantu-
lya, an infectious-disease specialist, revealed the cause of the
discrepancies between Uganda's HIV infection rate and those
of other heavily infected countries. Uganda had begun a program focusing on abstinence and fidelity instead of condoms.
While the rate of HIV infection in every other country continued to escalate, Uganda's fell dramatically. (Lest there be
any concern over the researchers' religious zeal, Mr. Green
describes himself as a "flaming liberal" who does not attend
church.)"[7]

Condoms do not always prevent pregnancy, let alone protect against the transmission of life-threatening STDs. With scientific facts like these, how can anyone imagine that condom use leads to "safe sex"? Has ideology blinded them to reality?

Touting the use of condoms as effective prevention against life-threatening infections is not only immoral, it's downright dishonest. And sex-education programs that encourage students to use condoms for "safe sex" go beyond dishonesty; they engage in the destruction of future generations by cheapening the authentic meaning of sex and promoting dangerous lifestyles.

Medical science agrees that the only 100% effective prevention against STDs is abstinence until marriage and then fidelity within that marriage, but to our modern-day ideologues that smacks of obscurantism, Middle-Ages morality, and unhealthy sexual "repression." Even though thousands of generations of our predecessors lived quite happily and sexually satisfied in that "unhealthy sexual repression", that fact doesn't seem to make it through their ideological interpretations of sex. When will they face the facts? When will they recognize that they are trapped in a fundamentalism that has to reinterpret all of reality to fit their preconceptions – and base passions?

Abortion

The sexual revolution brought us more than just a plague of new sexually transmitted diseases. It also established induced abortion in law and society as a women's "choice" and "right to privacy."

For more than thirty-five years, abortion has been one of the most divisive issues in America, not only in politics, but also in education, religion, and science. Opposing sides of the argument gradually dug into their trenches and warily watched for any movement from the enemy. Once again, a barrage of words characterized the initial hostilities. According to George Orwell, some language is "designed to make lies sound truthful and murder acceptable, and to give an appearance of solidity to pure wind." Nowhere was that more true than with the abortion debate.

Examine for a moment the change in the term "abortion." Everyone knows that murder is wrong and, like it or not, abortion has always been linked in people's minds to murder... at least until the past couple of decades. A 1970 article in the official journal of the California Medical Association proposed the linguistic strategy to follow for separating the two ideas, the only way in which abortion could possibly gain acceptance.

> *"The traditional Western ethic has always placed great emphasis on the intrinsic worth and equal value of every human life regardless of its stage or condition. This ethic has had the blessing of the Judeo-Christian heritage and has been the basis for most of our laws and much of our social policy. The reverence for each and every human life has also been a keystone of Western medicine and is the ethic which has caused physicians to try to preserve, protect, repair, prolong, and enhance every human life which comes under their surveillance. This traditional ethic is still clearly dominant, but there is much to suggest that it is being eroded at its core and may eventually even be abandoned. This of course will produce profound changes in Western medicine and in Western society."* [8]

The article goes on to highlight three factors in modern society that suggest a rationale for changing that "traditional Western ethic." The much dreaded population explosion, a reduction of natural resources, and new emphasis on "quality of life" (i.e., comfort) over life itself all called into question the old ethic.

> *"What is not yet so clearly perceived is that in order to bring this about hard choices will have to be made with respect to what is to be preserved and strengthened and what is not, and that this will of necessity violate and ultimately destroy the traditional Western ethic with all that this portends. It will become necessary and acceptable to* **place relative rather than absolute values on such things as human lives,** *[emphasis added] the use of scarce resources and the various elements which are to make up the quality of life or of living which is to be sought. This is quite distinctly at variance with the Judeo-Christian ethic and carries serious philosophical, social, economic, and political implications for Western society and perhaps for world society."*

The authors of this article were at least honest with themselves and their readers. The rationale is clear: in order to look out for ourselves in the long run, we've got to start planning ahead, dropping the birth rate, and getting rid of that obnoxious hang-up with the absolute value of life.

Nazi doctors using prisoners as guinea pigs agreed, just as did Stalin in his purges to advance the Soviet State. In the name of civilization, we must beat down the citizens; in the cause of "quality of life" we must end the "less-qualified" lives.

"The process of eroding the old ethic and substituting the new has already begun. It may be seen most clearly in changing attitudes toward human abortion. In defiance of the long held Western ethic of intrinsic and equal value for every human life regardless of its stage, condition, or status, abortion is becoming accepted by society as moral, right, and even necessary. It is worth noting that this shift in public attitude has affected the churches, the laws, and public policy rather than the reverse. Since the old ethic has not yet been fully displaced **it has been necessary to separate the idea of abortion from the idea of killing, which continues to be socially abhorrent. The result has been a curious avoidance of the scientific fact, which everyone really knows, that human life begins at conception and is continuous whether intra- or extra-uterine until death. The very considerable semantic gymnastics which are required to rationalize abortion as anything but taking a human life would be ludicrous if they were not often put forth under socially impeccable auspices. It is suggested that this schizophrenic sort of subterfuge** *is necessary because while a new ethic is being accepted the old one has not yet been rejected."*[9] [emphasis added]

What happened soon after this prophetic academic article is documented history. The currents of change already swirling about in society whipped into a storm that washed away the old ethic. The proabortion movement gained momentum, framed the abortion debate as a matter of "choice" and personal freedom, and moved their cause through the court system to establish a new constitutional "right" to abortion. The actual reality of abortion, the techniques used, and the consequences were ignored. It was all about "freedom" and "privacy."

"Deceptive" would be a good word to describe this manipulation of language, though "schizophrenic" might be even more appropriate. Scientific data showing that life begins at conception was shuffled under the table and experts were found to assure us that "no one really knows for sure."

Since the term "abortion" evokes negative feelings of death, other names were found for the same reality. "Voluntary interruption of the pregnancy," "evacuating the afflicted/infested (uterine) area" or "post-conception fertility interruption" sound quite professional, neutral, and most importantly, they remove the image of the lost child. It shows that the "ultimate objective of the anti-life mentality is not only the legalization of abortion, but to free consciences from blame."[10]

In the early 1980s, the balance of power threatened to shift. Public support for abortion in the United States continued to slip as the facts about it become more apparent: physical and psychological trauma (Post Abortion Syndrome), links to increased risk of breast cancer, militant feminist groups resisting even the most reasonable limitations, and advances in medical science that allow us to peer into the womb and observe the developing human life. The scientific advances were not the only cause of this shift in support; the millions of women who had experienced abortion firsthand knew — with that intuitive genius proper to women — that there was something terribly wrong with all this, no matter what verbal camouflage was used to cover it up.

From the 1960s on, abortion supporters had referred to "fetal matter" and "uterine tissue," to successfully blur the distinction between human life and disposable Kleenex. New scientific techniques, however, made it increasingly difficult to maintain that position, because when you can see an ultrasound of the fetus it looks decidedly human. Ultrasound is an amazing reality check. Before ultrasounds, maternal-fetal bonding often occurred after the fifteenth week of pregnancy, when the mother senses fetal movement for the first time. But with ultrasounds, bonding is possible within the first thirteen weeks, according to British researchers Stuart Campbell and Judith Lumley, because peering inside her own womb quickens a mother's emotional attachment to her unborn child.

Indeed, evidence that ultrasound helps to persuade women not to abort came in an unpublished study by Eric Keroack, medical director of A Woman's Concern, a crisis pregnancy center in Boston. Keroack compared two eighteen-month periods in the center's history, keeping data only on women who expressed interest in abortion. Without a sonogram, about 60 percent of 366 tracked women had abortions. But with a sonogram, 25 percent of 434 tracked women aborted. He estimated that 125 babies were born who would otherwise have been aborted.[11]

For many years it was assumed that children do not start smiling until several weeks after birth. Yet new developments in ultrasound technology changed that perception. Obstetrician and professor Dr. Stuart Campbell at the Create Health Centre for Reproduction and Advanced Technology in London developed 3-D ultrasound technology to show parents their unborn child moving, crying, blinking and even smiling. "Before birth, most babies smile frequently. This may indicate the baby's trouble-free existence in the womb and the relatively traumatic first few weeks after birth when the baby is reacting to a strange environment," stated Dr. Campbell.[12]

Campbell's high-tech window to the womb also shows the babies moving their limbs at eight weeks, leaping and turning by twelve weeks, curling their toes and fingers at fifteen weeks, and yawning at twenty weeks. The clients' reactions are overwhelming, Campbell said, "especially with fathers, who rarely get involved. Before, they sat in the corner. Now, they really show emotion. I enjoy scanning and looking at babies. It is so informative about babies and behavior. Every scan is an adventure."[13]

How have proabortion activists reacted to the photos of unborn babies smiling for the cameras?

Anne Karpf, a commentator for the British periodical *Guardian* who bills herself as a "medical sociologist," says the photos are "deeply disquieting," yet at the same time ridiculed the antiabortion lobby for being "intoxicated with evidence of a fetus' humanity." Australian Birth Control Services medical director Geoff Brodie complained that the photos "will be picked up by those groups that use anything and everything to stop terminations but ignore the fact that women have a right to choice."[14]

When General Electric began running ads last year celebrating the company's new innovations in sonography, a writer for the *American Prospect* complained the commercials were "a milieu of clever illusion" that "blur(red) the distinction between a fetus and a newborn infant." NARAL, the

National Abortion and Reproductive Rights Action League published a booklet titled "Unmasking Fake Clinics," warning that pro-life crisis pregnancy centers are buying ultrasound machines as part of a "new agenda" to deceive pregnant women.[15]

Deceive? Since when do pictures lie? Human beings smile, but it takes a truly cold heart to put a knife – or a suction machine – to an innocent beating heart. Can we detect something of ideological fundamentalism here?

The International Planned Parenthood Federation, the largest provider of abortion services worldwide, remains firmly dedicated to "reproductive health, rights and choices" despite the new data. Citing Jeffrey Kahn, Director of the University of Minnesota Center for Bioethics, it agrees that "although the images 'will certainly inflame the debate' over abortion rights and 'may change our emotional response to that foetus in the womb,' they will not change 'the *whole construct of how we've thought about abortion* [emphasis added], which is staked to the viability of that foetus outside the womb.'"[16]

Johnson & Johnson vice president Dr. Nancy Snyderman said abortion-rights supporters and abortion-rights opponents should not "use the *science for propaganda*, but to understand the significance and the beauty of it all, and to talk about the *interpretation of these movements* with great caution" [emphasis added]. Dr. Jacques Abramowicz, professor of obstetrics, gynecology, and radiology at the University of Chicago, said that the images do not necessarily mean that fetuses experience emotions, adding, "It's dangerous to jump to the conclusion that fetuses [sic] have feelings, but certainly you can see them moving and doing lots of things."[17]

Twisting reality to fit your "construct"? Adapting science to your propaganda? "Interpretation" of the facts? If this is not a clear case of ideological fundamentalism, what is?

Faced with the bare facts, and confronted with such clear manipulation, no wonder recent polls show a shift in public opinion. A *USA Today/CNN/Gallup* poll taken January 15, 2003 showed that "Eighty-eight percent of the respondents said they would favor a law or proposal that requires doctors to inform patients about alternatives to abortion before performing the procedure. And 78 percent said women wanting an abortion should be required by law to wait twenty-four hours before going ahead with the procedure."

"On the issue of prior notification, 73 percent said girls under eighteen should be required to have parental consent before an abortion. Seventy-two percent said a woman should be forced to tell her husband before she has an abortion." When it came to partial-birth abortion, "seventy percent said the gruesome procedure should be outlawed, except in cases where the woman's life is truly in danger."[18]

Part of this drop in public backing of abortion is linked to another branch of the biological sciences. In the 1980s, scientists began studying a possible link between abortion and breast cancer, analyzing data that had previously been unavailable. Abortion opponents vaunted the new scientific data, but abortion supporters hastily dismissed the information as being "circumstantial," "methodologically flawed," or "driven by antiabortion fanatics."

Yet as the abortion count rose and the years passed, the data kept coming in, and studies continued to issue forth.

Abortion and Breast Cancer

In 1996, City University of New York Professor Joel Brind published a report revealing that twenty-three of twenty-eight studies found a link between abortion and breast cancer. The analysis caused an uproar in Britain, where it was published in the *Journal of Epidemiology and Community Health,* and the editor was prompted to write: "I believe that if you take a view (as I do) which is pro-choice, you need at the same time to have a view which might be called pro-information without excessive paternalistic censorship (or interpretation) of the data."[19]

Yet paternalistic censorship is just what 12 US Congressman tried to do. On Oct 21, 2002, twelve House Democrats led by abortion advocate Rep. Henry Waxman, D-Calif, wrote Health and Human Services Secretary Tommy Thompson demanding the National Cancer Institute's Web site be edited to assert that there is no correlation between abortion and breast cancer.

The debate was heating up. Abortion supporters could smell the danger and those more interested in safeguarding their own ideas than in confronting scientific facts were not about to tilt the balance of power. Dr. Andrew von Eschenbach, appointed by President Bush to head the cancer agency, convened a February 2003 meeting of the National Cancer Institute to discuss the issue. The word "abortion" was avoided like the plague in the workshop entitled "Early Reproductive Events and Breast Cancer."

The workshop's introductions made it clear that this was a *scientific* conference that was to leave out all emotions and politics surrounding breast cancer and abortion. But those warnings were disingenuous, critics of the National Cancer

Institute said. "It serves their purpose," said Dr. Elizabeth Shadigian, an obstetrician and researcher at the University of Michigan-Ann Arbor. That purpose was to advance the institute's view that there is no link, she said."[20]

The 100 epidemiologists, clinicians, and doctors convened to review the evidence *quickly* agreed that a woman who terminates her pregnancy does not face a higher risk of the devastating disease later in life. "No link between abortion and breast cancer" was the headline that went out across America.[21]

The majority of the researchers convened agreed, with almost no debate and without time to study the data, that there was no link between the two. However, only scientists who disagreed with the link made official presentations and new data was cited that none of the other medical professionals present were able to verify or see either beforehand or even during the workshop.[22]

Despite the absence of clear scientific data, they concluded that most early studies of the relationship between abortion and breast cancer were compromised by a supposed methodological error known as "recall bias." Critics of the reports say that many of the healthy women in the studies were likely to have lied about having had abortions, whereas those with breast cancer – theoretically desperate for any explanation – were supposedly more likely to reply honestly.

Karen Malec, president of the Coalition on Abortion/ Breast Cancer, countered, "Scientists know there is no evidence of recall bias, a theory which says that more cancer patients honestly report their abortion histories than healthy women. The study, Howe et al. 1989, ruled out any possibility of recall bias because researchers used medical records and matched them to fetal death certificates. They did not use interviews. Yet Howe et al. found a statistically significant 90 percent increased risk."[23]

Pulling an error in method out of the air? Ignoring all the facts? Selective presentation of the scientific data? That sounds like scientific misconduct, the trumping of truth by ideological objectives.

That is nothing new to Dr. Angela Lanfranchi, a breast cancer surgeon, fellow of the American College of Surgeons, and clinical assistant professor of surgery at the Robert Wood Johnson Medical School in New Jersey. "Paternalistic censorship is what I experience every time I try to speak on the science supporting the abortion-breast cancer link.

"When I first heard of the link between abortion and breast cancer, in 1993, I thought it was a pro-life fantasy. 'That's crazy,' was my initial response. However, out of curiosity I changed the history form I used in my work as a breast surgeon, asking each woman the order and outcome of all pregnancies. The results surprised me.

"In the first six months I had two patients in their 30s with breast cancer; one had had seven pregnancies and six abortions, the other five pregnancies and three abortions. I continued to see more and more young women with a history of abortion, developing breast cancer. Of course, I may have been witnessing a statistical fluke."[24]

So she started studying the phenomenon. She found that miscarriages do not increase breast cancer risk, since they are associated with low estrogen levels that do not cause breast growth. However, when a pregnancy is terminated before the breast cells reach full maturity, a woman is left with more immature type 1 and 2 breast lobules (milk glands) than before her pregnancy started, and therefore is at increased risk. Her breasts never mature to type 3 and 4 lobules, which would have occurred in the third trimester and would have lowered her risk.

These medical facts combined with statistical analysis convinced Dr Lanfranchi. *The Journal of the National Cancer Institute* published in 2002 its data showing breast cancer rates between 1973 and 1998 increased more than 40 percent. The increase since the mid-1980s is entirely confined to women of the Roe vs Wade generation, not to the older group of women.

Ideology should not prevent the dissemination of this information. As Dr Janet Daling, who identifies herself as being pro-choice, says: "If politics gets involved in science, it will really hold back the progress we make. I have three sisters with breast cancer, and I resent people messing with the scientific data to further their own agenda, be they pro-choice or pro-life. I would have loved to have found no association between breast cancer and abortion, but our research is rock solid, and our data is accurate. It's not a matter of believing. It's a matter of what is."[25]

When science is used when it serves our purpose and tossed aside when it contradicts our preconceptions, it is time to ask some serious questions. What is more important: my ideas or the truth? My conception of reality, or real reality? My political position and status, or the basic demand of honesty with myself and others?

But unfortunately for us, we are not getting much of that truth. The same tactics used to smooth over consciences with regard to abortion are employed in the new bioethical battlefields of artificial insemination, birth control, stem-cell research, euthanasia, and human cloning.

Confuse the terms, sow a little doubt, throw in some benefits, get backing from a few prominent scientists, and *voilá*... public opinion turns to your side. Since people form their opinions from what they know, doctoring the flow of information and hiding the full facts will always modify people's opinions, even when it goes against common sense. And once public opinion has been won over, political power will soon capitulate; only the rare politician will risk his neck by sticking up for what is right despite the polls.

Our confusion about sex has also undermined our traditional understanding of the family.

SEX, MARRIAGE, AND FAMILY

Mother, father, children. It seems so simple. So how could anyone be confused about the meaning of family? Yet confusion is rampant nowadays, and much of it stems from dissociating sex from commitment. When sex is just a passing moment of pleasure without any deeper human meaning, without openness to life, without a pledge of "till death do we part," not only does sex itself become trivialized, marriage and the society based on family are undermined. In this process, the feminist movement has played a key role, though increasingly it is the homosexual rights movement that leads the foray.

Fringe forms of feminism have abandoned the movement's noble beginnings as a catalyst for achieving fairness in the home and workplace – which most of us would see as worthwhile goals – to claiming that the only path to happiness for women is to resist marriage and eschew the traditional family model. When they look at marriage, they don't see that the wives, husbands and kids involved live happier, healthier, longer lives, or that the children of united marriages learn more, avoid out-of-wedlock births, and have much lower rates of chemical addictions and crime.[26] They see oppression, misery and slavery.

Marlene Dixon, a sociology professor at the University of Chicago, declared in 1969 that "The institution of marriage is the chief vehicle for the perpetuation of the oppression of women; it is through the role of wife that the subjugation of women is maintained. In a very real way, the role of wife has been the genesis of women's rebellion throughout history."

Not to be outdone, that same year, author Kate Millett wrote *Sexual Politics*, affirming that "[wives'] chattel status continues in their loss of name, their obligation to adopt the husband's domicile and the general legal assumption that marriage involves an exchange of the female's domestic service and [sexual] consortium in return for financial support."

The language is direct, but one has to wonder just what marriage they are talking about. Yet even after the Age of Aquarius was well behind us, feminist opposition to marriage continued. By 1990, for example, the group Radical Women was claiming the traditional family was "founded on the open or concealed domestic slavery of the wife."

These strange conceptions of marriage are clearly derived from materialist ideologies and a Marxist mode of analyzing human life. They find much of their inspiration in Frederick Engels, who asserted, "The modern individual family is founded on the open or concealed domestic slavery of the wife, and modern society is a mass composed of these individual families as its molecules." He even proclaims war on the traditional family: "The first condition for the liberation of the wife is to bring the whole female sex back into public industry, and that **this in turn demands the abolition of the monogamous family** as the economic unit of society"[27] [emphasis added].

Modern critics of the family continue on the path of confusion. For starters, they claim that the traditional *Leave It to Beaver* style of family – mom, dad, and several children - is outdated. The new "family" isn't about having kids, or even about a man and a woman for that matter... it's about "love" and "commitment." How can we claim that marriage is about procreation when not all married couples have children, not all children are born within marriage, and with new technology even same-sex unions can have children? Could we be so coldhearted as to say that single moms, same-sex duos, and cohabitating couples are not a family? Would we deny them the same rights and legal benefits as a "traditional" family? Isn't it time to get up-to-date?

Homosexual activists have been especially enthusiastic protagonists in the debate to modify traditional definitions of "marriage" and "family" to admit same-sex unions. After Vermont opened the door to same-sex civil unions, activists shifted efforts to other states. In March of 2003, hearings opened up in the Massachusetts Supreme Court.

New England's Gay & Lesbian Advocates and Defenders (GLAD) filed a lawsuit on behalf of seven same-sex couples on April 11, 2001 under the title Goodrich v. Dept. of Public Health. The plaintiffs, who have been in "committed" relationships of seven to thirty-two years' duration, claim that they have the constitutional right to marry under the state's constitution. This Massachusetts case was not an isolated event. At the same time, five states were debating legislation proposing legal recognition, in various forms, to same-sex couples. And in New Jersey a legal action similar to the Massachusetts case was also being heard.

Behind this activity is what the Boston Globe calls "a well-planned national push to expand homosexual rights."[28] The first step is to achieve the same legal rights as heterosexual couples. The second is to challenge the 1996 federal Defense of Marriage Act (DOMA), which says marriage can only be between one man and one woman, and allows one state to refuse to recognize a homosexual partnership that is recognized in another state. Ultimately, the homosexual activists seek to change the definition of marriage.

The Reality of Homosexuality

Despite all the talk about tolerance, diversity, and equality for homosexuals, there is an incredible amount of confusion over just what homosexuality is. No one likes to examine these uncomfortable sexual matters, but if we really want to understand the rationale behind one of the strongest fundamentalist forces shaping the nation's understanding of the family and sexuality, then we must come to grips with what homosexuality *really* is, not what it is often painted to be.

To begin with, we should distinguish clearly between *tendencies* and *actions*. I may be tempted to shoplift a candy bar from the store. That temptation is bad, but I am not bad as a person until I actually take the candy bar, stuff it into my pocket, and walk out the door. My freely chosen action makes me bad, not the tendency. A person may be psychologically conditioned toward theft (a kleptomaniac), but the person is not a thief until they carry out those actions. Kleptomaniacs are not thrown in jail, but thieves are. So tendencies and actions are separate things.

Unlike irrational animals, we are free. Our tendencies and instincts do not make us what we are. As free persons we can choose what tendencies we will follow; we can choose what actions we will perform; we can choose what kind of person we will be. As human beings, we are not "determined" nor "predestined" to follow our animal instincts. We are free to accept or reject our tendencies, and that includes tendencies to homosexual acts (known medically as *Same-Sex Attraction*).

Homosexual activists often deny this distinction, claiming that you cannot separate who a person is from what they do. Yet while this is true in part (what we do does progressively make us who we are), the argument in the end is false because it adds a third element – *identity* – that is neither a tendency nor an action. Identity is the subjective identification with homosexual tendencies and actions.

A simple example can help make this clear:

- a man's desire to be a father is a natural *tendency* and desire
- having sex with a woman so as to generate a new human being and become a father is an *action*
- recognizing his child and assuming his personal responsibility as a father is *identity*

Tendencies, *actions*, and *identity* are three different realities. Homosexual tendencies are not the same as homosexual acts or the homosexual identity. This fact has long been recognized by psychiatrists and psychologists who distinguish between three categories: *Gender Identity Disorder* (GID),

Same-Sex Attraction (SSA), and *homosexual acts*. The first two categories are not homosexuality, but tendencies that can be accepted or rejected, albeit with varying degrees of difficulty.

In our investigation into the reality of homosexuality, what does science have to say about the causes and consequences of these three categories?

Tendencies: Gender Identity Disorder and Same-Sex Attraction

The Diagnostic and Statistical Manual IV of the American Psychiatric Association has defined Gender Identity Disorder (GID) in children as "a strong, persistent cross gender identification, a discomfort with one's own sex, and a preference for cross sex roles in play or in fantasies."

Some researchers have identified another less pronounced syndrome in boys – chronic feelings of unmasculinity. "This second type, while not engaging in any cross sex play or fantasies, feel [sic] profoundly inadequate in their masculinity and have [sic] an almost phobic reaction to rough and tumble play in early childhood often accompanied by a strong dislike of team sports. Several studies have shown that children with Gender Identity Disorder and boys with chronic juvenile unmasculinity are at-risk for same-sex attraction in adolescence."[29]

Scientists are still studying these phenomena, but current evidence suggests that GID can stem from difficulty in identifying with their own mother (in the case of girls) or father (in the case of boys). Children are born biologically female or male, but especially during the critical years of two- to four-years-old and the period of puberty they must identify with their sex, not merely on the objective level but also on the personal and subjective level. When this bonding does not occur, the risk of GID or SSA rises substantially. It is a nearly universal fact that no homosexuals claim to have had loving, respectful relationships with their own dad. Boys need to identify with their father and affirm their masculinity and when this does not occur, psychiatric difficulties arise.

GID is a treatable disorder. There is no "predestination" to homosexuality. When early identification and proper professional intervention are backed up by parental support, GID can often be overcome. Unfortunately, many parents who report these concerns to their pediatricians are told not to worry about them. In some cases the symptoms and parental concerns may appear to lessen when the child enters the second or third grade, but unless adequately dealt with, the symptoms may reappear at puberty as intense, same-sex attraction. This attraction appears to be the result of a failure to identify positively with one's own sex.

"While a number of studies have shown that children who have been sexually abused, children exhibiting the symptoms of GID, and boys with chronic juvenile unmasculinity are at risk for same-sex attractions in adolescence and adulthood, it is important to note that a significant percentage of these children do not become homosexually active as adults. For some, negative childhood experiences are overcome by later positive interactions... The labeling of an adolescent, or worse a child, as unchangeably "homosexual" does the individual a grave disservice. Such adolescents or children can, with appropriate, positive intervention, be given proper guidance to deal with early emotional traumas."[30]

Biological science is clear: children are born either male or female. However, children have to learn what it means to be a man or a woman and they "have to identify with – and be accepted by – their same-sex parents and peers. If they are going to grow up psychologically healthy they have to feel safe and comfortable with their masculinity or femininity. If, for whatever reason, they fail to pass successfully through this essential developmental stage, they may in adolescence develop same-sex attractions."[31]

Same-Sex Attraction (SSA) is a graver disorder than GID since it involves stronger impulses and the behavior that sometimes accompanies it brings greater consequences for the individual. What causes this attraction for persons of the same sex? Is it biological? Is it determined by a person's surroundings and their experiences, or is there a "gay gene" that "hardwires" people that way?

Two rival theories are jousting for preeminence in this search for the causes of SSA. The first insists that SSA and homosexuality are *biologically determined*, that a "gay gene" makes them the way they are. According to this theory, environmental factors may play a role, but the rules coming from nature force us irresistibly towards certain actions and lifestyles. The political advantages for homosexual activists in this theory are clear, since society is more likely to accept demands for changes in laws and religious teaching if people accept that homosexuality is genetically determined and unchangeable.

However, scientists of the second theory argue that the biological determination theory ignores the reality of human freedom and even manipulates science for political purposes. They propose instead – according to current evidence – that *environmental factors* play the greater part in influencing the "sexual orientation" of individuals. In this theory, everything

from friends, talents, social acceptance, successes and failures, relationship with parents, sexual experiences, abuse,
and permissiveness of society contribute to the formation of
a person's tendencies (including GID and SSA). These in turn
influence a person's actions and ultimately their identity.

Current studies indicate that individuals experience
same-sex attractions principally due to environmental factors. These factors do not "determine" the individual, but they
do exert a powerful influence. Undoubtedly each individual
has a unique background, yet there are similarities in the
patterns of development. The personal histories of those who
experience same-sex attraction often display one or more of
the following:

- alienation from the father in early childhood because
  the father was perceived as hostile or distant, violent,
  or alcoholic
- mother was overprotective (boys)
- mother was needy and demanding (boys)
- mother emotionally unavailable (girls)
- parents failed to encourage same-sex identification
- lack of rough and tumble play (boys)
- failure to identify with same-sex peers
- dislike of team sports (boys)
- lack of hand/eye coordination and resultant teasing
  by peers (boys)
- sexual abuse or rape
- social phobia or extreme shyness
- parental loss through death or divorce
- separation from parent during critical developmental
  stages

In a few cases, homosexual behavior appears later in life as a response to a trauma such as abortion or profound loneliness, and generally same-sex attraction or homosexual activity occurs in a patient with other psychological diagnosis, such as:

☐ major depression
☐ suicidal ideation
☐ generalized anxiety disorders
☐ substance abuse
☐ conduct disorder in adolescents
☐ borderline personality disorder
☐ schizophrenia
☐ pathological narcissism

This is not new information for psychiatrists. In fact, SSA and homosexuality were diagnosed and treated as psychiatric illnesses – abnormal behavior – until 1973. In that year, homosexual activists succeeded in pressuring the American Psychiatric Association (APA) into removing homosexuality as a mental disorder from the APA's *Diagnostic and Statistical Manual on Mental Disorders* (DSM). "Homosexuals had lobbied the APA since 1971 and began disrupting APA meetings, grabbing microphones and shouting down any psychiatrist who considered homosexuality to be a mental disorder. The tactics of 60s anti-war protesters worked. The APA caved and homosexuals have used this victory to proclaim that homosexual behavior is normal."[32]

Dr. Ronald Bayer, writing in *Homosexuality and American Psychiatry: The Politics of Diagnosis* acknowledged that the APA decision was based on politics, not science: "The result [of the APA removal of homosexuality from the DSM] was not a conclusion based upon an approximation of the scientific truth as dictated by reason, but was instead an action demanded by the ideological temper of the times."

Perhaps science will yet triumph over ideology, but that remains to be seen. Meanwhile, scientific studies continue to confirm that SSA is a psychiatric disorder. "Three recent well-designed scientific studies (Fergusson, Herrell and Sandfort) have shown that persons with same sex attraction (SSA) – the forerunner of homosexual activity – suffer from other psychological problems at a rate substantially higher than those without SSA. Some of these problems, such as pathological narcissism and borderline personality disorder are very difficult to treat. Additionally, men with SSA are more likely to suffer from substance abuse problems, sexual paraphilias, and sexual addiction."[33]

These conclusions are not limited to a handful of studies. Repeatedly, "homosexually oriented individuals have been found to exhibit a significantly higher level of psychiatric problems than the general population."[34] This fact is clear, even though science has not been able to clarify fully yet whether these psychiatric problems are part of the cause of homosexuality, or merely the consequence of homosexual actions.

Whatever their relation, it is clear that "if the emotional and developmental needs of each child are properly met by both family and peers, the development of same-sex attraction is very unlikely. Children need affection, praise and acceptance by each parent, by siblings and by peers. Such social and family situations, however, are not always easily established and the needs of children are not always readily identifiable."[35] When GID and SSA are not adequately treated, these tendencies will sometimes lead to homosexual actions.

Actions: Homosexuality

Homosexual actions include anal sex, reciprocal masturbation, and sexual intimacy that in general mimic heterosexual sex. These sexual acts are focused on personal gratification and include no intention of procreation... and occasionally no interest in the health or good of the partner either.

We should not lose from sight the reality of these homosexual actions. Homosexuality is not merely an "abstract social question."[36] It is a very real phenomenon that has *causes* and *consequences*.

When speaking about human actions, there is only one *cause*: the free human person. Unlike other animals, we are not irresistibly guided by instinct. While homosexual actions can be influenced by *tendencies,* it is always a free human being that chooses those *actions* (unless of course we are speaking of rape where freedom is violated). The only real cause of homosexual actions is a free human person, irregardless of whether biological or environmental factors predominate in forging the tendencies.

There are certainly circumstances, such as psychological disorders and traumatic experiences, which can seriously diminish an individual's responsibility for their choices. These conditions, however, do not negate our freedom.

Nor do they negate the *consequences* of homosexual actions. Whether they want it or not, individuals who engage in homosexual acts bring upon themselves consequences that are outside their freedom. Recent findings published in the *British Journal of Psychiatry* indicate higher incidences of illegal drug usage, alcoholism, psychological problems, and violence in the gay community than in the general population. There are serious medical, emotional, psychiatric, and societal consequences of homosexual actions.

1. Medical consequences

Unhealthy sexual behaviors occur among both heterosexuals and homosexuals, yet medical evidence indicates that homosexual behavior is uniformly unhealthy. Men having sex with other men leads to greater health risks, due both to the violent nature of anal sex, resulting in damage to body tissues, and to the promiscuity prevalent in the homosexual lifestyle. Statistics tell us that gay sex is often tied to substance abuse, promiscuity and unsafe sex practices, and a significant minority of gay men also participates in sadomasochism, public sex in bathhouses and group sex.

This promiscuity is rampant even among homosexuals who claim to have a stable partner. Dr. Robert L. Spitzer, a prominent psychiatrist most famous for his pivotal role in 1973 in removing homosexuality from the psychiatric manual of mental disorders, released a study in October of 2003 that was published in the *Archives of Sexual Behavior*.[37] According to data compiled in this study, 34 percent of male respondents (and only 2 percent females) had engaged in homosexual sex with more than 50 different partners during their lifetime.

This promiscuity leads to the spread of STDs and an extremely high incidence of contagion among homosexuals. According to an official report of the *Centers for Disease*

Control and Prevention, "Researchers estimate that men who have sex with men (MSM) still account for 42 percent of new HIV infections annually in the United States and for 60 percent of all new HIV infections among men. Several recent studies have pointed to high, and increasing, levels of other STDs among MSM."[38]

Yet the medical dangers are not restricted to AIDS and to common STDs. "Men who have sex with men account for the lion's share of the increasing number of cases in America of sexually transmitted infections that are not generally spread through sexual contact. "The list of medical diseases found with extraordinary frequency among male homosexual practitioners as a result of abnormal homosexual behavior is alarming: anal cancer, chlamydia trachomatis, cryptosporidium, giardia lamblia, herpes simplex virus, human immunodeficiency virus or HIV, human papilloma virus – HPV or genital warts – isospora belli, microsporidia, gonorrhea, viral hepatitis types B and C, and syphilis. Sexual transmission of some of these diseases is so rare in the exclusively heterosexual population as to be virtually unknown. Others, while found among heterosexual and homosexual practitioners, are clearly predominated by those involved in homosexual activity."[39]

Simply put, homosexual activity and the homosexual lifestyle are physically dangerous, even deadly.

2. Emotional and Psychiatric Consequences

Homosexual activity brings with it serious emotional and psychiatric problems, ranging from dissatisfaction, to incapacity to maintain stable relationships, to suicidal tendencies.

Ex-gays who underwent reparative therapy were asked why they sought to change. "The majority of respondents (85 percent male, 70 percent female) did not find the homosexual lifestyle to be emotionally satisfying."[40] On the contrary, following therapy, many former homosexuals experience a marked increase in both the frequency and satisfaction of heterosexual activity, while those in marital relationships note more emotional fulfillment between their spouses and themselves.

This dissatisfaction with the homosexual lifestyle can reach the point of despair and severe depression, leading to suicidal tendencies. In some studies, over a third of the participants who experienced homosexual attractions reported that at one time, they had seriously contemplated suicide. Two extensive studies appearing in the October 2000 issue of the American Medical Association's *Archives of General Psychiatry* confirm a strong link between homosexual sex and suicide, as well as a relationship between homosexuality and other mental problems.

One of the studies in the journal, by David M. Ferguson and his team, found that "gay, lesbian and bisexual young people are at increased risk of psychiatric disorder and suicidal behaviors. The youth suffering from these disorders were four times as likely as their peers to suffer from major depression, almost three times as likely to suffer from generalized anxiety disorder, nearly four times as likely to experience conduct disorder, five times as likely to have nicotine dependence, six times as likely to suffer from multiple disorders, and over six times as likely to have attempted suicide."[41]

Does "homophobia" and negative social pressure cause

this suicidal tendency and related disorders? Homosexual activists would claim so.

However, an extensive study in the Netherlands undermines the assumption that homophobia is the cause of increased psychiatric illness among gays and lesbians. The Dutch have been considerably more accepting of same-sex relationships than other Western countries for many years. In fact, same-sex couples now have the legal right to marry in the Netherlands and homosexual behavior is accepted on par with heterosexuality. The Dutch study, published in the *Archives of General Psychiatry*, did indeed find a high rate of psychiatric disease associated with homosexual behaviors, where there is little or no social rejection or "homophobia."

The study from the Netherlands does not stand alone. A December 2003 study published in the *British Journal of Psychiatry* found that "Gay men and lesbians reported more psychological distress than heterosexual women, despite similar levels of social support and quality of physical health."[42]

In fact, science finds links between homosexual actions and psychiatric problems repeatedly. "Compared to controls who had no homosexual experience in the twwelve months prior to the interview, males who had any homosexual contact within that time period were much more likely to experience major depression, bipolar disorder, panic disorder, agoraphobia and obsessive compulsive disorder. Females with any homosexual contact within the previous twelve months were more often diagnosed with major depression, social phobia or alcohol dependence. In fact, those with a history of homosexual contact had higher prevalence of nearly all psychiatric disorders measured in the study."[43]

J. Michael Bailey, in his commentary on the research on

homosexuality and mental illness concluded, "These studies contain arguably the best published data on the association between homosexuality and psychopathology, and both converge on the same unhappy conclusion: homosexual people are at a substantially higher risk for some forms of emotional problems, including suicidality, major depression and anxiety disorder."[44]

3. Societal consequences

At the risk of sounding pedantic, we must state the obvious: homosexual sex does not produce children. A society without children is destined to die, and homosexuality therefore constitutes a danger to the survival of society. Though this fact is obvious, it does not hurt to be reminded of it.

There are, however, other serious perils to the health of society instigated by homosexuality, including the rampant epidemic of STDs in the gay community. It isn't good for any society to have its members killed off by a plague.

Yet besides these clearly documented dangers lurks a much more imminent menace: child abuse and sexual predation of minors.

Homosexual activists deny any link between homosexuality and exploitation of minors, yet the evidence tells a different story. As Dr. Timothy J. Daily, Ph.D. notes, "Despite efforts by homosexual activists to distance the gay lifestyle from [sexual abuse of minors], there remains a disturbing connection between the two. This is because, by definition, male homosexuals are sexually attracted to other males. While many homosexuals may not seek young sexual partners, the evidence indicates that disproportionate numbers of gay men seek adolescent males or boys as sexual partners."[45]

Though certainly not all homosexuals are pedophiles

or sexual predators of minors, the disproportionate numbers who are is alarming. Perhaps the most tragic aspect of
the homosexual-abuse of minors connection is the fact that
men who sexually molest boys or young men often lead their
victims into homosexuality and sexual predation. Evidence
indicates that a high percentage of homosexuals were themselves sexually abused as children:

□ A 2003 study in the *American Journal of Public Health*
found that 39 percent of males with same-sex attraction have been abused by other males with same-
sex attraction. An earlier study in *Child Abuse and
Neglect* discovered that 59 percent of male child sex
offenders had been "victim of contact sexual abuse
as a child.[46]

□ The *Archives of Sexual Behavior* reports: "One of the
most salient findings of this study is that 46 percent
of homosexual men and 22 percent of homosexual
women reported having been molested by a person of
the same gender. This contrasts to only 7 percent of
heterosexual men and 1 percent of heterosexual wom-
en reporting having been molested by a person of the
same gender."[47]

□ A study of 279 homosexual/bisexual men with AIDS
and control patients discussed in the *Journal of the
American Medical Association* reported: "More than
half of both case and control patients reported a sexual
act with a male by age sixteen years, approximately 20
percent by age ten years."[48]

□ Noted child sex abuse expert David Finkelhor found
that "boys victimized by older men were over four

times more likely to be currently engaged in homosexual activity than were non-victims. The finding applied to nearly half the boys who had had such an experience… Further, the adolescents themselves often
linked their homosexuality to their sexual victimization experiences."[49]

□ A study in the *International Journal of Offender Therapy and Comparative Criminology* found: "In the case of
childhood sexual experiences prior to the age of fourteen, 40 percent (of the pedophile sample) reported
that they had engaged 'very often' in sexual activity
with an adult, with 28 percent stating that this type of
activity had occurred 'sometimes'"[50]

□ A National Institute of Justice report states that "the
odds that a childhood sexual abuse victim will be arrested as an adult for any sex crime is 4.7 times higher
than for people… who experienced no victimization
as children."[51]

□ *The Journal of Child Psychiatry* noted that "there is a
tendency among boy victims to recapitulate their own
victimization, only this time with themselves in the
role of perpetrator and someone else the victim."[52]

"The circle of abuse is the tragic legacy of the attempts
by homosexuals to legitimize having sex with boys. For too
many boys it is already too late to protect them from those
who took advantage of their need for love and attention. All
too many later perpetrate the abuse by themselves engaging in the sexual abuse of boys. Only by exposing the lies,
insincere denials, and deceptions – including those wrapped
in scholastic garb – of those who prey sexually on children,

can we hope to build a wall of protection around the helpless children among us."[53]

Yet instead of protection, our children are getting ideology. The educational establishment is often an active promoter of the homosexual agenda, and in their zeal to "make schools safe for young gay and lesbian people" they end up nurturing a new generation of sexual victims and victimizers.

Reality tells us that "bad" things exist. A free fall off a 37-story building, a constant diet of Big Macs, or the death of a friend are "bad" because they go against what is best for us, either spiritually, psychologically, or physically. When psychiatric tendencies – brought on by abuse, environmental influence, or family problems – lead people to behavior that is objectively dangerous for themselves and others, only a new fundamentalist could deny that this is "bad."

Cancer is another one of these "bad" things. Certain cells in the body rebel against their natural roles and mutate into forms that harm the person, sometimes even killing them. Cancer is a sickness that goes against our biological nature. So what would you think if someone suggested a "National Celebrate Cancer Day" to commemorate the spread of cancer, as if it were some great advancement? Wouldn't this "affirm" our cancer patients and testify to our tolerance of cell "diversity"? The idea is ridiculous, yet when it comes to homosexuality why should we celebrate and "affirm" unnatural and unhealthy behavior? Homosexual actions bring serious risks for the person acting on SSA and for society at large. How can we encourage what is objectively bad?

Certainly, a cancer patient or a person with Same-Sex Attraction has the same human rights as anyone else, but a cancer patient would never suggest that we should encourage cancer or suggest to school students that they should engage in behaviors that will lead to getting cancer.

The Agenda for Homosexual Rights

The distinctions and facts we have just reviewed will be construed by homosexual activists as homophobia, religious narrow-mindedness, and "fundamentalist," yet the scientific facts are clear and *not a single religious argument* has been used in the previous pages.

When this evidence is ignored or bullied into silence, we are without a doubt faced with an authentic fundamentalism: the secular religion of diversity. Homosexual activists are not concerned with refuting the evidence, but rather with manipulating science, silencing the opposition, and advancing their agenda. What do they want? The answer is quite simple: legitimize homosexual practice in *morality* and *law*. All the tactics and arguments in their agenda revolve around this goal of legitimization. The two motives that drive homosexual activists toward this goal are *equality* and *security*.

In the first place, they are propelled by a sense of injustice: they crusade for the noble cause of *equality*. As long as all lifestyles and opinions are not equally accepted by society and codified in law, they sense a cause for victimization and abuse of a minority. As the attorney for the homosexual activists in the 2003 Massachusetts case claimed, "The exclusion of the plaintiffs from marriage ... violates the fundamental right that these plaintiffs enjoy with all others in this commonwealth."[54] Homosexual activists seek the legal and social benefits of being able to call their unions "marriages." Tax cuts, adoption rights, legal testaments, and numerous other benefits can only benefit spouses or immediate family.

Modifying the definition of marriage is the key to unlock the candy closet.

According to these equality claims, homosexuality should be, not only decriminalized, accepted, and tolerated, but even supported, protected, and advocated. Where special abuse was prevalent in the past, they claim special treatment should now be given to compensate for the former inequality.

Yet secondly, and perhaps most importantly, there is a powerful underlying psychological need that homosexuals feel for *security and legitimacy*. No one likes to be labeled. No one likes to be scorned or called bad, and if the actions which you freely commit bring on the opprobrium, you can either change yourself or try to change reality. Since they are not ready to change their lifestyle, many homosexual activists are trying to change reality. This is the homosexual agenda: change society so that it accepts homosexual behavior. They follow six principal tactics in the implementation of this agenda.

1. First, they begin by framing the debate as a matter of "equal rights." If you can set the conditions and the direction of an argument, that's half the battle, so the arguments are set up in the framework of equality. The acceptance of heterosexuality as the only normal sexual "orientation" is "discriminatory," just as the traditional concept of marriage is. In our tolerant and egalitarian society, there is no room for discrimination.

2. Their second argument is based on biological determinism. If there is a "gay gene," that means homosexuals are what they are naturally, and therefore deserve special rights and legal recognition.

3. A third argument works on the notion of change.

Homosexual activists try to show that human nature can evolve... and some go so far as to argue that homosexuality is an upward evolution of mankind. In the same vein, they argue that marriage in not an institution set in stone. Because it has changed with the times – slaves were once forbidden to marry and that changed, interracial marriages were forbidden and those laws were overturned – in our times marriage should change again, modifying its definition so that laws against homosexual marriage can be removed.

4. From this argument, activists often develop a fourth: freedom. They claim that each person chooses his or her own orientation.

5. Homosexual advocates also resort to what in itself is the weakest argument, but in our disoriented society has become the strongest. They claim that the fundamental focus of sex is personal realization, not the good of the partner or the continuation of the species. Similarly, marriage is not about a man and a woman; it's not about bearing and raising children; it's all about "love and commitment."

6. Tolerance is the final argument for the legitimization of homosexual actions. Typical expressions of this one remaining virtue in American society include: "whatever floats your boat, man," "if that's what makes you happy," "I'm personally opposed, but I can't force my morals on others." As Justice William Kennedy wrote in the majority opinion for Lawrence vs. Texas, the July 2003 Supreme Court decision that overturned sodomy laws, "No state has the right to interfere with the private sexual activities of homosexuals."[55] The

acceptance of relativism as the basic operating system of American life has made us incapable of saying that anything is wrong, bad, or intolerable.

Why the Unnatural Can Never Be Natural

As Hegel once remarked, "You need not have advanced very far in your learning in order to find good reasons even for the most evil of things. All the evil deeds in this world since Adam and Eve have been justified with good reasons."[56] Homosexual advocates present plenty of "good" reasons for justifying their actions and for changing the definition of marriage, but each one of them can be found seriously lacking.

1. Equal Rights

The first argument – for equal rights – appears sound, but a closer examination finds fatal flaws. Take for example one popular equal rights argument, "A loving man and woman in a committed relationship can marry. Dogs, no matter what their relationship, are not allowed to marry. How should society treat gays and lesbians in committed relationships? As dogs or as humans?"

The conclusion is clear, but only if you accept the parameters. Should we treat gays as dogs or humans? Obviously as humans. The argument *seems* convincing, but even on a merely logical level we discover serious defects. The middle term – relationship – is used in two different senses and therefore the conclusion cannot be valid. It would be like arguing that since cats eat mice, and a mouse is a computer accessory, cats eat computer accessories. The conclusion sounds correct, but is factually and logically wrong… and a bit ridiculous too.

The equality argument falls into the same irrationality, even though it might *seem* it is solidly reasoned. Human relationships are completely different from dog relationships. The association that human beings have is based on what we are, our specific nature, namely our freedom *for* and spiritual intelligence (inference and creative capacity). The relationship between dogs is based on their specific nature, which is only freedom *from* and a limited animal intelligence. Human freedom is above and beyond animal freedom, and because this middle term is different, the entire argument is false.

But going beyond this mere logical level, why should we consider equality to be the king value to which we must all bow down?

Some authors would claim that equality is the only way to ensure a just society, since left to our devices we will always seek our own greatest good, even to the detriment of others. The end result would be the rule of might, not the rule of right. Faced with this choice, the only viable solution to our radical egotism is establishing the "veil of ignorance," whereby before we ever exist, we work out how to treat others. Since we don't yet exist, we do not know what qualities we'll have either. Since no one knows exactly what luck they will have in the draw – tall, short, fat, skinny, smart, or stupid – everyone's self-interest will lead them to give equal rights to everyone, just to make sure they don't get the short end of the stick.[57]

This is an attractive theory, and it *seems* convincing, but there are three main problems.

First, the assumption that man is always radically egotistical has no basis in philosophy or history. Undoubtedly, we all have a natural tendency to selfishness, to see things from our perspective, to arrange things to our greatest advantage, but tendencies are not actions. History is witness to countless saints, mothers, and rulers who put the needs of the weak and defenseless before their own.

Humans are not just rational animals; we are also social. We have natural ties to other people, not simply because I need them to survive and satisfy my own needs, but because I contribute to society and others depend upon me. The clearest example is from family life: a father who goes to office day in and day out – even though he hates his job – because he knows his family depends on him or a mother who stays up all night beside a sick toddler's bed, not because she doesn't like sleeping, but because her child needs her. Parents constantly put the needs of the weaker members before their own. The capacity to forget oneself to serve others is a sign of maturity, a testimony that we are not necessarily radical egotists. Heroism of this nature can come in packages as small as Mother Theresa of Calcutta.

The second problem with the "veil of ignorance" is that it is artificial. When will we ever not exist or not know what qualities we have? When has any such situation ever existed? The fact is that we only arrive to the possibility of debating such issues when we already know our own qualities and when we know what is right and wrong. In real life, the "veil of ignorance" is not total, but only partial. We do not know exactly what will take place or who will possess which qualities in the future, but we do know what is good for human nature. Consequently, human nature – not equality – is the only basis upon which to build a just future society.

The third difficulty with this theory of justice is that it neglects another basic fact: persons come before society (just like the horse goes before the cart). The problem with ideological systems like communism is that they dream of great advancements of mankind, promise the elimination of all injustice, and propose the progress of the peoples, but forget the individual in the process. What comes first, a single person or the relations between people? That question is the same as asking, "What comes first, a cow or the herd of cows?" Obviously the cow and the person come first, since you cannot have relations between individuals that do not exist.

We are not fulfilled by satisfying our whims or by doing what we feel like, but by living according to our spiritual nature (i.e., freedom). Through reason and will, this freedom sets our tendencies to self-love, pleasure, and happiness in order. The most radical freedom is not license and disorder, but rather self-discipline and order.

The purpose of society is to help each of its members to their fulfillment, to set up the necessary conditions so that each person can attain their greatest good. Equality is secondary to this goal: if it helps members of society reach their natural aim, it is good, but when a false application of equality begins discriminating against some and deviating citizens from their natural fulfillment, it is bad.

If we were to accept the framework of equality as the greatest good, then freedom for all, interests of the majority, the common good of society, truth, reality, and freedom of expression all become secondary. They can even be trampled on if they get in the way of "equality."

In the poignant short novel *Animal Farm* by George Orwell, the farm animals decide to rebel against the tyranny of the farmer and establish a truly just and egalitarian society. They are led into battle by the courageous horses and the crafty stratagems of the pigs, and after the successful rebellion, they set up a collective farm ruled by the animals, for the animals. Seven rules written in broad letters across the side of the big red barn guide their actions, beginning with the fundamental principle that "all animals are equal."

Yet little by little, the animals see the rules abrogated. First, they receive a new interpretation and the meaning of the words is "adapted to new circumstances." Then an "outdated" rule is crossed out from the barn wall. No one seems to notice at first until key animal leaders of the original rebellion start to disappear. The pigs reassure the other animals that all is under control, while at the same time instituting curfews, limits on education, a dog police force, and more work with less leisure.

The rules are again updated and one by one – always by night – they disappear from the barn wall. When one old horse grumbles that things may have been better under the old farmer, she is sharply rebuked. Finally, the animals wake up one morning to find only one rule scrawled in bold white letters across the red barn: "All animals are equal, but some animals are more equal than others." The pigs meanwhile have set up their headquarters in the old farmer's house, donned his clothes, and no one seems to be able to distinguish anymore between them and humans.

The animal farm story is often repeated in the modern struggle for "equality." Homosexual activists fight for what they call "equal rights," but end up repressing medical reality and the rights of other citizens to act and speak according to their convictions. The current attempt to push "equality" and "tolerance" on the rest of society ends up stifling freedom.

Where does equality draw its authority to rule over truth,

reality, and freedom? Why should equality be more important than liberty? Putting "equal rights" as the greatest good of society only brings greater evil, because authentic equality can only be attained when there is a proper relation to truth, freedom, and reality.

This principle becomes clear when we apply it to real life. If we have two high-school students, one who is extremely sharp, studies six hours every day, and turns in all his brilliant papers on time, and another who is dimwitted, never opens a book, and copies his homework from others, should the teacher give the same grade to both out of "equality"? Wouldn't this be a greater injustice?

Or in the business world, let's say that a man starts off an asphalt company with $2000 borrowed money, and over the course of twenty-five years through hard work, savvy deals, and quality service he builds up a multimillion dollar business. Another man starts a business as a false front to a credit card scam, raking in thousands of dollars through fraud and by stealing from unwitting customers. Both businessmen have multimillion dollar businesses. Are they equal? Is the one just as good as the other simply because the end result is the same? Both are defined as "multimillion dollar businesses," but saying they are the same thing or that one is just as good as the other is an affront to common sense and basic morality, just as it is ludicrous to define traditional marriage and homosexual "marriage" as the same thing.

These are questions that the advocates of "equality" rarely consider and the modern man loses sight of in a society infatuated with "tolerance." This was clearly the case in decisions of the Canadian Supreme Court in 2003 – it declared that the traditional definition of marriage is discriminatory

toward same-sex unions – and by the United States Supreme
Court in *Lawrence vs Texas* striking down Texas' ban on homosexual sodomy that same year.

The Massachusetts's Supreme Court ruling of November
18, 2003 redefining marriage as the "voluntary union of two
persons as spouses, to the exclusion of all others" borders on
the schizophrenic, since the new definition speaks of "exclusion," the very principle upon which the old definition was
rejected. Chief Justice Margaret Marshall's desire to advance
equal rights for all has only resulted in special rights for some.
It has become increasingly clear that the New Fundamentalists are not really seeking equality for all, but rather equality
for those who are "more equal than others." This self-inter-
ested justice is not justice at all, let alone *for* all. Equality that
ignores reality will only generate greater problems.

There is one final problem with the equality argument for
"homosexual rights." It hinges upon the assumption that the
Constitution's main purpose is to protect minorities from the
majority. In this concept, law keeps the big fish from eating
the little fish.

This is true, but only partly. The law is meant to protect
minorities, but this goal is secondary to the primary purpose
of law: to bring about the common good. The good of society isn't what is best for the government or for some vague
"Motherland" or "Fatherland"; the good of society is the good
of each of the members of society. And what is best for each
person is not granting their every whim or satisfying every
new appetite that comes along (every good parent knows
that); the best for each person is the fulfillment of what they
are, of their spiritual and rational nature.

That is why law is not merely *legal*; it is also *moral*. Law itself cannot determine what is moral (right or wrong), but what it establishes can be right or wrong inasmuch as it corresponds with moral law. Just law takes the conclusions of ethics (the science of what is right and wrong) and applies them in practical norms for the community.

Law both *reflects* and *influences* the morality of society: it is both child and parent. That is why a government cannot be tolerant of everything, just like a parent cannot tolerate every whim and temper tantrum of a child. It has to draw a line in the sand saying, "You can do this, but *that* is going too far." Why? Because some things are simply bad for you, even if it's what you want. A government *necessarily* legislates morality in every law and court decision, whether it is *laissez-faire* or Puritan morals. Every law has a foundation in some philosophical and ethical vision of the world and there is no such thing as an indifferent and neutral government.

2. Biological Determinism

The second argument – biological determinism – proposes that homosexual behavior is predestined by a "gay gene." While a number of researchers have sought to find a biological cause for same-sex attraction and the media promote the myth that a "gay gene" has already been discovered, the fact remains that SSA is a psychiatric tendency, not a genetic "predestination."

No firm scientific evidence has been found to validate the claim that homosexuality is biologically determined. Widely publicized scientific studies connecting the hypothalamus, genetic markers, hormones, or brain chemistry to homosexuality have all been dismissed as highly speculative and, in some cases, deliberately deceptive. In fact, all serious studies show that homosexuality is – simply put – deviant sexual behavior.[58]

Until 1973, the *American Psychiatric Association's Diagnostic and Statistical Manual* identified same-sex attraction (SSA, the precursor to homosexual actions) as a psychological disorder. Dr. Robert Spitzer of Columbia University, was instrumental in the removal of that section of the manual. Using early studies on the issue, he argued that homosexuality was "natural" and biologically determined behavior – therefore not chosen and not subject to change. And since it was "natural," it would also be morally acceptable for the person to act according to these natural dispositions.

Since Spitzer's early studies, many others have been published with similar conclusions. In spite of several attempts, however, none of the highly publicized studies has been scientifically replicated. In fact, many do not even make a claim for a genetic basis to same-sex attraction.

Take for example a study conducted at the UCLA School of Medicine in October of 2003 on the developmental differences between the male and female brains of mice. The results were touted as evidence that sexual orientation is hardwired into the human brain before birth. A reporter from the Reuters titled his article, "Sexual Identity Hard-Wired by Genetics" and opened with this sweeping statement, "Sexual identity is wired into the genes, which discounts the concept that homosexuality and transgender sexuality are a choice, California researchers said on Monday."

Psychologist Warren Throckmorton disagreed. "All this study really suggests," he noted in an opinion piece published by the Web site of Grove City College, "is that genes may play a role in creating the differences in male and female brains. This is not news; researchers have known this for a long time." But the study, Throckmorton said, has nothing to do with the formation of sexual orientation. "No wonder the public is confused about this issue. The reporting has made inferences that are not at all warranted by the study itself."[59] Even the lead researcher of the project put a damper on the journalistic joy: Dr. Eric Valain maintained that "This is not about finding the gay gene."

Surprisingly (or perhaps not so surprisingly), most of the news-service articles "overlooked" these facts... and even failed to mention that the study was conducted upon mice, not human beings. Anyone who thinks mice and men should have sex and reproduce in the same way needs a little more than a damper... they need a reality check.

But instead of facing reality, they start blinking. Yes, blinking.

Another 2003 study – based on blinking patterns – was published in the *Behavioral Neuroscience* journal and claimed to support the theory that homosexuality is directly caused by genes. Journalists were eager to trumpet the headline, yet, as in the past, the press reports and public statements misrepresented and propagandized the study beyond recognition.

The head researcher in the blinking study, Qazi Rahman, is adamantly against the idea that environment plays a fundamental role in the formation of same-sex attraction. In fact, he has conducted several studies to "prove" that homosexuality is destined by biological data, the blinking study being just one of them. According to Rahman's conclusions, the fact that fifteen lesbians on average blinked in a similar manner to fifteen straight men when startled "proves" that homosexuality is genetic.

However, what press releases failed to specify was that the study also found no substantial differences between the blinking patterns of straight and gay men. "Because a small group of lesbians blinked like a small group of straight men, the leap is made to assume being a lesbian is obligatory? The inference is confounded by the fact that it is well known that smoking can impact startle response, and Rahman's study did not take smoking status into account in choosing study participants. Hence, the headlines for the Rahman study could easily have read: 'Sexual orientation not genetic for gay men; might be for lesbians.' I must have blinked; I didn't read that anywhere."[60]

If same-sex attraction were genetically determined, we could expect identical twins to be identical in their sexual attractions. However, that is not the case. There are numerous scientific reports indicating quite the opposite. Case histories typically reveal *environmental factors* which account for the development of different sexual attraction patterns in genetically identical children, supporting the theory that same-sex attraction is a product of the interplay of a variety of environmental factors, not some "gay gene."

If same-sex attraction were genetically determined, it would be naturally eliminated from the gene pool. Homosexuals by themselves do not reproduce and without offspring, the "gay gene" would disappear. However, the facts again speak otherwise. Amazingly, same-sex attraction and homosexuality have not disappeared with time; instead, they tend to flourish in particular cultures and in certain periods of history, as can be seen in the history of the Persian kingdom, the decadent Roman Empire, and other sexually permissive societies throughout history.

If homosexuality were genetically transmitted, it would be inevitable, immutable, irresistible, and untreatable. Current evidence indicates quite the opposite.[61] The fact remains that irregardless of tendencies, a free human person can choose or reject homosexual actions. Yet studies are now indicating that even those *tendencies* can be changed.

Dr. Robert Spitzer, the doctor whose research helped achieve the declassification of homosexuality as a disorder in 1973, published a new study in October of 2003 on the results of reparative therapy with gay individuals. He humbly acknowledges that his former hypothesis was wrong and that new evidence invalidates his previous position. In fact Spitzer concludes, his newest study "clearly goes beyond anecdotal information and provides evidence that reparative therapy is sometimes successful."[62] SSA and homosexuality can be changed, not just resisted. In fact, this is perhaps the strongest argument against a genetic determination of homosexuality: it is possible to change same-sex attraction and homosexual orientation with proper treatment.[63]

As members of society, persons with homosexual tendencies have all the rights of other citizens. But to merit special protection, they would have to first show that they are different from normal citizens. Since they don't have blue skin, they don't belong to a separate race, and they don't share a common handicap or a minority religion, the search for a substantiating difference cannot be found in the genes. There is no solid evidence to show biological determinism – in fact quite the contrary – and what makes homosexuals different isn't their *nature*, it is their *behavior*.

Homosexuals may form a minority group in society, but their group is based on free *actions*, not nature. A gang of bootleggers in the 1920s wouldn't deserve special rights before the law, so why should homosexuals? Should heroin addicts receive special treatment under the law? Or perhaps prostitutes are entitled to special group treatment? Homosexuals are what they are because of their actions and choices. Their behavior, even though influenced at times by strong psychological forces, is freely chosen and acted upon.

Psychological factors such as environment, life experiences, or sexual exploitation may incline a person toward same-sex attractions, but the actions themselves remain wrong and contrary to nature. Psychological tendencies do not make something natural, nor do they make the actions coming from the tendencies good. We wouldn't decriminalize rape simply because a sadistic rapist has psychological tendencies towards victimizing and strangling his victims. We give him therapy to redirect his tendencies, and if he can't control himself we put him behind bars in order to protect the rest of society.

We don't reassure kleptomaniacs that stealing is fine just because they have a psychological tendency towards theft. We send them to therapy and look for ways to control and redirect their negative tendencies. If he can't control the itch by himself, then the government steps in to offer a cozy prison cell.

The psychological factors might mitigate the sentence, but they don't change the fact that rape and theft are wrong. Same-sex attraction might decrease culpability, but it does not make homosexual acts good or natural.

The law does not exist to protect freely chosen misbehavior (i.e., bad behavior). If a man robs a bank, the law punishes him. If a man sexually assaults a little boy, the law punishes him. The law is meant to protect first the common good of society, not the private good of every individual. A serial killer might claim that he is denied "equal rights" and "discriminated" against when sentenced to prison, but no one would take him seriously – so why do we take homosexuals seriously?

The real reason they are being taken seriously is because our society has lost its sense of what is right and wrong. Our crisis is moral... and more precisely ethical. We are afraid to stick up for what is good and "discriminate" against what is bad. We are enslaved by our own relativism and tolerance.

3. Change

Along with the "natural" arguments, homosexual activists often claim that everything is subject to *change*. Human nature can change, society changes, and our definitions of things like marriage and civil rights can change. Despite its pseudoscientific appearance, the argument for homosexuality from change is on just as flimsy a foundation as biological determinism, both *historically* and *conceptually*.

Any serious student of history will find the same reflections, fears, passions, and desires at work in Hesiod, Virgil, Dante, Montesquieu, or Dostoyevsky. Man has not changed. There is an incredible diversity in their approaches and fluctuations in historical conditions, yet human nature remains a constant. Any attempt to deny its existence is self-contradictory, just as is the claim that human nature changes.

While it is certainly true that historical circumstances do change, human nature does not. The application of basic principles of reality can change, but not the principles themselves. Similarly, while it is certainly true that the application of marriage laws has changed over the centuries, it is completely false to say that marriage itself has changed. Marriage has always been between a man and a woman. The fact that certain people were denied the right to marry or that intermarriage between religions, races, or nationalities was discouraged has nothing whatsoever to do with the core reality of marriage. Marriage has always been between a man and a woman.

On a conceptual level the argument falls apart also. Marriage is not an arbitrary institution, something that we invented and can change according to our whims. In the case of basketball, we invented the game and we can change the rules as we see fit. In the case of marriage, we did not invent it and we cannot change the rules arbitrarily. Marriage is a *natural institution* that depends on the interrelational aspect of human beings, the complementarity of the sexes, and the biological need to continue the species. These are all scientific facts and unchanging realities. Evolutionary, historical-anthropological, psychoanalytical, and structuralist interpretations of marriage can never adequately explain away these facts. On the contrary, as the past forty years of social experimentation have shown, these theories help create the chaos of broken families, dysfunctional homes, and a new generation of children without the necessary support of a solid family.

In a June 2003 article in the *Population and Development Review*, Linda Waite and Evelyn Lehrer give an overview of the research literature on marriage, unambiguously stating: "We argue that both marriage and religiosity generally have far-reaching, positive effects."[64] Among their main points, which they back up with five pages of bibliographical references, are these:

- Married people are less likely than unmarried people to suffer from long-term illness or disability, and they have better survival rates for some illnesses.
- Getting married, and staying married to the same person, is associated with better mental health. Marriage is also associated with greater overall happiness.
- A large body of literature documents that married men earn higher wages than their single counterparts.
- Children raised by their own married parents do better, on average, across a range of outcomes: infant mortality; health; schooling; and avoiding having children as unmarried teenagers. Studies also document that parenting styles formed by religious affiliation are better for children's welfare. And kids who are religiously active themselves seem to do better at school and manage to avoid dangerous behavior.
- Emotional and physical satisfaction with sex are higher for married people.
- Married couples have notably lower levels of domestic violence.

Trying to explain the causal factors behind these results, Waite and Lehrer observe that both marriage and religion lead to positive outcomes by providing social support and integration. They also encourage healthy behaviors and lifestyles. Notably, the benefits from marriage apply to those who make a lifetime commitment while both divorce and cohabitation significantly reduce the positive effects.

So is this an argument for homosexual marriage? After all, if marriage brings so many positive personal and social benefits, shouldn't it be open to homosexuals also?

Perhaps if marriage were a man-made institution, the argument might have some weight... maybe. But marriage is not man-made. It is a *natural* institution,[65] as old as recorded history, and because it is natural it cannot be changed arbitrarily. To make this clear, take the example of gravity. It is a fact of nature, and no amount of wishful thinking can make it disappear. Social planning won't change gravity, and even if everyone in the world agreed that gravity no longer existed, it would still exist. Gravity is a natural fact, just as human nature and marriage are. We cannot change them according to our whims. This is not discrimination or close-mindedness... this is reality.

Even if we were to open "marriage" to homosexuals, it would not really be marriage (the natural institution) and it consequently will not bring the benefits that marriage brings to a married man and woman. There simply is no rational basis for changing the definition of marriage to include homosexual unions.

Homosexuals have a right to live as they choose (this is their God-given freedom, even if they use it poorly), but they do not have the right to choose what is good or bad, what is true or false. They do not have the right to redefine marriage for the rest of society so as to satisfy their own selfish goals. They do not have the right to abuse children and minors, or to change the definitions of abuse and pathology to cover up abuse. They do not have the right to mislead people into thinking that homosexual actions are simply another "lifestyle" choice just as good as any other.

4. *Freedom*

Are we free then to choose our "gender"? Can we choose our "sexual orientation"?

Yes and no. We certainly can affirm our tendencies – whether they be heterosexual or homosexual – and thus identify psychologically with them. A kleptomaniac can identify with his tendency to steal, thus affirming his personal identity as a thief. He may even think that this is good for him. After all, he's just following his "natural" tendency.

Yet this subjective identification will only be natural and good when it corresponds to human nature. Our psychological development can be impaired or deviated, but that does not change human nature. The circumstances change, not the nature, so homosexual actions and the homosexual identity or lifestyle will always be objectively wrong even when subjectively accepted by the individual.

No matter how much this is denied, it does not change the facts, any more than denying gravity eliminates its existence. This dichotomy between identity and nature brings consequences in the psyche, including the fierce drive for legitimization.

5. *"Love and Commitment"*

Faced with the clear rational evidence against the gay lifestyle, activists often turn to more subjective arguments. "But we love each other." "We're committed to each other." Blaise Pascal was certainly right when he said, "The heart has its reasons, of which the mind knows nothing." Love does not always follow reasons.

Yet we can still permit ourselves a few questions: Can love be wrong? Is there such a thing as disordered love?

Homosexual activists claim that their mutual love and commitment justify their relationships. If human life is fulfilled in love, it would be wrong to deny homosexuals the chance to happiness simply because we don't approve of their way of loving.

Love is an ambiguous word. Do I mean affections, sentiments, part-time commitment, or lifetime commitment? Is it the love I have for ice cream or the love of jelly beans? Is that love just about sex, or is it also about "in sickness and in health till death do we part"? Our difficulty in speaking about love is tied to the confusion about what love really is.

Is love a feeling? No, because our feelings and sentiments change from one day to the next, but that doesn't mean I stop loving. Is love just a personal preference? No, because even love has limitations and must follow the laws of nature. A person can love a country, a dog, a child, or a friend, but in none of these cases is it sexual. When a person tries to have sex with a country, we call him nuts; with a dog, bestiality; with a child, molestation or abuse; with a friend, sick. Sex can be disordered and wrong in these cases because it is misdirected. Love is much more than just sex: it is the gift of oneself, not just a feeling, not just sex. Love is not about getting; it is about giving. To love means to give yourself to the one who is loved, but always within the framework of what is good according to our spiritual nature.

Marriage is not just about "love and commitment" in a generic way. It is about authentic love that follows reality and about serious commitment. It is about children, personal and social relations, education, and social stability. Marriage follows the rules of nature. A dog and a cat cannot produce offspring, nor can two bulls produce a calf. The natural law is that animals must be of the same species and of the opposite sex in order for their sexual union to be natural and fruitful. Even in the rare cases where two different species can bear offspring, these are always sterile (e.g., a horse and a donkey can bear a mule). Infertility is a sign of failure in nature.

Yet the fact that some married couples don't have children either because of infertility or personal decision doesn't determine the purpose of marriage. If an apple tree doesn't bear any apples, we don't stop calling it an apple tree. We check to see if an early frost nipped the blossoms or if insects infested it or if an internal disease is eating it away from within. It is still an apple tree and under normal conditions it will produce apples (not oranges or grapes or tomatoes). It is a fact of the science of horticulture.

The science of biology is equally demanding when it comes to humans. Marriage between a man and a woman will usually result in children, unless there is some disease, infertility, or other secondary reasons. However, homosexual unions will never result in children without outside intervention. No shift in the realm of ideas, social trends or new technologies can change the biological facts.

Despite the biological facts, though, many homosexual activists keep up their efforts to change the definition of "marriage." If a marriage is about love and commitment, why can't homosexuals get married? If they love each other, why not seal that love with a lasting commitment? And if they can marry, they deserve equal rights with any other marriage; they should be recognized by the state, receive equal taxation, and have all the same opportunities. Failure to recognize these rights amounts to repression and injustice.

Let's change the case a bit. I have a friend who loves her

German shepherd. They've been together for five years and have a deeply committed relationship. They go everywhere together and even share the same room. So why can't they marry? Why can't they solidify that love and commitment with a more solemn bound?

Sound ridiculous? Perhaps in fifty years we will look back at the current debate about same-sex marriages and think the same thing.

Marriage is intrinsically both *personal* and *social,* and when one aspect is lacking we do not have an authentic marriage. What is legally and socially recognized is not only the *personal* love and commitment of the individuals, but also the *social* impact of their relationship. It is in the best interests of a society to have healthy families. It stabilizes the economy, increases happiness of individuals, fosters initiative, and sets a steady foundation for education and discipline. Though some would argue that the purpose of marriage has evolved from an "instrument of social stability" to "an expression of commitment," the intrinsic nature of marriage has not and cannot change. What has evolved is the desire of some same-sex partners to change the definition of marriage in order to have access to the institution.

Marriage between a man and a woman is the basic unit of society, the social nucleus in which most children are born and raised. This function has an irreplaceable role in society, and in return for this contribution, marriage is recognized and protected by civil authority. This reciprocity has demographic, economic, social and intergenerational consequences that we as a society ignore at our peril.

No doubt some marriages are imperfect and children can be looked after outside of traditional marriages. But a stable and lasting marriage remains the best environment to raise children. For their psychological development, a child needs both parents – father and mother. Society is paying a huge price from the effects of divorce and the damage will only increase as same-sex marriages and adoptions multiply. Traditional families are the most reliable and stable foundation for the future of society.

That is why divorce was illegal – or at least much harder to attain – in most nations until the past century. That is part of the reason why adultery, incest, bigamy, and polygamy are (or were) outlawed – they undermine healthy families. Individuals are "free" to act in that way, but society cannot be indifferent towards these practices any more than you could be indifferent to someone cutting off your left foot. Even before any legal penalties, these practices bring very negative moral consequences for those caught up in them. These splashes ripple throughout society.

6. Tolerance

When their previous arguments don't work, the activists pull out their trump card: tolerance. "Treat us with compassion and open-mindedness! You might not like us, but let us live as we choose." According to this rationale, gays and lesbians shouldn't be judged by their tendencies or by their actions – they simply shouldn't be judged at all. They reject that you can love the sinner while hating the sin. After all, that distinction doesn't leave them free to act like they want.

There is really no problem with tolerance... if that were really what homosexual activists are asking for. But it is not.

Tolerance originally meant allowing people with different beliefs to live accordingly without fear of reprisal. It then mutated into the idea that all beliefs are equally valid. This was mistaken, but at least it allowed for the possibility that people might publicly express their beliefs. People could still openly and rationally debate what they thought was good and true. This tolerance still separated *belief* from *actions*. You were free to believe that polygamy is a God-given practice, but you were not free to practice polygamy. You were free to believe that Catholics were the scum of the earth and deserved to be tarred and feathered, but you were not free to carry out those actions in society without facing the consequences.

But the "tolerance" that homosexual activists are after isn't this kind. Their "tolerance" means that no one – except for those who oppose homosexual acts – should ever hear anything that contradicts what they think, or otherwise upsets them. It means that they are out to get their "rights," even if everyone else has to suffer because of it.

They do not want tolerance of their *beliefs*; they want tolerance of their *actions*. This distorted vision of tolerance is radical, egotistical, and extremely dangerous to a free democratic society. If we cannot say that certain actions are wrong, why do we have prisons? Why do we have a penal and legal structure at all?

That is why Senator Rick Santorum's controversial statement in April of 2003 caused such uproar. He exposed the hypocrisy and the danger of the "tolerance" argument. "We have laws in states, like the one at the Supreme Court right now, that has sodomy laws and they were there for a purpose. Because, again, I would argue, they [acts of sodomy] undermine the basic tenets of our society and the family. And if the Supreme Court says that you have the right to consensual [homosexual] sex within your home, then you have the right to bigamy, you have the right to polygamy, you have the right to incest, you have the right to adultery. You have the right to anything. Does that undermine the fabric of our society? I would argue yes, it does."[66]

Does the "right of privacy" establish a constitutional right to practice homosexual sex? Why not a constitutional right to bestiality? After all, the practitioner in question will ensure that his acts are performed in private. Does the fact that it is done privately make it all right? If we accept the argument anyone can do whatever they want, as long as it's private, we lose any rational basis for denying polygamy, bestiality, and pedophilia. Are these good for society?

A healthy society cannot tolerate every action. It must clearly stand up for morality and right reason or risk its gradual disintegration.

Is this "fundamentalism" perhaps a bit too extreme? Yet how can standing up for the promotion of society's common good be called "fundamentalist"? With all the clear evidence indicating the serious physical and psychological consequences of a gay lifestyle, couldn't we claim that the real fundamentalists are those who refuse to face the facts?

To be compassionate does not mean lying to individuals about the consequences of their aberrant behavior. True compassion entails the desire to alleviate the cause of someone's distress. To confirm someone in their vice – which is the real cause of their problems – is the opposite of compassion. Why is this truth so hard to see? Perhaps because "compassion" has been redefined by militant homosexual advocates to mean confirming, not alleviating, the distress.

Perhaps one day, history will recognize that the real homophobes are those affirming the homosexual lifestyle...

and thus condemning these people to an epidemic of STDs, AIDS, psychiatric complications, and death.

And the Agenda Marches Forward...

Close examination of these arguments for homosexuality and homosexual marriage finds serious rational deficiencies. In fact, the arguments used by homosexual advocates can often be quite irrational, even fundamentalist. Is it any wonder then that they must turn to irrational methods and to the use of power to get what they want?

The name-calling begins first. Anyone who opposes "homosexual rights" is labeled intolerant," a "hate-mongerer," a "bigot," or a "homophobe." And it does not matter what arguments are used against them. They are not there to listen to opposition arguments, but to justify their lifestyle. Any opposition is automatically "discrimination" and every argument is "religious," thereby making it null and void in the secular world of law. It doesn't matter to them that God or religious faith has nothing to do with most of the arguments at hand.

The activism rarely stops with the name-calling. Homosexual advocates take the battle to the legislature and to the power of law. Progress in passing laws for the homosexual agenda has gone very slowly. After a few failed efforts in liberal states like Massachusetts and California, activists realized they would have to change tactics. That's why they have increasingly turned to court decisions and judicial advocacy to get their way.

As one homosexual activist declared, "The number of people who oppose equal rights for gays and lesbians is far greater than the number of homosexuals. Few politicians are willing to alienate 50 percent of the population in order to extend equal rights to, say, 5 percent. Change will probably have to come through the courts."[67]

And that is exactly where the activists have turned their attention.

They began the campaign for homosexual rights in rural states – less educated and involved citizens are easier to manipulate – where judges and state Supreme Courts smiled upon their advocacy efforts. After legal challenges to existing marriage law in Hawaii and Alaska, they managed to get favorable rulings for homosexual marriage, despite overwhelming public disapproval. However, voters quickly showed their resolve to protect marriage to one man and one woman by passing state constitutional amendments. Disheartened, but not beaten, they resolved to take new measures to advance the agenda.

Vermont proved to have all the favorable conditions. With a mix of progressive city dwellers, rural farmers less involved in politics, and a small population, the activists figured it would be easier to work public opinion. And even more important, the state did not have a mechanism by which the voters could easily overturn the decision of the courts via a statewide referendum.

With all the conditions in place, a same-sex couple sued the state for discrimination and won a court ruling in their favor. The Vermont Supreme Court, in a broad sweep of judicial legislating, *ordered* the state legislature to either allow gays and lesbians to marry, or create a new form of government-recognized partnership for gays and lesbians equivalent to marriage in terms of benefits, obligations, and rights.

This ruling has opened a floodgate. Since then, dozens

of lawsuits have been launched by gays and lesbians who obtained a civil union in Vermont and then "found out" that their home state refuses to recognize their status. According to one activist Web site, "many gays and lesbians... will request the same rights, benefits and obligations... the states will refuse, lawsuits will be filed in many states, and one of these will eventually be appealed to the Supreme Court who will authorize civil unions across the U.S."[68]

Yet equal rights and civil unions aren't enough. Homosexual activists have their sights set higher: marriage, adoption rights, reduction of the age of consent, and decriminalization of child rape. This agenda is further advanced in Europe where activists have succeeded in marriage rights in the Netherlands, some form of adoption rights in Sweden, Belgium, and the Netherlands, and the age of consent as low as thirteen. Closer to home, in June of 2003, the Canadian Supreme Court mandated "marriage rights" for homosexuals throughout the nation. Not long after, the Massachusetts Supreme Court issued a similar ruling, mandating marriage for homosexuals.

Where will it stop?

To answer that question, we have to examine the agenda's motor. What motivates the strategy? Homosexual activists seek equal "rights" because they feel the pressure and opprobrium of being "different." They know their behavior is not accepted by society, and deep down there's an inkling that there is something more than just not being accepted by society; they sense that something is morally wrong with their actions... but they don't want to change that behavior. And since they are not going to change, society will have to change. At the core of the motivations for the homosexual rights movement is the urgent desire for legitimization.

That is why they will not stop until society is formed in their image and likeness. Nothing short of total acceptance of their actions and lifestyle will satisfy.

The key that unlocked the door to their current success was the 1973 decision by the American Psychiatric Association (APA) to remove same-sex attraction (SSA) from its list of psychological disorders. Now they are grinding another key in the same workshop, but for a different door. In May of 2003, members of the APA met in San Francisco to hear arguments for the declassification of pedophilia, fetishism, transvestism, voyeurism, and sadomasochism from the *Diagnostic and Statistical Manual of Mental Disorders* (DSM-IV-TR).

Dr. Charles Moser of the San Francisco Institute for the Advanced Study of Human Sexuality (IASHS) and Dr. Peggy Kleinplatz with the University of Ottawa, presented a paper entitled: *DSM-IV-TR and the Paraphilias: An Argument for Removal*. Their sophisticated jargon and pseudoscientific terms cloak the two basic arguments they propose:

1. Since these various "sexual interests" are culturally or religiously forbidden, they should not be considered mental illnesses.
2. Since psychiatry has no foundation for determining what is normal or abnormal behavior, these sexual behaviors should no longer be stigmatized.

Does the fact that religion and culture frown upon cannibalism and murder take away the fact that they are wrong?

Religion opposes them because they are contrary to nature, to God's order of things, but we don't need to invoke God to tell us that cannibalism and murder are contrary to the best interests of mankind. God has given us intelligence so that we use it.

Furthermore, if psychiatry has no foundation for determining what is normal or abnormal, what are they doing calling themselves scientists? Of course there are criteria for normal and abnormal behavior! The problem is that those criteria go against the agenda of pro-pedophilia groups like the North American Man Boy Love Association (NAMBLA), the Christian Boy-Love Forum, Girl Love Garden, and Philia. The problem is that psychiatrically disturbed people are trying to justify their disordered sexual interests, cloaking outright perversion in pseudoscientific jargon.

"If pedophilia is deemed normal by psychiatrists, then how can it remain illegal?" asked Linda Ames Nicolosi of the National Association for Research and Therapy of Homosexuality (NARTH). "It will be a tough fight to prove in the courts that it should still be against the law." In previous articles, some mental health professionals have argued that there is little or no proof that sex with adults is necessarily harmful to minors. Indeed, some have argued that many sexually molested children later look back on their experience as positive, Nicolosi said. "And other psychiatrists have written, again in scientific journals, that if children can be forced to go to church, why should 'consent' be the defining moral issue when it comes to sex?" Nicolosi said.[69]

Is this ridiculous or what? Where will this activism stop? It will not stop until we've all agreed that homosexuality, bisexuality, and pedophilia are socially acceptable behavior... or until the activists recognize their disorders and change.

The root of homosexual activism is a moral problem. Homosexual acts – even when they follow acquired psychological tendencies – are contrary to our human nature. Though the sexual infatuation of our society makes this harder to see, it does not make it any less true. Many people long ago made the disconnect between sexual activity and procreation. This is why logically the privacy cases went from contraception for married couples, to contraception for any couple, to limited abortion, to abortion on demand, and now sodomy. Once you accept the legitimacy of non-procreative sexual activity, the logical basis to exclude homosexuality disappears. Once you have separated marriage from procreation, there is no logical basis to exclude homosexual marriages.[70]

Things contrary to nature bring pain. It hurts to stand on your head or to cut off a finger because it is contrary to nature, but the pain is even sharper when we are dealing with what is *specific* to human nature: our reason and our spiritual transcendence. That is why moral pains like slander, imprisonment (taking away freedom), or the death of a loved one are harder to bear than physical pain. The deep dissatisfaction and pain that comes from sin naturally moves us to change, to remove the source of nuisance. We can turn away from the cause of the pain (i.e., conversion) or sink more deeply into it with the hope that the bother will go away. When we choose to sink in, the sludge hardens around us. We get used to the stench and even begin to justify it, using all the rationalizations possible to affirm our partial and twisted picture of reality.

The New Fundamentalism

When partial pictures of reality are affirmed, an ideology is born. The "diversity" ideology that transforms the push for homosexual rights into a broad political movement is no different; in fact, it is a core manifestation of the new fundamentalism. The idea of equal rights for all, of multiculturalism, and of diversity began as a visionary goal for humanity. Now, diversity and the accompanying political correctness have morphed into a quasi-religious civic ideology, a broad belief system, a new fundamentalism.

As author Peter Wood writes in his book, *Diversity: The Invention of a Concept*, the diversity movement is an attempt to alter the root assumptions on which American society is based, chiefly by downgrading individual merit and common standards in favor of separatism and group rights. In other words, diversity is a political position, not just a feel-good term or a call for hiring more minorities.[71]

For its more radical adherents, diversity goes beyond a mere political position. "Political correctness is not, as many of its critics claim, a movement that reduces everything to politics. It is a form of religious fanaticism that attempts to eliminate politics, as is the case with other totalitarian regimes."[72]

As *New York Time's* columnist Richard Bernstein wrote: "In investigating multiculturalism over a period of two years, I have rarely met a multiculturalist ideologue who bothered to learn anything beyond a few heartwarming clichés about another culture, or who even evinced much curiosity about a people other than his own. The ideological multiculturalists are not interested in inclusion or diversity. Indeed, they are so uninterested in ideological diversity that they are among the leading proponents of legislative codes to punish "offensive" speech, thereby helping them in their real goal, which is empowering more people who think as they do."[73]

Political correctness, rooted in relativism and advocating tolerance, thus becomes a self-perpetuating fundamentalism. Authentic freedom is denied in the effort to advance the "rights" of special interest groups enslaved to their own passions. Diversity training in school rooms, on campuses, and in the corporate world are thus "quite simply, an attack on freedom and autonomy for people to be pressured, or required to attend chapel and told what it is proper to think, to feel, and to believe. The whole point of the liberal revolution that gave rise to the 1960s was to free us from somebody else's dogma, but now the very same people who fought for personal liberation a generation ago are striving to impose on others a secularized religion involving a set of values and codes that they believe in, disguising it behind innocuous labels like 'diversity training' and 'respect for difference'."[74]

The irony of this situation is that the multiculturalists are those quickest to warn Americans of a "vast right wing conspiracy" and of "radical Christian fundamentalists." This is an authentic case of mistaken identity: the wolf in sheep's clothing has managed to convince the flock that the shepherd is the wolf.

In the midst of so much confusion and manipulation of terminology regarding sex, family and life issues, evangelical Christians, Muslims, and Catholics have found themselves in an odd alliance, battling together for the survival of the family. Almost always at odds – and even at war – during the past centuries, these religious believers joined efforts during the United Nations conferences in Cairo on population and development (1994) and the Beijing conferences on women (1995 and 2000) to defend the basics of life and liberty.

As a result of this experience, the Catholic Church was compelled to write a *Dictionary of the Family* of nearly 1000 pages to help clear up the clouds of confusion scattered at UN conferences and in national legislatures and courts. Cardinal Alfonso López Trujillo, president of the Vatican's Pontifical Council for the Family, said that the project was carried out at the request of several governments that participate in U.N. conferences and Catholic nongovernmental organizations. "Ambiguous terms and concepts impede a real understanding of the speaker's intentions," he explained. "Everyone will see that it is a serious and systematic effort to engage in a clarifying dialogue."

"We do not engage in crusades nor do we go against institutions," he said. "Rather, we try to use the instruments of truth that develop between faith and reason, and in this case, we wish to carry out a dialogue with everyone, educators, politicians and lawmakers."

Can we find a positive echo in our educational system, media and law to that openness to dialogue and truth?

"The problem with consensus – even communitywide consensus – is that it is malleable, manipulable, and subject to strange changes over time. It is amazing what we can get used to, given enough time and given enough confusion about identity, experience, values and tolerance."[1]

— GEORGE CARDINAL PELL

Spreading the Contagion

EDUCATION

At bottom, the pathology of new fundamentalism afflicting the nation – and indeed the entire culture of the West – often stems from education and through education infects new generations of students. Schools help to create and re-create ideas, culture, beliefs, and practices. As John Dewey wrote, "Etymologically, the word education means just a process of leading or bringing up. When we have the outcome of the process in mind, we speak of education as shaping, forming, molding activity – that is, a shaping into the standard form of social activity. ...we are concerned with the general features of the way in which a social group brings up its immature members into its own social form."[2]

About this there is no debate. The real conflict is in the realm of ideas about *what to teach* and *how to teach it*, and ultimately about reality, about what is true and good. *What to teach* is dictated by what you consider important, which in turn is determined by your philosophical principles. *How to teach* is dictated by what you think will help persons to learn best, which in turn is determined by your conception of the human person. This is why the problems in education are directly tied to the crisis in philosophy itself, especially in epistemology (how and what we know), anthropology (concept of human being), and ethics (what is good).

American educational theory rested for nearly two hundred years upon the realist philosophical basis of Aristotle, though the ideas of Hume, Locke, and other Enlightenment philosophers were mixed into the foundation. At the beginning of the nineteenth century, John Dewey revolutionized educational theory by shifting emphasis toward a subjective, pragmatic, relative, and "democratic" model of education. The educational "experts" who followed Dewey – and they still dominate the educational establishment – exude an air of sophisticated skepticism and turn their nose up at the simpletons who stick to the old-fashioned ideas like truth. They speak of the "Copernican Revolution of Immanuel Kant," the fresh insights of John Dewey, Nietzsche's demolition of traditional values, the scientific advances of cognitive sciences, the "new geopolitical sphere" requiring greater "open-mindedness," and on and on.

At the base of these pseudoscientific and philosophical ideas lies the premise that we cannot know reality as it is; we know only what things **appear** to be, but not what they really are. Some even assert that there is no reality, no truth, no values. Since they do not exist, each person must create their own; education's role is reduced to accepting and confirming these personal values or truths. There is no room left for judging the comparative worth of values or determining right or wrong. That is why equality and tolerance – and not truth or freedom – become the highest values.

Few people ever really think about these problems; most of us simply absorb basic assumptions from our surroundings and live by them. Precisely on this point, the university world is different. Professors are supposed to think about problems, to examine ideas and evaluate their validity, to search for the truth, and to discover the answers to mankind's deepest questions – and then pass their insights on to students in their charge. That approach was the glory of a liberal arts education.

But that glory has faded. Now *technology*, *pragmatism*, and *ideologically driven philosophy* have almost completely replaced the search for truth at the university level. Since any educational establishment, by necessity, takes its direction from this highest level, is it any wonder that every school level down from this top one exhibits the same characteristics?

The *technology* and communication revolution has dazzled university faculties around the world, and whole programs have been fundamentally altered to cater to technical courses, methods, and applied science – while pure science, philosophy, and the classical humanities have been progressively neglected. "'Knowledge for power,' for 'man's conquest of nature,' has replaced knowledge for truth... The goal of education suddenly becomes utilitarian, pragmatic and instrumental."[3]

Pragmatic and practical results replace truth. What matters it to get ahead, to succeed. You've got to make it big, get rich, and make your mark on the world. Physicists make money, philosophers don't, and college alumni that make money are more likely to win renown and give back financial support for their alma mater. University administrations tailor their programs towards these practical results, and students are quick to pick up that what really matters is money, not truth. This money meritocracy encourages flexibility and openness. It does not reward those who are stubborn, argumentative or affixed to notions of absolute truth. Instead of outdated ideas of character and honesty, it encourages secondary virtues like industry, geniality, enterprise – and also certain sins like shallowness, sycophancy, and phoniness.[4]

When the search for truth is neglected, fundamentalism often fills the spiritual vacuum. Partial truths get blown up into the whole truth, and science – even when lacking any real scientific basis – purports to answer all the world's problems. The rapid spread of Marxist and socialist theory (whose supporters always claimed to be *scientific*) among the intellectual elite is one manifestation of the truth vacuum being filled by an attractive system of abstract ideas divorced from reality. The repercussions for education will continue to be felt for decades.

We would fail to understand what is happening in education—and thus in society—if we did not grasp the nature of the deep conflict between the realist and the relativist worldview. Indeed, we would not exaggerate if we were to speak of an authentic "culture war" being waged on the campuses of our schools and universities. Though the manifestations of this war are many, we focus our attention on two of the most representative theories that show symptoms of the new fundamentalism and spread the epidemic of relativism.

Constructivist Theory
Professional educators claim that their treatment of chil-

dren in school rests on a scientific foundation. Advances in the cognitive sciences have guided the design of a new course of study designed to help children learn better and achieve their fullest potential as individuals. Of course, these modern claims to a scientific basis for education are nothing new.

> "Horace Mann, the 19th-century father of the public school system, was one of the first educators to claim that the process of schooling is based on science. Without verified scientific knowledge of how a child's mind develops, he said, 'one would have no right to attempt to manage and direct . . . a child's soul.' But Mann's belief that he possessed such knowledge was unjustified. The 'science' on which he based his theory of education was phrenology, the now entirely discredited pseudoscience of bumps on the skull."[5]

Is this new educational theory of "constructivism" any more scientific? Examine the evidence for yourself. By constructivism, we mean the theory that students *construct* knowledge for themselves as they learn. Each learner individually (and socially) *constructs* meaning and values. According to this basic idea:

1. We have to focus on the learner in thinking about learning and not on the subject/lesson to be taught.
2. There is no knowledge independent of the meaning attributed to experience (constructed) by the learner, or community of learners.

Constructivism is opposed to instructivism. Proponents of the theory set up this basic dichotomy:

<u>Constructivism</u>	vs.	<u>Instructivism</u>
Pedagogy of Choice		Pedagogy of Control
Situated learning		Teaching as telling
Experience		Instruction
Student Centered		Teacher Centered
Nonauthoritarian		Authoritarian
Divergent		Convergent (only one right answer)

Instead of a teacher setting the curriculum, directing the class, and authoritatively teaching the students in order to converge on one answer, constructivism promotes student friendly curricula. Teachers are encouraged to ask their students what they want to learn; by finding out their interests we are sure to keep their attention. Hands-on experience and field trips are more important than classroom instruction since students learn by "experience and contexts" and through "spiral organization" and need such experiences to "facilitate extrapolation."

Beautiful words and theories aside, constructivism faces two major challenges.

First of all, it flies in the face of reality. There is no doubt that education is personal and that we do learn by experience and association as well as from the surrounding environment. Family, peers, community, and culture all influence the educational process. Our growth in knowledge is a decisively dynamic project: we never stop learning. Even so, our experience is always of reality and within the framework of reality. We know what is. The difference between a schizophrenic mental patient and a psychologically healthy person is that the impaired person can't tell the difference between his ideas and reality. Telling our children that they can *construct* their own reality is like telling them to become nutcases.

Again, there is no doubt that in a certain sense we do *construct* our own world. Our everyday experiences and choices make up who we are. There is also no doubt that we can influence reality – this is part of our freedom – but this is always within the parameters of the real world. Certain things simply do not change in this life.

Rape is always wrong, even if some pervert constructs in his own imagination the idea that rape is good. Should we let him "*construct* his own reality"? Constructivism gets off to a bad start when it ignores the real world.

The dichotomy set up by constructivists is too cut and dried, too black and white. The real option is not between taking into consideration your students or forcing doctrine down their throat; the alternative is not one of choosing between an interesting or a boring class for students. The real issue – which is not fully faced by constructivist theory – is: what is reality really like?

The second major flaw of constructivism is in the results. It simply has not worked as an educational system, no matter how much money has been thrown at it.

Between 1967 and 1976, a program called Project Follow Through charted the educational process of more than 70,000 kindergarten through third grade students in 180 schools ranging from rural to urban to determine the effectiveness of different teaching models. The project evaluated education models falling into two broad categories: those based on child-directed construction of meaning and knowledge, and those based on direct teaching of academic and cognitive skills (DI).

"In only one approach, the *Direct Instruction* (DI) model, were participating students near or at national norms in math and language and close to national norms in reading. Students in all four of the other *Follow Through* approaches – discovery learning, language experience, developmentally appropriate practices, and open education – often performed worse than the control group. This poor performance came in spite of tens of thousands of additional dollars provided for each classroom each year."[6]

"Researchers noted that DI students performed well not only on measures of basic skills but also in more advanced skills such as reading comprehension and math problem solving. Furthermore, DI students' scores were quite high in the affective domain, suggesting that building academic competence promotes self-esteem, not vice versa."[7] Though the study was designed just to compare academic performance, the *Direct Instruction* students also outperformed the control group in fields such as attendance, college acceptance, and retention in all studies with statistically significant results.

Basically, the constructivist models compared miserably to classic teaching methods. The old "instructivist" model prevailed... yet unfortunately common sense did not. Faced with this overwhelming evidence, we would have expected educators to set aside the failed programs and embrace the classic direct instruction method. But that was not about to happen.

On the contrary, even before the *Follow Through* study

was officially released, the Ford Foundation commissioned a critique of it; educational professionals were quick to claim that "the audience for *Follow Through* evaluations is an audience of teachers that doesn't need statistical finding of experiments to decide how best to teach children. They decide such matters on the basis of complicated public and private understandings, beliefs, motives, and wishes."[8]

Translated, that means "we have our ideology and no amount of scientific data or reasoning will change that." The problem is not simply that some educators have false ideas; it's that many are blinded by their abstract *a priori* system, ignoring any hard evidence that contradicts those ideas. Despite their lackluster performance, constructivist models of education have continued to dominate the public school system since the 1970s. This lack of common sense has resulted in some pretty stunning educational failures. Here is a just sampling:

- In 1997, the Democratic Leadership Council found only 3 percent of Americans gave the nation's public schools an "A" grade, while 43 percent chose between "D" and "F."[9]
- American students consistently score at the bottom of international tests in math and science despite the fact that we pump more money into public education ($6,857 per pupil) than any other nation.[10]
- While students in lower grades score above the international average, "the longer they stay in our school system, the further they fall behind the rest of the world."[11]
- According to the *National Assessment of Educational*

Progress released June 19, 2003 by the National Center for Education Statistics, 36 percent of fourth-graders cannot read at what the test defined as a "basic" level. The figure for whites is 25 percent, for Latinos 56 percent, and for blacks 60 percent. The same report reveals the steady decline of all reading skills in the upper grades. One in four 12th-graders cannot read at a basic level, down from one in five in 1992.[12]

□ Since 1962, national average SAT scores (indicators of verbal and numerical readiness for college work) have steadily dropped, a decline that authorities claim is not related to changes in the tests. In fact, during the same period the tests have been simplified.[13]

□ Of the 70 percent of all students who graduate from American public high schools, only 32 percent qualify for college. Of the 51 percent of blacks who graduate, only 20 percent qualify for college; of the 51 percent of Hispanics who graduate, a mere 16 percent qualify for college. "The main reasons these groups are underrepresented in college admissions is [sic] not insufficient student loans or inadequate affirmative action," researchers found, "but the failure of public high schools to prepare these students for college."[14]

□ An April 2002 comparative survey of 400 of today's *college* seniors found that they score the same or only slightly better than *high school* seniors of the 1940s and 1950s. When given a test covering four areas of general knowledge, American *college* seniors score at about the same overall level as did *high school* graduates of fifty years ago. Today's seniors do better on questions pertaining to literature, music, and science;

about the same on questions about geography; and worse on questions dealing with history. By almost every measure of cultural knowledge in the survey, today's college seniors appear to rank far below the college graduates of mid-century.[15]

☐ In Massachusetts 1795 applicants who wanted to *teach* in public schools were given mandatory basic tests in reading and writing. Fifty-nine percent of them failed. What did the Massachusetts Board of Education do? It promptly lowered the standard for a passing grade.[16]

The contrast between these dire results and the facts associated with traditional education could not be greater. This becomes especially clear when we compare public to private education (where discipline and classic educational models tend to prevail).[17] Study after study, like this one of the *National Center for Education Statistics*, show the consistent difference, even when other factors such as race and income have been accounted for.

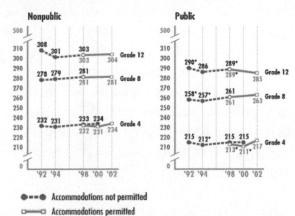

In addition, children who study at home consistently score above the national average on standardized testing; they learn more and outperform their public and even private school counterparts. "According to official reports for the American College Testing Program (ACT), home schoolers have scored higher on average than students in public and private schools. In 2000, the average composite ACT score for high school students was 21, while home school students scored 22.8."[18] In 2001, a U.S. Department of Education survey "shocked the education establishment by revealing that homeschoolers as a whole do better on the SAT... than students who go to schools outside the home. The survey found that home schooled students average 568 on the verbal test (out of a possible 800), whereas the rest of the schooled population averages 506. For math, home schoolers average 525, while others average 514."[19]

Dr. Lawrence M. Rudner conducted a study in 1998 that included 20,760 students in 11,930 families. He found that in every subject and at every grade level (K-12), "homeschool students scored significantly higher than their public and private school counterparts." Twenty-five percent of all homeschool students at that time were enrolled at one grade level or more beyond their age and according to the same study, the average eighth grade homeschooler was performing four grade levels above the national average.[20]

Homeschooling scores high marks in other areas as life as well. A recent study[21] of homeschooled graduates revealed the following characteristics:

□ Homeschoolers attain more post-secondary education than do their non-homeschooled peers. Over 74% of home-educated adults ages eighteen to twenty-four have taken college-level courses, compared to 46% of the general United States population.

- □ 95% of the homeschool graduates surveyed are glad that they were homeschooled.
- □ 59% of the subjects reported that they were "very happy" with life, while only 27.6% of the general U.S. population is "very happy" with life.
- □ Only 4.2% of the homeschool graduates surveyed consider politics and government too complicated to understand, compared to 35% of U.S. adults.
- □ The study found much greater political involvement of adults who were homeschooled. 76% of homeschool graduates surveyed between the ages of eighteen to twenty-four voted within the last five years, compared to only 29% of the relevant U.S. population. The numbers of homeschool graduates who vote are even greater in the older age brackets, with voting levels not falling below 95%, compared to a high of 53% for the corresponding U.S. populace.

Despite the surprising success of home education – even in the realm of "socialization" – teacher unions continue to adamantly oppose the growing trend of homeschooling. But if the primary goal of educators *really* is education, why the opposition to homeschooling? Perhaps there is something more to add to the equation? The loss of state funds when students withdraw from public schools certainly is a factor. Receiving a symbolic slap in the face for failure to educate is undoubtedly another; no one likes have a "nonprofessional" doing their job better than them. These factors play a role in the animus against homeschooling, yet oftentimes, the biggest factor is simply that educational professionals have other goals besides learning.

Critical Theory

Constructivist theory explains some of the ridiculous things going on in modern educational practice, yet there are other wacky systems hiding in the halls of our schools following in the *constructivist* tradition, though with a Marxist twist.

Without question, one of our chief ideological scourges is Marxism, and, like a deadly virus, it is highly adaptable. Though the red banner of communism may be discredited, the socialist interpretation of reality has loosened neither its hold nor its influence over American intellectuals. The names of Marx and Engels may not be heard nearly as often, yet Freire, Marcuse, Dewey, Gramsci, Derridà, and Chomsky are on the tip of nearly every college professor's tongue.

These professors begin with the presuppositions of Marx and apply them to race, sex, and gender. Few areas of university studies have steered clear of the new theory. Applied to culture, language, and law, it has taken on the name "critical theory" or "critical pedagogy." It interprets every aspect of modern American society as a tool of power, a means for the ruling power structure to impose its view of reality upon the masses.

Critical theory makes three basic assumptions:

1. Firstly, it assumes there is no such thing as truth. We cannot know reality as it is, just as it appears to us. Since I cannot know reality in the same way someone else knows it, there is no objective truth.

2. Secondly, it assumes that life is all about power. Even
    so-called disinterested relationships like love, parent-
    hood, and friendship are inherently power structures,
    masked by altruistic feelings.

3. Thirdly – and as a logical consequence – it assumes
    that inequality of any sort is the greatest evil to be
    eradicated. As long as any person is in control or has
    more power than others, we can expect only hard-
    ship, discord, and confrontations. For this reason,
    critical theory and modern Marxists assume that the
    ideal society is the egalitarian, tolerant democracy.
    Total freedom and total equality for all (no matter
    how self-contradictory that may be).

Given these three pillars, critical theory looks at our
modern society and discovers that there is an unequal social
stratification based upon class, race and gender. Naturally,
those of high power and status at the top of society control
the rest (hegemony), even if the oppressed do not realize it.
Supposedly, these elites work quietly to maintain the status
quo – to maintain their power structure and the unequal conditions, because this allows them economic and social benefits. Their tools for maintaining power are the mass media,
education, politics, religion, and even language. According
to these critical theorists, the seamless hegemony virtually
compels the "oppressed" to give their tacit permission to be
oppressed by those in power. The control is subtle, almost
imperceptible, and both oppressors and oppressed believe
the current system is the only way, the right way.

But, magically, the critical theorists have not been fooled.
In an intellectual, gnostic move, they style themselves free of

the hegemonic control under which everybody else suffers in mental darkness. The goal of the critical theorists is to raise the consciousness of those who are being oppressed and lead the revolution against the current power structures.

Critical theory is applied especially to literature (critical literacy) and to law (critical legal studies – which are very popular at Harvard Law School). "The main notion of critical legal studies is that the law, while appearing to be a neutral and impartial set of rules, actually functions to help maintain the domination of society by the dominant group. Critical literacy holds that reading and writing do pretty much the same thing."[22] As one professor put it, "people with authority to name the world dominate others whose voices they have been able to suppress."

In critical theory, education is no longer about learning facts, numbers, and skills, or about absorbing the intellectual content of a country's cultural and political traditions. These things belong to an outdated model of education that is completely unfit for the new age of critical theory and the political advocacy this brave new world requires.

As one popular social studies textbook directs: "We must stop exhorting students to be 'good citizens' according to our own unquestioned view of good and help them instead to ask 'good questions' about their own values and those of others. Controversies, rather than fixed knowledge and values, will play a central role in the structure of social studies education."[23] Yet how can students create "controversy" when they do not know the subjects they are criticizing? Why should they advocate for something they have not even understood?

Education theories like this help explain the phenomenon witnessed in American classrooms during the 2003 conflict in Iraq. While many professors and teachers displayed their support for American troops, others were turning classrooms into propaganda centers, organizing walkouts, school-wide demonstrations, canceling classes in protest, or parading around the cafeteria with antiwar slogans. Perhaps this education for advocacy principle explains why students – especially in elementary grades – are taken out of school to join rallies, protests, and political events. Cute little faces attract sympathy for the cause. Columnist Thomas Sowell agrees:

> *"That was certainly true of a recent photo of a little seven-year-old boy holding a sign demanding more money for the schools and holding his fist in the air. He was part of a demonstration organized by his teachers, and including parents and other students, all of whom were transported to California's state capital in Sacramento to protest budget constraints brought on by the state's huge deficit.*
>
> *"There was a time when taking children out of classes to fight the political battles of adults would have been considered a shameless neglect of duty. But that was long ago.*
>
> *"The little boy with the sign and his fist raised in the air is just one of the millions of victims of a shameless education establishment. It is not just that he is not in class learning the things he will need for his own mental development. He is out in the streets learning dangerous lessons for the future.*
>
> *"The most dangerous lesson of all is that he doesn't need to know what he is talking about, that what matters is venting his feelings and being an activist.*

"He is learning to let himself be manipulated by others, setting him up for all sorts of pied pipers he is likely to encounter in later years, who may lead him into anything from personal degeneracy to movements like the Taliban or the cult that Jim Jones led to their doom at Jonestown.

"What can a seven-year-old boy know about the issues that he is carrying a sign for or shaking his fist about? Has he even heard – much less understood – any other side of the issue he is being used for?"[24]

Many of those directing the course of American education find no problem here. After all, if education is for learning to be a good citizen, to participate, to advocate, this boy was learning what it means to be an active citizen. Who needs to know what they are talking about?

As critical literacy professor Linda Brodkey[25] writes in her book, *Writing Permitted in Designated Areas Only:*

"If composition can be said to abet the middle-class illusions of meritocracy, then the ***deregulation of writing*** is about replacing that empty promise with pedagogy that honors the First Amendment by teaching students that freedom of speech is meaningful only if the citizenry is literate. Not just functionally literate. Literate. Not just fluent. Literate. ***Literacy is attitude, entitlement,*** the entitlement that middle-class privilege masks in prescriptions but that writing lays bare in the ***sheer force of the desire*** to see and to get readers to see what can be seen from where the writer stands."[26] [emphasis added]

Like much of obscure academic writing, this paragraph needs to be translated into English. Brodkey seems to advocate three premises here:

1. Writing doesn't need to be good (meritorious) to be published; it just has to follow her idea of literacy.
2. Literacy doesn't mean being able to read and write; it means to subscribe to her political views and interpretation of reality (namely, that all is power and entitlement).
3. Ideas don't need to be logically proven or true, just forcefully stated.

(Conclusion: everyone should follow Linda's ideas even if her ideology is flimsy and her writing is as logical as the arrangement of spaghetti on a plate.)

Critical literacy is really not very complicated. "It means that language is not a neutral something that is available in equal measure to everybody, or even that it is consciously used and shaped by an author to reflect reality. Language is a creation of society that serves the holders of power, enabling them to maintain that power by controlling the very way in which thought and ideas are expressed – even while, of course, giving the impression that the way things are, the status quo, is entirely rational, inevitable."[27] As James Sledd, professor emeritus of the Department of English at the University of Texas, Austin, affirmed, "(Standard English is) an instrument of domination by the privileged."

Ridiculous as all this may sound, there are kernels of truth in critical theory. Language is a power; about that there can be no doubt. Even "the analysis of the use of language as an instrument of social order is not farfetched; nor is it original. Incorrect grammar excludes people just as bad manners do."[28] The problem lies in assuming that language should not be based on truth (since this no longer exists in their system) and in affirming that life is all about power. Yet critical theorists don't often think about the foundations of their theory. They are too busy transforming the culture, creating a "brave new world."

So let's subject critical theory to a brief critique. What structure does it propose? Why is it right, true or better than the current system?

These are the questions that are rarely discussed – if not completely ignored – by critical theorists. It rejects objective truth, and in the process loses any rational basis for determining what is true or false, good or evil. That is why critical theorists have to settle for secondary principles such as equality, tolerance, or peace. These become the cornerstone of their "critical" structure. But if there is nothing objectively good or evil, how can we affirm those secondary principles so dear to the modern multiculturalists?

Why should we practice equality? Certainly not because it is true; that's not an option in our postmodernist society. And I can't say it is good because we have eliminated that possibility as well. Why should I be tolerant? Simply because it is the right thing to do? But how do I know it is the right thing to do? Who's to say that an intolerant Islamic extremist isn't right? Do I go by my feelings? But his feelings tell him he is right. And why should peace be our great goal? Does that mean I should let myself be beaten up, raped, tortured, or shot just to keep the "peace"? When we eliminate the possibility of finding the truth, we no longer have a foundation for our key ideas. Rational debate disappears. We have to fall back into the savage struggle for power and control.

In the end, this is the fundamental flaw of Critical Theory: it fails to justify the new structure it proposes. In fact, there is ample discussion about *how* to bring about the "new order," but little about *why* that new order is better. By eliminating any reference to truth or goodness, language and education become no more than tools of power. Young teachers are instructed that literature is a tool of oppression and "teaching as a way of proselytizing for their gender, their race, or their radical – most often specifically Marxist – political beliefs."[29]

Public education has become a primary political and cultural battleground where "enlightened" administrators and teachers impose the new structure regardless of reality and what is best for students. In the end, critical theory is not about offering something objectively better; it's about imposing a new ideological structure. It's a matter of power.

A famous quote from George Santayana comes to mind: "Fanaticism consists of redoubling your efforts when you have forgotten your aim."[30] In this ideologically-charged atmosphere, education has become just another tool for spreading the contagion of the new fundamentalism. Children learn the group thinking and socialist values needed for "global citizenship"; self-esteem and socialization – not academic proficiency – have become the primary goal of education.

According to educational consultant Peggy McIntosh, schooling should work for the abolition of right/wrong, that "faulty paradigm in which children are encouraged to accept the authority of correctness versus wrongness… It's the either/or, right/wrong, you got it/you didn't, you can be graded high or you can be graded low…" Since all of that is 'damaging' for the child's psychology, "you have to put the child in a lateral position to her own learning, beyond win-lose…In this case learning is seen not as a mastery but as our connection with the world, as we grow and develop as bodies in the body of the world."[31]

With such irrational goals, it's no wonder many educators ignore the facts, even as new generations of students get a shoddier education and a truncated future. For those whose sole goal is to change society, education is too powerful a tool to lose just because the facts stand against their ideology. As Alan Charles Kors, a University of Pennsylvania history professor and coauthor of *The Shadow University*, makes clear in his book, many university orientation facilitators believe the university cannot be content to educate students, but "must become a therapeutic and political agent of progressive change."[32]

The National Education Association, the teacher's union that describes itself as "America's largest organization committed to advancing the cause of public education," has taken that mission to heart. In 1996, it employed more political operatives than both major political parties combined, and its annual meetings deal more with political issues than education.

The political bent of the NEA is clearest when it comes to the "multicultural" and "diversity" agendas. During its 1999 convention the NEA affirmed its commitment not only to "diversity"-based curricula, but urged that it be introduced in early childhood (from birth through age eight) education programs. One of the resolutions stated "that a diverse society enriches all individuals." That clearly can be true, but finish reading that resolution and the clarity disappears. According to the NEA, encouraging people with different "sexual orientation" is all part of this "enriching diversity."

On Feb. 8, 2002, the organization went further, adopting a plan to make schools "safe" and hospitable for gay, lesbian, bisexual and transgendered students and education employees. The plan was ostensibly targeted at punishing "harassment" and "discrimination."[33]

With all the challenges current educators have to face in improving educational performance, one has to wonder why they devote so much time to advocating faulty theories and dubitable social changes. Shouldn't they be more worried about math skills, the literacy rate, and helping more students graduate with proficiency for college? In short, shouldn't they worry about education?

Yet let's not make a simple mistake here. It would be easy to demonize the educational system, accuse teachers, rage against the faulty system, and complain about the current flaws in education... and perhaps in many cases we would be justified. The great majority of teachers, however, just want the best for their students. They are an incredibly dedicated and hard-working group; they sacrifice time, sleep, and other promising professions simply because they love to teach. They feel it is a calling.

A recent study, "A Sense of Calling: Who Teaches and Why," reflects the thoughts of teachers who have been in the profession for five years or less.[34] Among the findings:

- Teaching isn't a career of last resort, since 96 percent of those surveyed say teaching is what they love.
- Eighty percent said if they were starting over, teaching

is the career they would choose.

- □ Three-quarters, well above the proportion for most other professions, say they expect teaching to be their lifelong career.

Yet at the same time, a large majority say they were taught little about the ABC's of teaching such as how to run a classroom, maintain discipline, deal with the routine pressures of the profession and even – amazingly – how to teach effectively. Given the reigning ideologies among teachers' unions, education colleges, and teachers of teachers, there should be little wonder why.

"For much of the past century, the leader's of the nation's education schools – an eclectic mix of progressive pedagogical experts and psychometric experts – have seen themselves (sometimes heroically) as the vanquishers of the academic tradition. In every subject field, progressive educators have assailed the established order, whether it be the teaching of literary classics in English, the study of events in chronological order in history, or the mastery of computational skills in mathematics."[35]

These intellectuals – backed with systems like Critical Theory and Constructivism – transformed the face of education and have turned in stunning results… mostly bad. Instead of the search for truth, education became training for advocacy, which often turns into thinly veiled indoctrination of teachers, educational texts, and students. The already difficult task of teaching students effectively is only made harder by the ideological fundamentalism that has infected the system.

MEDIA

The only social force with more power than education is the mass media. The average American student spends more time watching television, surfing the web, or playing video games than attending school. Here are a few facts to give you an idea of the media's formative power:

- According to the *Boston Globe*, the average American child watches twenty-five to thirty hours of television weekly. By the age of eighteen, a child has viewed some 15,000 hours of television. This compares to 11,000 hours spent in the classroom. The only thing a child does more than watch television is sleep.
- By the age of six, the average American child will have spent more time watching television than he will spend speaking to his parents in an entire lifetime.
- From the ages of three to five, the average preschooler put in more hours before the television set than he or she will spend in a college classroom.

We are what we eat. And when we are fed through the television tube, there should be no surprise when our attitudes and behavior are more and more like those we watch. We form our outlook on life from what we know. So is mass media giving us the whole picture?

The Real Picture?

What we know depends either on our direct experiences or on the testimony of others. I know that I like jelly beans because I experience it directly. I am convinced of who my parents are because I lived with them for eighteen years. My knowledge is direct and sure.

When we lack direct experience, our knowledge must rely on the testimony of oth-ers. Have you ever been to Kosovo? Do you *really* know that Madagascar exists? Have you ever seen an electron or proton or quark? Our in-formation – our knowledge – about these places and things comes from trust in others. It is a *human faith*. I put my confidence in the testimony of someone else who *has* seen and experi-enced these things. I trust that they are telling the truth and presenting me the whole picture.

Yet pictures can be gar-bled.

In the fall of 2000, *The New York Times* published a

An Israeli policeman and a Pales-tinian on the Temple Mount.

photo with the caption, "An Israeli Policeman and a Pales-tinian on the Temple Mount." The picture showed a bloody, dazed youth stumbling to the ground with an angry police-man in the background, shouting and shaking a club. The obvious message was that he had just beaten the young man and was threatening him with more. No accompanying story, no further explanations.

The "obvious" message couldn't have been further from the truth. The young man was actually a twenty-year-old Jewish student from Chicago studying in Jerusalem. He had been yanked from his car by a furious mob of Palestinians who had beaten, stabbed, punched, and kicked him until he nearly lost consciousness and blood streamed down his face. He managed to break away, running for his life up a hill to an Israeli police outpost. The threatening policeman was protecting the young man, shouting back the angry mob that wanted to finish off their victim.

The reality of this picture was twisted.

As the young man himself attested, "When a photo gets published, there are many links in the chain, and in this case, I don't know where the fault for the garbled caption lies. But it is deeply disturbing that the *New York Times*, the *Associated Press* (and everyone else in-between) assumed that if it's a victim, it must be a Palestinian. ...this event highlights the power of the media to influence public opinion. If truth is to prevail, we can't just "read" the newspaper. Be discerning and become part of the process. Otherwise, you're just a passive object of someone else's agenda. Who are the innocent victims and who are the aggressors? The truth is often the opposite of how it appears."[36]

"Neutrality"

Mistakes are bound to happen. Mislabeled captions, faulty information, and outdated data all make for mistakes in the media business. They shouldn't happen, but even the best sources will sometimes err.

Yet what happens when the "error" is not a mere mistake? What if someone were to color the news by selecting what is and what is not printed or reported on, by twisting words to mean something other than what we normally understand them to mean, by carefully selecting the sources of information and order of its presentation to advance their particular point of view? Is this really so farfetched? Is it possible that someone could be more interested in an ideology than in the truth?

My high school Journalism 101 affirmed that the goal of a journalist is to neutrally inform. News reporting has to be objective, "telling it like it is." A good writer is supposed to detach his own ideas and beliefs from what he is reporting so that "just the facts" come through. Any honest journalist, however, will tell you this is not the case. "Neutral" journalism simply does not exist, even with those who pretend to exercise it. In fact, when someone strives to be neutral, they end up representing a certain viewpoint, namely, that all sides of the argument are equal.

Admittedly, some topics like the weather are more "neutral" than others. About these topics, neutrality is possible. But in more serious issues – the things that really matter in life – everything is not equal: some things are good, others are bad; some things are *true* and others are *false*. Is the slaughter of 500 innocent women and children a neutral fact? Would the theft of stockholder's benefits by shady administrative manipulations be neutral? Does it really matter if I report that 500 demonstrators show up for a rally instead of reporting the 50,000 that really turned out?

About these issues, there is no neutrality. There is truth. And the mass media has the *mission* and the *responsibility* to tell the truth. "The fundamental moral requirement of all communication is respect for and service of the truth. Freedom to seek and speak what is true is essential to human communication, not only in relation to facts and information but also, and especially, regarding the nature and destiny of the human person, regarding society and the common good, regarding our relationship with God. The mass media have an inescapable responsibility in this sense..."[37]

True heroism in the mass media exists. Think of the reporters who expose repressive regimes, corrupt business deals, unjust sentences, or genocide despite the danger to their own life and liberty.[38] Note the journalists who seek out the noble and uplifting elements of human life and testimony. Champions of truth continue their struggle for a better world, and freedom of speech and of the press are necessary conditions for that ideal.[39]

But neutrality? Is it possible in the mass media?

"Bias"

Much has been said and written about media "bias" from both sides of the political spectrum. Recent bestsellers such as *It Ain't Necessarily So: How the Media Make and Unmake the Scientific Picture of Reality*[40] and *Mobocracy: How the Media's Obsession with Polling Twists the News*[41] add to a list of other classics on media bias beginning with *The Media Elite* in 1980[42] and continued with more recent works such as *Bias: A CBS Insider Exposes How the Media Distort the News*[43] and *Arrogance: Rescuing America from the Media Elite,* by Bernard Goldberg. Or take Brent Bozell's work entitled *And That's the Way It Isn't.*[44] Not only these books, but countless other reports, surveys, and studies corroborate the evidence that the media is "biased."

Even thinkers on the left side of the political spectrum

aren't content with the media: it's not liberal enough. Re-
nowned scholar Noam Chomsky makes that clear in *"Manu-
facturing Consent: The Political Economy of the Mass Media.*[45]
Eric Alterman argues in his work *What Liberal Media?* that
the "liberal media" doesn't exist at all. "The myth of the liberal media empowers conservatives to control debate in the
United States to the point where liberals cannot even hope
for a fair shake anymore."[46]

So who's right? Is there a media bias or not?

Moderates Abound, But Few Newsroom Conservatives				Values Gap on Social Issues			
	General Public*	Nat'l Press	Local Press		General Public*	Nat'l Press	Local Press
Ideological self-rating	%	%	%	Belief in God...	%	%	%
Liberal	20	34	23	Is necessary to be moral	58	6	18
Moderate	41	54	61	Is not necessary to be moral	40	91	78
Conservative	33	7	12	Don't know	2	3	4
Don't know	6	5	4		100	100	100
	100	100	100	Homosexuality should be...			
				Accepted by society	51	88	74
				Discouraged by society	42	5	14
				Don't Know	6	7	12
					100	100	100
*Public figures from may 2004 Pew Media Believability Study (N=1800)				*Public Figures from U.S. component of the 2002 Pew Global Attitudes Project (Aug. 19- Sept. 8, 2002, N=1,501)			

At this point, we should clarify what exactly we mean by
"bias." The old Oxford dictionary calls it a "predisposition, prejudice, influence" and modern usage indicates "an unfair preference for or dislike of something." Bias is a slant on reality.

In this sense, every human being has a "bias." We all
see reality from a different perspective. And there is nothing
wrong in having a perspective. However, those values have
to be justified, judged, and compared to reality to make sure
they are true and good. It isn't enough just to have "values."

A May 2004 study of journalists' "values" has revealed just

how different they are from society at large.[47] While 33 percent of the general public declared themselves political "conservatives" and only 20 percent "liberals," a mere 7 percent of national journalists considered themselves conservatives and a surprising 34 percent labeled themselves liberals.

Yet even more revealing were the views of journalists regarding belief in God, morality, and homosexuality. Fully 91 percent of media professionals in the national press agreed with the statement that "Belief in God is not necessary to be moral," while just 6 percent of the general public agreed. When asked if homosexuality should be accepted by society, 88 percent of national journalists agreed, and a mere 5 percent thought it should be discouraged.

This bias often sneaks out unwittingly. Take for instance the lopsided treatment of two murder cases. In 1998, three men at the University of Wyoming tied Matthew Shepard, a homosexual, to a fencepost out in the countryside and tortured him to death after he propositioned them in a bar. In 1999, Jesse Dirkhising, a 13-year-old boy, was raped, tortured, and strangled by homosexuals. In a 2001 *New Republic* article, gay-rights advocate Andrew Sullivan wrote: "In the month after Shepard's murder, Nexis recorded 3,007 stories about his death. In the month after Dirkhising's murder, Nexis recorded 46 stories about his. In all of last year, only one article about Dirkhising appeared in a major mainstream newspaper. The *Boston Globe*, the *New York Times* and the *Los Angeles Times* ignored the incident completely. In the same period, the *New York Times* published 45 stories about Shepard, and the *Washington Post* published 28. The discrepancy isn't just real. It's staggering."[18]

As Bernard Goldberg, CBS reporter for twenty-eight years,

commented in a *Wall Street Journal* editorial that eventually lost him his job, "The old argument that the networks and other 'media elites' have a liberal bias is so blatantly true that it's hardly worth discussing anymore. No, we don't sit around in dark corners and plan strategies on how we're going to slant the news. We don't have to. It comes naturally to most reporters."[49]

Yet should this really be all that shocking? Bias in the media is nothing new. In fact, it is *intrinsically unavoidable*, because even journalists are human beings, and every person has a viewpoint on reality. The only reason bias surprises us is because we have bought into the myth of neutrality.

"Bias" in unavoidable. A certain "discrimination" of facts is a natural part of life: if you ask an Italian who the greatest soccer player is, he might reply Totti or Biaggio; ask a Brazilian, and they will assure you it is Pelé or Ronaldo. People interpret the facts according to their experiences and outlook on life. Just as there is no neutral view on life, there is no such thing as a perfectly neutral news source.

Bias is present in even straightforward reporting. In a study cited in *The Media Elite,* journalists were given a "neutral" sample story filled with many different perspectives, and asked to pick out the key elements. When their answers were compared to those of a control group to see what differences emerged, there was a clearly distinct interpretation of the story.

The "bias" began at the scene: reporters chose what facts seemed important to them. They take the pictures from their perspective and then select which ones are most representative – according to their subjective criteria – or will catch the audience's attention better. They carefully screen whom to interview and then choose the interviews that will make the news.

If neutrality in raw data is impossible to attain, it disappears completely when this data is selected and filtered by the studio crews, writers and editors. Even in the presentation to the public a certain "bias" comes through in the order of presentation (page 1 or page 18b), what topics are deemed "newsworthy," the sarcasm or emotion injected into neutral words, the time given to each of the opinions presented.

Even an "objective" reporter who tries to get both sides of the story sometimes ends up with a certain bias. In an effort at neutrality, everyone with a different opinion is given equal space to air their views. Yet precisely in this supposed objective balance bias creeps in. Take for instance an article on the discovery of a new moon of the planet Saturn. If the story claimed to be objective by quoting an astrophysicist of MIT explaining the data and a truck driver debunking the discovery based on his acute studies of the night sky, would that article be neutral and balanced? Or in a story about sexual abuse of children, would it be more neutral and balanced to contrast the authoritative viewpoint of an expert in the field with the reaction of someone on the street? If the national director of Catholics for a Free Choice – representing 25,000 disgruntled Catholics – is given equal time and importance as the pope – representing 1,000,000,000 Catholics around the world – does that equal balanced reporting?

Equal time for diverse opinions is no guarantee of accuracy and objectivity. It is necessary to weigh the arguments, the validity of different opinions, the authority of certain individuals and then discern. Not to weigh the differences means to lose objectivity because we present as equal two things that really are not so – that is an injustice. And in weighing the differences we lose neutrality because we realize that the arguments for one side are stronger than those of the other. It is impossible to ride the fence. We cannot escape a choice and this choice is already a certain "bias."

Some news shows, journals, or newspapers claim neutrality by publishing now and then stories from a different point of view. Yet even this is a silent recognition that there is a general angle that they usually take on the issues. It is important to recognize that *all* media has a "bias." It doesn't matter whether it purports to be liberal, conservative, or neutral. There is no real neutrality in the issues that really matter.

Mainstreaming the Media

Since we can't eliminate bias in its broadest sense, some would argue that the role of the media is to represent as closely as possible the will of the majority. The media should be "mainstream." In this approach, journalism should reflect the feelings, ideas, and prevailing opinions of the people.

"That's exactly what we do," is the media reply. But do they? The evidence suggests not.

When media elites are questioned about their personal positions on the issues, they like to think of themselves as "mainstream" and "centered." In a 1998 report examining claims of "liberal media," the Virginia Commonwealth University Department of Sociology and Anthropology gathered the following self-image impressions from people in the media.[50]

Q#22. On social issues, how would you characterize your political orientation?	Q#23. On economic issues, how would you characterize your political orientation?
Left **30%**	Left **11%**
Center **57%**	Center **64%**
Right **9%**	Right **19%**
Other **5%**	Other **5%**

Gathering people's subjective impression of themselves is like asking a woman if she is beautiful. No woman likes to call herself ugly, just as most media professionals shy away from straying out of the "mainstream." The global data of social indicators, however, tells a story quite different from the mirror on the wall. The famous Lichter-Rothman study in 1980 found these glaring differences between media professionals and the mainstream, confirmed by several subsequent surveys:

Demographic	Media	Public
White	98%	61%
Male	92	49
From Northeast corridor	61	38
From metropolitan area	68	65
From "professional" family	39	6
College graduates	77	21
Postgraduate study	37	6
Personal income	$135,000	$17,700
Family income	$186,000	$23,700

Political Outlook	Media	Public
Self-described liberal	65%	27%
Self-described moderate	18	41
Self-described conservative	17	32

Religious Factors	Media	Public
Agnostic or atheist/none	45%	9%
Protestant	14	56
Jewish	24	2
Catholic	8	28
Other	6	2
Attends church weekly	6	42
Attend church seldom/never	89	25

Though the definition of liberal or conservative has changed over the years, the basic conclusion of these facts does not. Those in charge of supplying our information, our lifeline to the world, do not think the same way as the general public. "Too many news people," writes Bernard Goldberg, "especially the ones at worldwide headquarters in New York, where all the big decisions are made, basically talk to other people just like themselves...they can easily go through life never meeting anybody who has a thought different from their own."[51]

When all your friends hold the same views there is no real diversity. Perhaps a certain diversity of race or creed, but not of opinion.

Since the 1980 study, the diversity of opinion in the media has seemingly *decreased*, as the May 2004 "Pew Media Believability Study" cited above indicates. In 1996, the Freedom Forum and The Roper Center released a survey of 139 Washington bureau chiefs and congressional correspondents. Not only was diversity of opinion almost nonexistent, but the Washington journalists turned out to be quite unlike the "mainstream" American. While the American public is divided just about 50/50 between the two parties, 50 percent of the journalists polled said they were Democrats while *just 4 percent* said they were Republicans.

Their actual voting patterns betray that total lack of diversity.

Political leanings (1992 election)	*Media*	*Public*
Voted for Bill Clinton	89%	43%
Vote for George Bush	7%	37%
Voted for Ross Perot	2%	19%

Whenever any politician gets 89 percent of the vote in one sector of the population, it's either because it was his hometown, he paid off the voters, or there was just a "free" election in Venezuela for Hugo Chávez.

Media and Religion

This discrepancy between the media and general public is especially obvious in the area of religion. Only 6 percent of media professionals in the Lichter-Rothman survey attended weekly church services, compared to 42 percent of the population. Though the statistics have changed slightly over the years, journalists are still often disconnected from religious practice and at times even embrace moral or political positions hostile towards organized religion.

In his 2002 book *From Yahweh to Yahoo!: The Religious*

Roots of the Secular Press, Professor Doug Underwood examines attitudes toward religion in the press and the religiosity of the professionals in the newsroom. Underwood, for many years an active journalist and then associate professor of communication at the University of Washington, carried out extensive research on journalists' religiosity.

"His surveys discovered that religion *does* play a part in shaping journalist's views and that it is a mistake to write off the profession in general as irreligious or unaffected by religious values. But, he adds, a common attribute in the journalistic profession is a skeptical and empirical mentality that can blind them to the importance of the spiritual dimension so important in many people's lives."[52] This scientific mentality often leads journalists to disdain the religious beliefs and practice of churchgoers, or simply ignore professionally what they do not understand personally.

Surveys and polls consistently show that the media is not like the people it informs. The media is clearly not "mainstream" in the normal sense of the word.

Yet why should conformity to the majority be the ideal of the press in the first place? To accuse the media of not being mainstream — even though it may be true — is an improper indictment. The media is not called to be mainstream nor to reflect perfectly the mainstream. Its vocation is to proclaim the truth.

Many columnists, journals and media outlets are honest enough to recognize their approach to the news: they willingly accept the label of conservative or liberal. They are not afraid to argue their point of view and put forward reasons for what they believe and hold as the true picture of reality. This contribution of different points of view enriches public debate and our understanding of the issues... as long as journalists are searching for the truth.

But when the ideal of the press is not to proclaim the truth—because, as the education establishment has taught all of us from early youth, truth does not exist—the media becomes a tool of affirming one opinion over another; it becomes a tool of power; it becomes propaganda. In this respect, much of the mass media has volunteered itself as a willing accomplice to the spread of ideological fundamentalism. It has become another weapon in the arsenal of the culture war.

Take the reporting on religion, a reality of great concern to most Americans and, as such, worthy subject for truthful reporting. Yet, by and large, the nation's newspapers and broadcasters largely refuse to take religion seriously. Some journalists go beyond passive indifference to religion – they can be downright hostile. Ted Turner, head of CNN, publicly called Christianity a religion "for losers." Though he later apologized for the statement, this did not seem to change his attitude in the least. On Ash Wednesday of 2001, Ted noticed some of the Catholic members of the news crew with ashes on their foreheads. "I was looking at this woman and I was trying to figure out what was on her forehead. At first I thought you were in the [Seattle] earthquake, but I realized you're just Jesus freaks."[53]

Nicholas Kristof, writer for the *New York Times*, while declaring his personal disagreement with evangelical Christians, acknowledged that the national news media treat the religiously and politically conservative evangelicals through the filter of the Northeast educated elite. "Liberal critiques sometimes seem not just filled with outrage at evangelical-backed policies, which is fair, but also to have a sneering tone about conservative Christianity itself. Such mockery of religious faith is inexcusable."[54]

Even though such overt antireligious sentiments are not a widespread epidemic, there is a real plague of shoddy reporting on religious themes. Uninformed reporters are too often lazy about getting their facts straight when assigned to cover religion stories. For example, western media routinely omit anti-Christian motivation in acts of violence overseas. In Nigeria in the fall of 2002, Muslims destroyed churches and beat and murdered Christians. Yet in many of the press accounts, there was no mention of who started the violence (Muslims), and who the victims were (Christians). The incidents were reported as "religious violence between Muslims and Christians." The *New York Times* reported on a Protestant missionary who was murdered in Lebanon with the headline: "Killing underscores enmity of evangelists and Muslims." But that "enmity" unmistakably goes only one way. "Whoever did this crime, I forgive them," the victim's husband said at her memorial service. "It's not easy. It took everything I have, but I can forgive these people because God has forgiven me."[55] A local Muslim leader testified that the missionary was murdered because her teachings of forgiveness sapped the will of the children to fight the Jews.

When religions are mentioned, the message is often distorted. In an investigation conducted by students at the University of Rochester in the summer of 2003, they found that nearly half of all 314 religion stories studied from 12 newspapers were actually about political, legal or criminal activities. Only 28 percent of the stories treated religion exclusively in terms of beliefs and values.

The study noted that coverage of Islam was mostly associated with crimes or violence, and one-third of all Catholic stories referred to crimes. A February 14 obituary of a priest in the *Boston Globe*, for instance, included many details about sex abuse in the Catholic Church, even though the priest in question had nothing to do with any scandal. "Coverage of Catholics and Islam was unbalanced everywhere," said Curt Smith, an English department lecturer who codirected the study. "If you were from another planet, you'd think all Muslims were terrorists and all Catholics were pedophile priests."[56]

How should we respond? Licking our wounds and crying foul? If a new brand of fundamentalism has taken a strangle hold on wide sections of the mass media, we have no one to blame but ourselves. There's no room for handwringing and victims here. We need to roll up our sleeves and get to work.

We need citizens to sharpen their critical sense and not believe every story, opinion, or fact that is printed or spoken. We need principled men and women with sense and savvy to fill the positions of top reporters, columnists, and commentators. We need intelligent scriptwriters, honest advertisers, and discerning viewers.

We need a revolution of truth.

GOVERNMENT

Though the media is often called the fourth branch of government, there are still officially only three: the executive, the legislative, and the judiciary. These three branches together have the noble goal of promoting the common good of their citizens, of guiding the *res publica,* of providing a stable system for the advancement of culture.

This great ideal of government can only be achieved if rooted in truth, in the truth about God and about man and about the world. "Democracy must be based on the true and solid foundation of nonnegotiable ethical principles, which are the underpinning of life in society."[57] Without reference to unchanging truths and the fundamental dignity of the human person, democracy cannot long prevail. Neither democracy nor capitalism by themselves are enough to respond to society's need for a stable operating system.

Unfortunately for us, the new fundamentalism has infected our politicians and civil servants with a relativistic mindset that rejects truth as intolerant, "fundamentalist," and antidemocratic. "However, in reality this exclusion of truth is a type of very grave *intolerance* and reduces essential things of human life to subjectivism. In this way, in essential things we no longer have a common view. Each one can and should decide as he can. So we lose the ethical foundations of our common life."[58] Without a common foundation and clear principles, a secularist, powerful ideology– perhaps under the guise of democracy and capitalism – will assert its reign.

The National Socialist government in Germany is just one of the many examples. The Nazi party was legitimately – and democratically – elected to power. In 1933 the new minister of education, Mr. Schemm, declared publicly to an assembly of university professors: "From this day on, you will no longer have to examine whether something is true or not, but exclusively whether or not it corresponds to the Nazi ideology."[59] Truth was abandoned and abuse of power was not far behind.

To guard against just such totalitarian systems, the founding fathers of America established the separation of powers and a system of checks and balances to guarantee the rights and freedoms of all citizens. For over two hundred years, that constitutional system has protected us from the oppression of tyrants, the scourge of dictators, and the living hell of totalitarian rule. Two dangers, however, are eating away at that foundation: stupidity and advocacy.

Stupidity

Human persons are not naturally stupid: we have the capacity to learn. That is why Aristotle defined man as a "rational animal." Animals are not rational – even if they might show some signs of "intelligence" – but human beings are. Dolphins might "sing," but they don't organize choirs and compose symphonies. Dogs might "cry," but they don't write eulogies or attend funerals. Chimpanzees can learn a few words to communicate," but they don't give parliamentary speeches or write books on their jungle experiences. Human beings are animals, but more than animals because of reason

Human beings are not "dumb animals," though when we don't use our reason there seems to be little difference. Our reason makes us different... and it makes us naturally moral (i.e., not like animals that just eat, reproduce, and die). Our actions are not predetermined by instinct or by the rules of fate; through our actions we show that we can change the world around us, we can influence the course of history, and we can make ourselves good or bad. Human beings are animals, but much more than animals because we are moral and can be virtuous or vicious.

A democratic republic works only with human beings, i.e., with *well-educated* and *virtuous* citizens. Democracy cannot work with animals... nor with people who act like animals. Education is not enough by itself, nor is virtue. Unfortunately for us, though, we seem to be losing both. And as Thomas Jefferson warned, "If a nation expects to be ignorant and free, it expects what never was and never will be."

The educational system – as we have already seen – is captivated by ideologies and the quality of teaching has plummeted. Yet even the content has changed, giving students less exposure to the rational foundations of democracy.

A 1998 article in *Harper's* summarizes the evidence:

- 59 percent of 4th graders do not know why the Pilgrims and Puritans first voyaged to America. (religious freedom)
- 68 percent of 4th graders can't name the first thirteen colonies.
- 90 percent of 8th graders can't recount anything about the debates of the constitutional convention.

According to a National Assessment of Educational Progress report, three-quarters of fourth, eighth and twelfth graders are not proficient in civics knowledge, and one-third of them do not even have basic knowledge. That makes one-third of our students "civic illiterates." "Children are not learning American history and civics because they are not being taught it, or at least they are not being taught it well. American history has been watered down, and civics is too often dropped entirely from the curriculum. Today, more than half the states don't have a requirement for students to take a course – even for one semester – in American government."[60]

Should we really be surprised? When some teachers routinely insult western civilization as racist, sexist, and the product of "dumb white males" it is no wonder children grow up ashamed of their heritage. When multiculturalist schools remove the names of George Washington and Thomas Jefferson from textbooks simply because they owned slaves, forgetting that the principles upon which they established the nation led to the elimination of slavery, we really shouldn't be surprised.

"Only one out of the top fifty universities in the country required undergraduates to take an introductory history course, such as Western Civilization, in 1993, down from 60 percent of the same universities in 1964."[61] We no longer know our own history, the foundations of our society, the reasons for being what we are... or were. And those who do not study history are doomed to repeat its failures.

A poll commissioned by the American Council of Trustees and Alumni tested seniors from the top fifty-five liberal arts *colleges* in the United States. The poll consisted of questions from a high-school-level exam (or what used to be high-school-level work). Eight-one percent received a grade of D or F and only one student got every question right.

"Thirty five percent thought that "From each according to his ability, to each according to his needs" (the Marxist nostrum) was in the Constitution. Thirty-four percent didn't know. More than half thought Germany, Italy, or Japan was a U.S. ally during World War II... Forty percent could not place the Civil War in the correct half-century... Only 42 percent knew to whom the words "first in war, first in peace, first in the hearts of his countrymen" referred (George Washington). Fewer than one quarter could identify James Madison as the "father of the Constitution," and only 22 percent recognized

the words "government of the people, by the people and for
the people" as belonging to the Gettysburg Address."[62]

Our citizens know less history and civics now than ever.
The shift from a general liberal arts education to specialized
technical skills has further debilitated our competence in citizenship. We have experts and specialists who can program
a computer, but lack a broader knowledge that protects them
from having the wool pulled over their eyes.

Perhaps even more important than the crisis in education
is the crisis in morality. Every person is moral – they know
deep down that some things are right and good while others are just plain wrong. Yet as we clearly saw in the pages
regarding sexual ethics, there are enough conflicting theories
about what is good or bad that confusion reigns supreme.
There are voices to justify every horrendous act, from bioeth-
icists supporting infanticide to the NAMBLA (North American Man-Boy Love Association) not only advocating sexual
relations between men and boys, but urging the government
to protect such behavior.

We are encouraged to act more like animals, to follow
our lowest instincts. Reason is ignored to give way to passion, satisfaction, and titillation. Is it any wonder, then, that
stupidity is ever more prevalent, eroding the very possibility
of a stable democratic government?

Advocacy

But stupidity is not the only enemy to the survival of democracy. As we examined in the chapter on education, the
little civics instruction that does arrive to our students increasingly focuses on democracy as advocacy. It is not necessary to reason your position or engage in open debate – heck,

you don't even have to know what you're talking about. What matters is the tactics, the methodology you use for asserting your position, for supporting your minority group, for securing "equality" and "rights" for your special interest group. You don't have to reason your arguments, just *feel* strongly about them.

Thinking is hard work. Discerning what is right and what is wrong is difficult. Shirkers will always avoid the strenuous for the comfortable, and in our entertainment culture whatever feels good and any personal opinions become more important than what is right and true.

Working for particular interests is not good or bad in and of itself. Everyone wants to work for some "cause" that they see as a good thing. But we have to answer a key question: is that "good" thing *really* a good thing? Is it a true good? Should some "goods" be subjected to other more important ones? How do we establish this hierarchy of goods?

Just because I determine some goal to attain does not make that goal automatically good, nor does it allow me to take any means whatsoever to attain it. That is irresponsible advocacy. To fall into this pattern of mindless advocacy would be the death of reason and of democracy.

Nowhere is this deadly tendency more obvious than in the realm of law.

The Power of Law

The legal framework of Western society was firmly established on the basis of Roman jurisprudence, Christianity, and the legal system of England. The rule of law was a great improvement over the rule of the club – less bruises and greater justice for all – since it appeals to our higher reason while brute force treats us as animals. A law-abiding society fosters progress because it provides stability and a climate of trust.

The great advancements attained through the legal system helped establish a society of law-abiding citizens. The law was established for the good of all and since virtuous, well-intentioned men made the laws based on common Christian principles and values, the laws generally turned out well. Just laws promoted the well-being of all citizens, and people naturally began to associate what was *legal* with was *right or good*. Law and morality were intertwined.

However, law is nothing more than a man-made series of rules. "That is all it is. In and of itself, law is entirely amoral. There are moral laws and immoral laws. Both decent and vicious governments make laws. The Holocaust began legally. Nazis and communists had judges and lawyers who respected their societies' laws. In our country, slavery was entirely legal, as was the racial segregation that followed it. The notion that obedience to a society's laws is always moral is itself immoral."[63]

Society has changed. The Christian principles and values that once guided our decisions and public discourse have been watered down or abandoned. The search for truth has been replaced with expediency, the "everyone wants to be a millionaire" syndrome, and couch potato comfort seekers. In this new atmosphere, law has also become detached from truth. It becomes simply a tool of power.

Take for example the case of NOW's (National Organization for Women) legal efforts to protect abortion services by law. In early December of 2002, the United States Supreme Court debated the case of *Joseph Scheidler vs. the National*

Organization for Women. The case became a forum on what sorts of protests are allowable in the public square. Abortion protesters within Joseph Scheidler's organization regularly engaged women in conversation before the entrance to abortion clinics in an attempt to dissuade them from aborting. They considered this a legitimate exercise of their First Amendment rights. Abortion clinic directors, whose clients were dissuaded or who shied away, found that such tactics hurt their bottom line and so claimed this was not free speech, but extortion. By bringing Scheidler to court, they hoped to silence that speech.

The first lawsuit was filed in 1986 by NOW under the RICO (Racketeer Influenced and Corrupt Organizations Act) statutes designed to attack organized crime. NOW alleged that minor "criminal" conduct - jaywalking, trespassing, standing on the steps of an abortion clinic - constituted extortion under RICO. Even parking in front of an abortion clinic - in a public parking space – was being called "an extortionate act," and NOW argued that protesters were using force, violence and intimidation to obstruct the rights of doctors to perform abortions and the rights of women to have them. When both the U.S. district court in Chicago and a federal appeals court dismissed the case in 1991 as unfounded, NOW began seeking another route.

In 1998, a reconstituted NOW vs. Scheidler case began making its way through the court system. That April, a jury held the Pro-Life Action League of Scheidler guilty and charged penalties of $257,000 in damages and at least $1 million in attorney's fees. In July 1999, U.S. District Judge David Coar in Chicago issued a nationwide injunction prohibiting sit-ins outside of abortion clinics and other *nonviolent* acts of

civil disobedience. This ruling was based on NOW's assertion that pro-life protesters were responsible for hundreds of
violent incidents.

And the violent incidents?

In 2000, NOW issued a news release calling a sidewalk
prayer vigil led by Cardinal Francis George of Chicago an
"act of aggression." (Little old grandmas with rosaries are
dangerous, you know.) There was no violence at the vigil –
unless you count the insults and threats hurled by the abortion clinic staff – but when people feel threatened, that turns
protest and displays of any different ideas into an "act of aggression."

And the dangerous racketeers?

NOW claims there have been hundreds of examples of
real violence and extortion by pro-life demonstrators, such as
a 1989 demonstration in which four abortion clinic staffers
in Chico, California, said they were crushed against a glass
wall for four hours until the glass gave way.

That is what they claimed…at least until the evidence
proved otherwise. A videotape of the entire Chico demonstration was found showing no anti-clinic violence, but plenty
of verbal attacks and thinly veiled threats against the pro-life
demonstrators by clinic personnel. Violence against abortion
providers and clinics unfortunately has occurred, but it certainly did not in this case.

The court transcript exposes even more. In oral arguments before the Supreme Court in December of 2002, NOW
attorney Fay Clayton defended the use of the term "violence"
to explain the actions of pro-life demonstrators.

Justice Scalia interjected, "You've used the term

'violence' several times. That's not what the instruction required. As your argument to the jury itself indicated, it was enough if they obstructed the entrance and 'failed to part like the Red Sea' if somebody wanted to go in."

"Not true," Clayton insisted.

Scalia then read aloud Clayton's own words from the trial transcript. She had told the jury that the defendants would be guilty of an extortionate act unless they were to "part like the Red Sea, and let a woman through" to the abortion clinic. "In other words," said Scalia, "you told the jury that you could find an offense... by the mere blockade. It wasn't smacking people around. It was just not letting people in."

"No, your honor," Clayton insisted.

"So," said Scalia, "you're changing your position here."

"No, your honor."

"I see," said Scalia skeptically.

Even caught in the act of verbal manipulation, advancing the agenda trumped honesty.

Teaching Relativism

The roots of this loss of truthfulness can be found in law schools themselves, where students learn to argue both sides of an issue regardless of their personal convictions or what they know to be true. They learn to control their emotions and passions, tailor an argument to fit their agenda, and undermine the position of opponents. First year students are presented hypothetical cases to help shake up their "antiquated" ideas of right and wrong. For example, the professor might check for reactions in this case:

"Imagine that a three-year-old boy falls into a swimming pool. An Olympic swimmer happens to be standing on the side, watching the whole situation. The child screams for help, splashes, and thrashes about wildly, trying to keep afloat. As he swallows water and his head dips under the surface, the bystander observes all without moving a finger. The little boy drowns. What is wrong with this picture?"

Student reactions are varied. One shocked student replies, "That was wrong. You can't just stand by and watch someone die."

Another young woman chimes in, "There was no danger at all for that swimmer. He could have saved the kid without even breaking a sweat. That loser deserves fifteen years in prison!"

The jubilant professor takes advantages of these natural reactions to show that morality means nothing in law. There is no law against what the Olympic swimmer did (or didn't) do; he would not be liable in any way under the law. They shouldn't think in terms of right or wrong, but just of legal and illegal. This case is typical of law school instruction, where morals are transformed into legal categories. Morals – what is right or wrong – are separated from the law in legal analysis.

There are advantages and disadvantages to this approach.

On the positive side, this legal training helps protect lawyers from judicial activism. In the above example, the legal question concerned not what was moral to do, but what were the obligations imposed by law on our hypothetical bystander. *Morally*, the Olympic swimmer should have saved the child's life, but *legally* he had no obligation whatsoever under current law. The question here is not what I think that the law should be (a moral question) but what the law is. The judicial activist is more concerned with what the law should be (his own moral sense) then with what the law is that he is charged to apply to the case before him. The question of what the law should be is proper to the legislative branch of government.

Unfortunately, this dichotomy between moral/legal seems to have succeeded only in divesting law students of traditional morality, but not the morality of relativism. Proponents of this new morality are not averse to judicial advocacy. As a result, we cannot protect a baby's life five minutes before its birth, but we guard by judicial decree a woman's "choice" to kill her child in order to protect her "privacy." As a result of this advocacy, the Massachusetts legislature must humbly obey the dictates of its court to "redefine" marriage to include homosexual unions. Some judges, trained in the schools of modern law, are standing morality and common sense on its head.

This type of legal training treats moral arguments as irrelevant or unimportant. It encourages moral relativism and acts as if there were no higher law than the law of the land. This might be a judicial necessity, but it is morally deadly, especially when we consider that the great majority of our elected politicians who make the laws received their first training as attorneys. When we forget about the great moral questions and the duties that spring from our human nature, we run the danger of losing our humanity.

That was precisely the case at the Nuremberg war crime trials held from 1945 to 1949. Those who came to the trials expecting to find sadistic monsters were generally disappointed. What is shocking about Nuremberg is the ordinariness of the defendants: men who were good fathers, kind to animals, even unassuming… and yet committed unspeakable crimes. Not legal crimes, but moral crimes. The torture, euthanasia, forced sterilizations, and executions were all perfectly legal under the Third Reich. The Nuremberg defendants – military leaders, doctors, and lawyers – never aspired to be villains. Rather, they were either swept along by the ideology of the day or suffered from career driven nearsightedness.

The Justice Trial[64] is one of the most interesting of the Nuremberg proceedings. Sixteen defendants, all members of the Reich Ministry of Justice or People's and Special Courts, raised the issue of what responsibility judges might have for enforcing grossly unjust – but arguably binding – laws. These lawyers and judges merely followed the laws… but laws that led to unjust executions, imprisonments, and genocide.

A law is not good because it is law; all law must answer to a higher law. And even when a law is just, unjust men who lose sight of the truth can manipulate the law to their favor. When the training of lawyers – as in the case of our drowning toddler –uproots them from morality to plant them in the soil of legality, we should not wonder at the proliferation of amoral lawyers more interested in making a buck, winning a name for themselves, or advancing their cause than in the truth and in what is best for society.

Alan Dershowitz, the Harvard law professor most famous for getting O.J. Simpson off the hook,[65] exemplifies the confusion in the judicial profession. In a September 2000 debate at Franklin and Marshall College, Dershowitz urged that we do things "because its the right thing to do," yet in the next sentence declared that he didn't know what was right or wrong and that no one can know that because there is no higher law, no unchanging truths. In his personal confusion, he denied any truth, any standard outside of what we ourselves determine.[66] Statements like that from one of the most prominent trial lawyers in the United States are sobering, but when that same lawyer is also training the top lawyers of the future, such a statement is truly frightening.

Denying the truth might work out well for powerful people like O.J. Simpson, but when truth is eliminated, the rest of the world will suffer. And precisely at this point we find the root of the rot in the legal system: the loss of truth.

Judicial Advocacy

When reference to truth is lost and relativism becomes the operating system of our laws, tyranny will follow not far behind. That is precisely what we witness in the new forms of judicial advocacy.

Passing a law is a slow process. It can takes years of effort and loads of money to research a topic, write the legal structure, garner support, advocate its implication, and succeed in convincing the public and other legislators of the law. The process is open to criticism and public scrutiny, and the politicians who pass unpopular laws don't stand much chance of reelection. New laws and social change come very slowly through the legislative branch of government, but this protects the nation from mob rule, shortsighted laws, and the consolidation of powers into a dictatorship.

It can also be a very frustrating process for advocates of social change.

From the beginning of the United States, politicians and special interest groups on both sides of the political spectrum looked for shortcuts in the system through increased executive power or by stocking the legislatures. However, it was the 1803 *Marbury vs. Madison* case that opened the biggest loophole for the quick road to power and change.

Initially the role of the courts was limited to simply interpreting the laws and applying them to cases, whether the laws were "constitutional" or not. The landmark *Marbury vs. Madison* case granted the Supreme Court the power of "judicial review," the ability to review laws and decide if they are "unconstitutional." All laws were subjected to the Constitution – or rather to the *judge's interpretation of the Constitution*. This case transformed the role of the judiciary, giving the courts increased power over the executive and legislative branches of the government.

Conversatives point to this case as the source of all our current judicial ills. But while it is certainly true that a judge or court can abuse this power of review, it is also true that Congress can abuse their legislative power by passing unjust laws. Laws are dead, and if applied generically without the human touch of a judge, they can be very unjust. That was the case with the laws of segregation; they were unjust and contrary to principles in the Constitution. So how do we go about changing these unjust situations? How do we maintain the balance of power between the executive, legislative, and judicial branches?

The question is complex, and upon the answer hinges the future of our civic freedoms. Alexis de Tocqueville addresses part of the solution when he wrote prophetically: "The president, who exercises a limited power, may err without causing great mischief in the State. Congress may decide amiss without destroying the Union, because the electoral body in which Congress originates may cause it to retract its decision by changing its members. But *if the Supreme Court is ever composed of imprudent men or bad citizens*, the Union may be plunged into anarchy or civil war."[67]

For over a century, this new power of judicial review was rarely exercised, but in the 1940's a new group of progressive Supreme Court justices began using it to bring about social change.[68] The Supreme Court decided a series of cases on prayer in school, religious schools, and display of religion in public that effectively introduced the phrase "separation of church and state" into the common speech of Americans. Privacy rights were first created and then gradually extended[69] to include contraception and abortion, while primary rights proclaimed in the Declaration of Independence and at the foundation of the Constitution – such as the right to life – were subjected to secondary rights such as "choice" or "privacy."

Social activists took the cue. If you want to get things done your way, fill the bench with judges on your side. "Repealing an unenlightened law is characteristically more arduous and less Mercury footed than a court edict. Persuasive arguments must be marshaled. Citizens must be educated and stirred from indifference or lassitude. The arts of legislative lobbying and tactics must be mastered. All this bother of active citizen involvement in self-government can be obviated by litigation implicating a handful of parties that culminates in a Supreme Court decree overriding the legislative process."[70]

The power of judicial review and the activism of new judges give the judiciary branch power it was never meant to have. It creates a political power above and beyond the President and Congress.

No wonder the appointment of judges has become such a politically charged event. Neither side in the culture war wants to lose one of the greatest weapons for change. In this partisan atmosphere, judicial nominees are increasingly subjected to meticulous probing, and if they fail to meet the ideological (not political) standards of the examiner, an *ad hominem* slur campaign begins.

There's been a lot of talk about liberal and conservative judges in politics and media. But can we really label judges that way? Everyone has their own opinions, but those opinions are not the law. That's why there are really only two types of judges: *law-interpreters* and *lawmakers*. Those who judge according to the law – both the letter and the actual spirit in which it was written – are the *law-interpreters*. Those who use the law to hand down rulings according to their own opinions become *lawmakers*. That is judicial activism; that is an abuse of a power never meant to be in their hands. Elected representatives and congressmen were meant to make laws, not judges and lawyers.

Whether liberal or conservative, judges are not there to impose their own ideology but to enforce the laws passed by others, including the supreme law of the Constitution of the United States. Judges are not chosen to settle political issues, but to carry out the law. Nevertheless, many liberal judges and justices, especially beginning with the Warren court, have made only the thinnest pretense of carrying out the law, when in fact they were imposing liberal ideology in their decisions.

"While liberal judicial activism and conservative judicial activism are equally contrary to the rule of law, they have not been equally prevalent in our times. Despite determined efforts in recent years among liberals in the media and in academia to create such equivalence, what have been called 'conservative judges' in our times have usually been judges who stick to the law as written. 'Conservative activism' has become a clever slogan, seldom documented with concrete examples among contemporaries."[71]

"Conservative" or "liberal" judges can both be good judges if they stick to interpreting the law, not making the law. (Whether or not they can be a good *person* by sticking to the law is another question.) Yet unfortunately, it seems as if the spirit of advocacy for social change has possessed a much larger portion of the liberal judges, making them bolder in their lawmaking pronouncements. Judicial advocacy has become one of the most effective tools for imposing social change.

When a democratic government forgets the truth about God and man as the basis for our common good it falls into serious problems. We are not so far from the abyss, and the justification of torture by prominent civil libertarian and Harvard professor of law Alan Dershowitz is just one example. While agreeing that torture is bad, he argues that it is already used in some cases; it would be better to legalize and regulate it openly rather than hide it behind our backs since "having laws on the books and breaking them systemically just creates disdain... It's much better to have rules that we can actually live within. And absolute prohibitions, generally, are not the kind of rules that countries would live within."[72]

So in the process of legalizing torture, perhaps we should eliminate speed limits – after all, who really follows them? And while we are at it, we should probably repeal laws against murder, rape, and theft because it is obvious from statistics and our prison population that many of our citizens are just not going to follow those unrealistic "absolute prohibitions."

For Dershowitz and other modern followers of "the end justifies the means," there is no natural law, no underlying rules in reality, no absolute truth, but just whatever we set up by our own laws. Since the Constitution and current law leave open the question of using torture, Mr. Dershowitz poses the question of under what circumstances it could be used. Perhaps for common criminals? What about for a terrorist with a ticking bomb?

As a good lawyer, he covers his tracks by posing what he thinks as an open question. "[W]hat if imprisonment is insufficient to compel him to do what he has a legal obligation to do? Can other techniques of compulsion be attempted? ...Could judges issue a "torture warrant," authorizing the FBI to employ specified forms of nonlethal physical pressure to compel the immunized suspect to talk?"[73]

Yet if judges can issue torture warrants, then why not terrorism, rape, or murder warrants? Why not go in and allow terrorists to come forward and make their case for why terrorism should be allowed? Why not establish a government agency for granting rape permits?

When the end justifies the means and we forget the truth about human dignity, common sense quickly disappears and an ideological monster is born. Unfortunately for us, modern law practice is forgetting the example of Nazi Germany and the Nuremburg trials. A new ideology – a new fundamentalism – has taken hold of advocates of the new social order. Judicial activism and the power of law have become key weapons in their battle to reform society in their own image and likeness, to enforce their will upon a reluctant populace.

Testimony to Truth

But the new ideological fundamentalism need not infect nor implicate all politicians, judges, or associates. History has known heroic lawyers who stood up for truth and the principles of just law in the face of tyranny, ideologies, and great personal danger. Men like Sir Thomas More in Henry VIII's England and Dr. Lothar Kreyssig in Nazi Germany.

In 1928, Dr. Lothar Kreyssig was appointed as judge at the Court of Guardianship in the town of Brandenburg in northern Germany. His superiors considered him to be a first-rate judge – until after the 1933 elections that brought the National Socialist's to power he began a series of minor insubordinations: slipping out of a court ceremony when a bust of Hitler was unveiled, publicly protesting the suspension of three judges who failed to follow the interpretation of "Aryan laws" favored by Nazi authorities, and referring to Nazi church policies as "injustice masquerading in the form of law."

Reassigned to the Petty Court in Brandenburg, Kreyssig continued to be a thorn in the Nazi side. When the judge discovered that inmates at a local mental hospital were secretly being removed and killed, Kreyssig sent a letter of complaint to the president of the Prussian Supreme Court in which he complained about the "terrible doctrine" that "placed beyond the reach of law" concentration camps and mental institutions.

Officials at the Reich Ministry of Justice summoned Kreyssig in an effort to straighten out his thinking on matters of civil liberties. It didn't work. Kreyssig returned to Brandenburg and promptly issued injunctions to several hospitals prohibiting them from transferring wards of his court without his permission. The final straw for the Reich Ministry came when Kreyssig brought criminal charges before the public prosecutor against a Nazi party leader who headed the regime's euthanasia program, "T4."

When efforts to persuade Kreyssig that the euthanasia program was "the will of the Fuhrer" and that the Fuhrer was "the fount of law" in the Third Reich failed, Justice Minister Franz Gurtner demanded that Kreyssig withdraw his injunctions against the hospitals. Kreyssig refused and was forced into early retirement. A criminal investigation was opened against Kreyssig, but closed without prosecution.

In his book, *Hitler's Justice: The Courts of the Third Reich*, Ingo Muller writes of the courageous judge: "No matter how hard one searches for stout-hearted men among the judges of the Third Reich, for judges who refused to serve the regime from the bench, there remains a grand total of one: Dr. Lothar Kreyssig."

Will our own court system prove to have judges of valor and principle?

Relativism and Democracy

Under our current condition of advocacy and relativism, we would do well to reflect on the nature of our government itself. Democracy is a form of government based upon rule by officials elected by the people, following the will of the people and seeking the good of the people. As Abraham Lincoln expressed it in the Gettysburg Address: "of the people, by the people, for the people."

Since this type of government has to juggle the will and ideas of all the people, we have come to accept the notion – particularly dear to the relativistic mindset – that a democratic government should be like the referee in a basketball game. He can't take sides. If the referee isn't neutral, he can't be a good referee. In fact, if he took sides the fans would start to boo, the coach and team discriminated against would start to complain, and formal complaints would be lodged with the conference officials to remove the referee from the circuit.

According to relativism, government should be "neutral," not embracing any ideas, religion, or moral stance. It should be the referee between the citizens, trying to maintain the equality, freedom, tolerance, and tranquility of all without taking sides. Government should be tolerant, and it would seem that the only way to be tolerant is to put all ideas, beliefs, and moral behavior on the same level. Nothing is "better" than anything else. We won't even mention that "T" word (truth). And as far as good or bad, well, those are pretty judgmental words and a democratic government has no business pushing morality on anyone.

In fact, it's not unusual to hear the opinion that ethical pluralism (everything goes, as long as it doesn't hurt someone else) is the very condition for democracy.[74] "There is a tendency to claim that agnosticism and skeptical relativism are the philosophy and the basic attitude which correspond to democratic forms of political life. Those who are convinced that they know the truth and firmly adhere to it are considered unreliable from a democratic point of view, since they do not accept that truth is determined by the majority, or that it is subject to variation according to different political trends."[75]

But can a government really be neutral? Is the role of government just to be a referee? Wouldn't it closer to reality to see that government is not like the referee, but more like the coach? Let's use the distinction between a referee and the coach to give us a better idea of what the purpose of government is, and consequently, how it should work.

Both the referee and the coach are on the basketball court and came there for the game. But after that, their ways part. The goal of the referee is to arbitrate between the teams and individual players to make sure the game is played clean and fairly, respecting the rules. He has an actively neutral role. He has to be active in seeing and judging every single play, following the score and players, noting rising tempers or hidden cheap shots, and calming the tempo. At the same time, his role is neutral, but this neutrality is based on principles. A referee who is neutral towards the rules of the game, who doesn't care if a player runs with the basketball down the court or if the players are hacking each other to pieces would be a horrible referee. The referee is neutral, but not towards the principles and rules of the game.

The coach's role is completely different. He is there to win a game. If he is a good coach, he'll do everything possible within the rules to organize the players, try new formations, run plays, and change the line-up in order to win. He'll motivate, encourage, scream, hop up and down, and maybe even throw a chair or two when he really gets heated. The coach can't be neutral about the game or about his players. And he isn't neutral about the rules either. He knows he has to play by them and respect them, even though his main goal is to win.

How does government match up to the referee and the coach? It depends on what your view of the purpose of government is. Is government the system that will bring us happiness in this life, a sort of heaven on earth? Or more realistically, is government the way we try to organize ourselves for the common good? Or is it simply a necessary evil, a burden that we put up with, and something that should put as few limitations as possible on personal freedoms?

Since government is the organization of individual persons, we can know the purpose of it when we know the final end[76] of a person. The purpose of a person is the *good*, and not just any good, but their personal good. And what is this good? Is it what he thinks is his good, or what is really his good?

Everyone can agree that we want to be happy, but hardly anyone seems to agree on what makes us happy. This problem has two solutions. First of all, happiness is a personalized experience, and each unique person will prefer certain things over others. There is nothing wrong with that. If my friend likes anchovy ice cream, even though it might make me sick to the stomach, he can go on loving it. If that helps makes him happy, then great.

But happiness is more than just pleasure and subjective preferences. We share a common humanity, a human nature in which certain elements of life unite us. This is clear on the purely physical level. While a 350° oven might be great for cooking chicken or for growing certain types of fungus, a human being will quickly die at that temperature. There are certain parameters outside of which we cannot thrive, nor even survive. The same is true on the moral level. A rabbit can mate with its own relatives without any moral implications, but in human beings we call that incest and it is the cause of serious family, societal, spiritual, and psychological problems. These survival parameters for human existence are just as important on the spiritual level. A prison inmate can have all the television, books, visits, and food he could ever want, but the fact that his freedom is denied is a serious punishment.

The task of the government is not to ignore these natural parameters, pretending that a man can be happy sticking himself in an oven, raping his daughter, or living in a box cut off from society. The government has to make value decisions. These should be based not on prevailing opinions, but on solid principles of what we are and what will make us truly happy.

The purpose of government then is justice and the *common good* of all the individuals under its care. "Justice is both the aim and the intrinsic criterion of all politics. Politics is more than a mere mechanism for defining the rules of public life: its origin and its goal are found in justice, which by its very nature has to do with ethics."[77]

Justice and common good do not mean lumping together all the good things each individual wants. That would be naïve socialism. The common good is a whole package of small goods, all those conditions that make it possible for every individual citizen to fulfill himself, to be truly happy. Government for justice and the common good means giving the players freedom to play the game according to their abilities and style, but always within the rules of the game and the rules of the team.

In this sense, we can see that government has elements both of the referee and of the coach. Like the referee, a democratic government often has to arbitrate between certain parties or factions. Its neutrality is like that of the referee: it does not choose sides, but always stays on the side of the rules. Government has to promote respect for these rules, these guiding principles, or anarchy will break out. When a government does not respect human rights or denies private property, it has begun to ignore the rules of the game. Like a bad referee, that government needs to be booed.

Going a step further, any government, even a democratic one, cannot be impartial towards the success of the nation. Every government is like the coach who wants to win. A government should look out for the good of the citizens, promote their culture, protect their physical safety with a national defense system, expand trade, etc. A government that neglected the good of its citizens would be worse than a bad coach: a coach only influences a few players but a government sways the destinies of millions.

Yet a government cannot forget that it is subject to the rules of the game. Just like a team cannot invent its own rules, a government cannot change the basic principles of human life and what is good or bad, true or false. A coach is free to organize his team as he sees fit, run different defenses, and follow varied strategies, but he is *not* free to make up rules that go against the rules of the game. He is not free to cheat, lie, or use underhanded means to win.

When a democratic government forgets the rules of the game, imagining that natural law, unchanging principles, and truth do not exist and that its own man-made laws can determine everything, then that democracy is headed for trouble. Wherever someone loses reference to absolutes, regardless of the formal nature of the regime, the abuse of power follows right behind.

Religion and Democracy

A real democracy is never neutral. There have to be some common values and principles that guide the nation; all the citizens have the right to be heard, to express their opinions, and to contribute to the formation of these common values and principles. "The life of a democracy could not be productive without the active, responsible and generous involvement of everyone."[78]

For democracy to work, all proposals must be freely discussed and examined. If we were to allow everyone to speak their mind, *except* people who work at McDonald's or Wendy's, would that be democracy? Would that be fair and just? If everyone could vote except registered Democrats, would that be a legitimate democracy? Of course not! The Civil War, the Women's Rights and the Civil Rights movements were fought for this equality.

But oftentimes, the value of tolerance is disingenuously invoked when a large number of citizens are asked not to base their contribution to society and political life on their particular understanding of the human person and the common good. Basically, you can say what you want as long as it is not related to Christianity at all; and if it is, hide it.

The "separation of church and state" is invoked to claim that the Constitution forbids any mix of religious ideas with government. Politicians should be neutral, and if they have faith they better make sure to keep it out of politics. Live the double life; keep your faith hidden. John F. Kennedy set the precedent during his campaign for the presidency: he assured the American people that his Catholic religion wouldn't interfere at all in government. Many politicians have taken his cue and aren't ashamed to say, "I'm personally against 'X,' but I can't let my personal opinions into the picture."

Yet isn't this a bit schizophrenic? Should we act on our knowledge or not? If a doctor discovers a cure for diabetes and keeps that knowledge to himself, wouldn't that be wrong? If a military scout sees an ambush ahead and neglects to warn his fellow soldiers, wouldn't we judge he is partially responsible for their deaths?

When we possess information that can help others or save them from danger, we have a responsibility to pass on that knowledge. To keep it to ourselves is wrong. It does not matter if that knowledge comes from religion, philosophy, biology, sociology... if it is true we have the duty to pass it on. In reality, there should never be a conflict between your creed and your legislation; after all, both should be oriented toward the good and what is best for society.

Unfortunately, there are some politicians who fiercely maintain that dichotomy between "faith" and real life. Afraid of any association with religion and wilfully ignorant of moral truths, they show that they are more worried about keeping their job than about serving the people; they keep up the appearances of doing what is best for society, but they are really looking out for "number one," They are puppets yanked to and fro by opinion polls. The whims of the populace – not principles or solid values – define their legislative agenda.

Elected officials have to decide, based on the information available to them, what is best for the good of society. Just like parents, politicians should not satisfy every whim of their children, but use their broader knowledge and acquired wisdom to do what is best for them in the long run. Politicians owe first and foremost their best judgment to their electors; by ignoring what they consider to be true, deferring or capitulating to public opinion, politicians do a grave disservice to society.

Many people seem afraid of a politician who admits to

being influenced by his religious beliefs. Nowadays, the government will "tolerate" religion as long as it stays quiet, but if it starts getting active, influencing people's ideas, or involves itself even indirectly in politics, then "Big Daddy" will have to step in to protect the legal order of the Constitution.

But when did religion become so dangerous? Did the framers of the Constitution really seek separation of church and state? The last time I checked, "establish" was not the same as "separate." You can establish a new restaurant, establish yourself in the medical profession, or establish a fact in an argument. Establishing is positive action to set something in place. But separation is quite different. I can separate the sheep from the goats, separate the facts in a court case, or separate whites and darks for the laundry load. Separation is negative distinguishing of disparate things. Establishing and separating are two very different actions.

The fact is, this "separation" is a new idea that has gradually worked its way into legal practice and the minds of citizens. The Constitution mentions nothing about separation of church and state, though the First Amendment of the Constitution states clearly that "Congress shall make no law respecting an establishment of religion, or prohibiting the free exercise thereof..." If we examine the period in which this Amendment was written, it is clear that this clause refers to the fact that the government should not set up an official state religion. This was the case in European nations of the period, and the practice had spread to several states where it often led to repression of other religions and to "prohibiting the free exercise" of believers.

The idea of "separation of church and state" would have seemed ridiculous to men who recognized the importance of religion for the success of a free nation. John Adams wisely proclaimed: "We have no government armed with power capable of contending with human passions unbridled by morality and religion. ... Our Constitution was made only for a moral and religious people. It is wholly inadequate to the government of any other."

The Founding Fathers all recognized the vital importance of religion in public life because they knew that religious values give the most solid basis for law and politics. But here even their Enlightenment conception of religion was deficient. For them religion is good because it is useful in creating ethical citizens. Religion was reduced to an ethical system. That is a bit like saying a gold bar is good because it is an excellent paperweight. While it is technically true, it fails to grasp the full merit and truth of the gold ingot, just as limiting Christianity to an ethical system fails to do it justice[79]

However, even that circumscribed understanding of religion's role in society has been so twisted that today "freedom *of* religion" really tends to be taken as freedom *from* religion. The institutional separation of church and state becomes the unworkable separation of anything religious from anything political – and religious values must dare not inform any public moral debate.

Government is urged to be "neutral" toward religion, so the State does not target religion for suppression, but it often acts in callous disregard of it. The "neutrality" of the state might be called into question if the State were to accommodate religious expression. But as we saw above, government can never be completely neutral. Neutrality towards religion would mean ignoring part of the rulebook of reality – the profound anthropological reality that all people are religious

– and leaving human reason to the easy deceptions of power and special interests.

"Here politics and faith meet. Faith by its specific nature is an encounter with the living God – an encounter opening up new horizons extending beyond the sphere of reason. But it is also a purifying force for reason itself. From God's standpoint, faith liberates reason from its blind spots and therefore helps it to be ever more fully itself. Faith enables reason to do its work more effectively and to see its proper object more clearly."[80] The Church's role is not to supplant government, but to enlighten consciences and reawaken the spiritual energy for seeking a just and good society.

A state hostile to religion sentences itself to death; precisely because it is inhuman, there has never been a fully atheistic society that has long survived. Religions, though divergent in beliefs, have always been present throughout the history of mankind because people yearn for truth, thirst for the transcendent, and seek some higher meaning in their life. If the state ignores this religious nature of humanity, it cannot fulfill its task of promoting the common good of its people. In fact, the government must acknowledge, accommodate, and support religion – but not a particular religion. That was the original meaning of the First Amendment clause on the "establishment" of religion.

Alexis de Tocqueville noted in 1831 that "There is no country in the whole world in which the Christian religion retains a greater influence over the souls of men than in America; and there can be no greater proof of its utility, and of its conformity to human nature, than that its influence is most powerfully felt over the most enlightened and free nation of the earth."[81]

Religion, particularly the Christian faith, has always exercised great indirect influence upon politics in the United States because it instructs citizens in authentic freedom. When people with religious convictions speak of morality, this is not a question of "confessional values" or pushing religion on others, because such ethical precepts are rooted in human nature itself and belong to the natural moral law. These principles aren't just for Christians. They do not require the profession of the Christian faith, although Christian teaching "confirms and defends them always and everywhere as part of her service to the truth about man and about the common good of civil society."[82] Promoting the common good of society according to one's conscience has nothing to do with confessionalism," interference, or religious intolerance. There is a rightful and necessary autonomy of the political sphere from that of religion – but not from that of morality.

So why then should those who, following their individual conscience, propose moral arguments or are influenced by their Christian faith be disqualified from political life?

Should they be denied the legitimacy of their political involvement because of their convictions about what is best for the common good?

That wouldn't just be ignoring part of the rule book; that would be like the most biased of referees. That denial would be the most *intolerant* secularism. "Such a position would seek to deny not only any engagement of Christianity in public or political life, but even the possibility of natural ethics itself. Were this the case, the road would be open to moral anarchy, which would be anything but legitimate pluralism. The oppression of the weak by the strong would be the obvious consequence. The marginalization of Christianity, moreover, would not bode well for the future of society or for consensus among peoples; indeed, it would threaten the very spiritual and cultural foundations of civilization."[83]

In a world sick with relativism, even the obvious becomes obscure.

> "Reawaken the spiritual energy without which justice, which always demands sacrifice, cannot prevail and prosper."[1]
>
> — BENEDICT XVI

The Remedies: Beyond Tolerance

THE TRUTH ABOUT GOD AND MAN

Having examined at length the genre of fundamentalism, the genesis of a new secular ideology and its manipulative tactics, and some of its contagion in culture, this work would remain incomplete if we did not make some attempt at providing a few answers to our troubles. Indeed, an examination of the symptoms of our society has made it clear how much the denial of truth (relativism) has led to an outbreak of new forms of ideological fundamentalism.

When enough citizens adopt indifference towards truth and shirk their responsibilities, either society will drift into decay, or a fundamentalism will step in to establish its "truth." As these pages have made clear, new forms of secular fundamentalism are tightening their grip on our common life.

This new fundamentalism poses a double danger. Like the old totalitarian systems, it destroys freedom from the *outside* – gradually stripping away rights and subjecting the individual to the state, class, race or gender. But what is more dangerous about this new fundamentalism is the relativism which threatens to destroy freedom from the *inside*, corrupting our capacity to recognize and choose what is good and true. When we embrace relativism, we gradually become slaves to instinct, passions, and the manipulation of publicity campaigns. These two dangers have a common root in the "denial of truth in the objective sense."[2]

This denial of truth rejects God to propose instead real or practical atheism; it rejects individual freedom to gain "equality"; and it rejects man's spiritual nature for a crass materialism and worship of pleasure and comfort. When there is no truth outside of us, all is relative, the rule of law becomes a farce, and the strongest will always prevail.

When there is no truth, we quickly lose the motives for life itself: Nietzsche was right on this point, and all becomes "will to power" and the death of God. Nihilism is the rational conclusion to the seemingly innocent premise that there is no truth. Many lives now are running in this operating system of relativism and it's no wonder there are so many freeze-ups, crashes, and breakdowns. Suicide rates have risen 400% in the past thirty years in the United States alone, not to mention the ex-communist countries where an atheistic ideology succeeded in eradicating faith from large sectors of its population. When God and absolute values are abandoned, despair creeps in.[3] This is the danger America faces: the denial of the truth about God and about man.

There is merit in this analysis, but pointing out the problems is not enough. There is so much more yet to be done. The problems remain to be solved, consciences stirred, and apathy overcome. Now that we have seen the religious, irrational, and radical nature of this new fundamentalism, we have to do something about it. It is time to act.

I will sketch here the general lines of the solution to the fundamentalist problem, but the responsibility to act remains in your hands. The sketch of a solution is worthless if you do not take concrete action. Take these general principles and apply them to your own life, to your own circumstances, and to your family, workplace, and community. This book will have been a waste of my time and yours if you are not resolved to do something about what you have read.

A Human and Religious Sickness

When someone runs a fever of 103°F, convulses with cold chills, and loses control of their bodily functions we can safely assume that they are sick. If our body doesn't work as it was designed to, it is ailing. In a similar way, when a person misdirects their spiritual thirst, misuses or disuses their intelligence, and then attempts to coerce the will of others to join or accept their misguided decisions, we can be sure that they are sick. This is the fundamentalist phenomenon. It is a human and religious sickness.

Fundamentalism is first of all a human sickness. What separates us from other animals is our reason, our capacity to think, reason, love, and communicate. We are rational animals by nature, and because we are rational we are also social, with the need to communicate and to coexist peacefully in society. Fundamentalism undermines these needs by cutting off rational debate and trivializing discussion of the issues. Instead of being truly open-minded and trying to understand the position of others, the fundamentalist tendency picks out whoever doesn't agree with me and sticks a label on them. It undermines trust in others who are not of our party, union, faction, or denomination without ever really trying to understand them. This is not only irrational; it is unjust.

Yet when ideology resorts to radical measures – and when does it not? – whether name-calling, ostracizing, political leverage, coercion, or brute force, it is even more clearly a human sickness. We are not just like other animals and we shouldn't act like them. We are free in the fullest sense, but pressure tactics of name-calling, slander, intimidation, and threats are not addressed to the freedom of the other individual. They ignore the dignity of the person and focus on getting one's own way. Radical measures used to assert my own will ignore human dignity, poison our mutual relations, and make authentic peace impossible.

Fundamentalism – whether in the form of fascism, Marxism or radical multiculturalism – is a human sickness, but even more fundamentally it is a religious malady: it is a warped solution to man's search for ultimate meaning.

Instead of broadening our horizons and accepting the evidence of reality as it is, the fundamentalist tendency locks in on narrow elements of truth... but not the whole truth. Ideology cuts short the search for ultimate truth by putting on blinders; it narrows in on partial truths as if they were the ultimate truth.[4] This is a religious problem, and for a religious sickness, we need a religious solution that builds upon a solid human base.

The Human Remedy
On the purely human level, the remedy for the sickness of ideology is *mutual respect, dialogue, honesty*. This

trio is the foundation for any society that wants to guide its members to authentic happiness. Respect, reason, and honesty are fully human, and only the society that guides itself by them can lead us to develop our human lives to the full.

Socrates, the great teacher of Greek philosophy, summed up well the human foundation of *mutual respect*, "I am not an Athenian, nor a Greek, but a citizen of the world." We all share the common lot of humanity. As Martin Luther King, Jr. said, "We may have all come on different ships, but we're in the same boat now." Recognizing this common bond of humanity should foster respect for others and enable me to sympathize with the struggles of my fellow travelers in the journey of life. It facilitates understanding of others' viewpoints. I don't have to agree with them, but I can respect their stance not because of what they stand for, but because of what they are. They are fellow human beings, deserving of my respect and esteem.

Rational *dialogue* enables us both to discuss the merits and defects of our positions, confident that many issues can be resolved by sorting out misunderstandings and clarifying what we mean. I once got into a light argument with a Mexican when I affirmed that there were no animals in the forest of a state park. "What do you mean there are no animals here?" was his surprised reply. "There are animals everywhere. Don't you see that beetle crawling through the underbrush? And look, there's a finch perched in those brambles." He kicked at a decomposing log beside the path and pointed out the worms, larvae, and termites that scurried among the fragments. "This forest is full of animals," he assured me.

"But those aren't animals!" I replied. "Those are insects and birds, not animals. I haven't seen any rabbits or squirrels or deer. Now those are animals."

My friend's face scrunched up in a look of bewilderment. "I think we have a confusion of terms here. When I say animal, I'm talking about any big or little creature of the animal kingdom. What do you mean by animal?"

"An animal for me is a mammal, any size from mouse to elephant," I replied. "I don't really consider fish or birds as animals; they are... well fish and birds. And insects definitely aren't animals for me."

A smile flitted across my Mexican friend's face. "Then we are both right," he laughed. "The forest is full of my kind of animals, and so far we haven't seen any traces of your animals."

Only rational dialogue can bring opposing sides to reconciliation and mutual understanding. If we had each blindly asserted our position, we never would have agreed nor understood what the other meant. Without maturity, that dialogue will never happen and without authentic open-mindedness, that dialogue will never bear the fruit of understanding and peace.

The third – and perhaps most important – treatment for fundamentalism is *honesty*, to sincerely seek the truth as we see it. This is a human need, not a religious argument.

It is possible to lie to ourselves, even without realizing it. We can be close-minded and arrogant, blindly asserting that whatever we think is the truth, and that what someone else believes is just their opinion. This arrogance and foolishness stagnates us in our beliefs, blinding us to any other possibilities and blocking the road to progress in knowledge. This laziness makes us prefer the intellectual comfort of knowing something – even if small and imperfect – to the daunting task of seeking out the truth. This is insincerity and dishonesty.

It is not enough for me to be sincere in what I know. We naturally want to know that we know, and to know that what we know is true. This search for truth applies equally to the scientist scouring far reaches of the galaxy with the Hubbell for clues to the birth of our world or to your teenage daughter who tests her boyfriend to see if he really loves her. Even those who scoff at truth invariably continue to search for it in one form or another: honesty and the search for truth are intrinsic to human life. To cut that search short is not only inhuman, it also leads to an infection of ideological fundamentalism.

The Religious Remedy

Is there such a thing as a religious remedy to ideological fundamentalism? It's been insinuated and stated to us in every public debate that the more deeply religious people are, the more likely they are to be bigoted, closed-minded, and, in general, a threat to civic peace. We've heard it repeated so often that we often take it for granted. But nothing could be further from the truth.

The Gallup polling organization developed a twelve-item scale to measure the segment of the American population that is "highly spiritually committed." Gallup reports: "While representing only 13 percent of the populace, these persons are a 'breed apart' from the rest of society. We find that these people, who have what might be described as a 'transforming faith,' are more tolerant of others, more inclined to perform charitable acts, more concerned about the betterment of society, and far happier."[5] Simply put, serious religious commitment makes people not only truly open-minded, but also better citizens.

"Another study by Gallup shows that 83 percent of Americans say that their religious beliefs require them to respect people of other religions. Put differently, religion is the foundation of religious tolerance. Be prepared to take cover when you try that out on the secular bigots who rail against the bigotry of religion."[6]

But not just any religion will do. Not all of them practice mutual respect, nor do they all fully respect the human search for truth; a quick look at the heresy trials for Christians in Pakistan or the intolerance towards religions other than Islam in Saudi Arabia makes that clear.

Eighty-three percent of Americans said their religion fosters "tolerance." What religion does that 83 percent affiliate with? Were Muslims or Jews responding? Perhaps a few were, since these religions make up .5 and 1.3 percent of the US population. Were they Buddhists or Rastafarians? Maybe a tiny percentage, since they are less than 1 percent of the population. Without a shadow of a doubt, the vast majority of those respondents were Christians. Christianity is the religion of more than 75 percent of the American population and Christianity is the primary reason for our attitudes of religious tolerance.[7] Not just any religion will do when it comes to religious freedom.

Because the ideological fundamentalism we have examined is at root a spiritual sickness, the only lasting cure will come from authentic religion. If all we want is mere "tolerance" – just putting up with others – then we really don't need religion. A set of laws and a strong police force are enough to enforce that type of tolerance. Just look at the "success" of UN peacekeeping troops that enforce "peace" between peoples. But if we want authentic tolerance, that is, mutual respect and peaceful coexistence, religion is indispensable. To be truly tolerant, we must go beyond tolerance to respect for the person and respect for the truth, values which are upheld specifically in and by religion.

But what exactly is religion? It is a bit like time: if you don't ask me what it is, I know. Most of us have grown up with Christianity, but the longer we live, the more we travel, and the more globalization transforms society, the more we realize that we really don't know what religion is. Despite the volumes written about religion, the immense production of writings within religions, and the innumerable references you will find to it in newspapers and magazines everyday, few people seem to know what religion really is.

What Is Religion?

Part of the confusion stems from the diversity of religions. We call Hinduism, Christianity, Islam, Zoroastrianism, and sometimes even the New Age movement "religions," but they are all extremely different from one another. What is it that makes a certain association of people a religion? Common interests? Certain rites or beliefs? The same uniforms?

For many, religion is just like their racquetball club or bridge circle: religion is nothing more than another club. Changing churches to find a stimulating preacher, less judgmental people, or some novelty is no big deal – after all, it's just another social group. No doubt religion is social, but it is much more than social. I can eat a hot dog in my kitchen or in the baseball stadium, but only a very shortsighted person would say that it is the same thing. The hot dog in the stadium is juicier, full of flavor, and is only part of a much bigger reality, where there is a game to be won or lost and heroes to be made.

Religion is more than a club. It is our search for truth, for meaning, for purpose in our lives – not just any truth, but the Ultimate Truth. In this sense, religion is the expression of what is most important for man. We can live without a hot dog, but we cannot live a truly human life without meaning.

Religion always involves three elements: the subject, the actions, and the object. Whatever its particular expression, religion must always have a subject – an individual person – with his intelligence, will and sentiments. This person experiences the need for self-transcendence, a sense of inadequacy, a thirst for the Absolute. This in turn is expressed in actions, whether stories, rites, prayers or sacrifices which are always directed towards some object – variously conceived by different religions as the Immanent, Transcendent, Holy One, Absolute, Infinite.

If we looked at religion from the outside, we would see that it is the complex of symbols (rites, myths, etc.) or of norms by which men manifest and actuate a relation of submission and dependence on the Divinity. Put in simpler terms, "Religion is a life-transforming world perspective which affects every aspect of life."[8] It is man's discovery of meaning and how he acts upon it.

Viktor Frankl, the Austrian doctor who survived a Nazi concentration camp during World War II, wrote about the need for purpose in his book, *Man's Search for Meaning*. Men died and lived – if you can call the forced labor, beatings, and a few ounces of weak soup for sustenance "living" – every day in the concentration camps. And it was not the physically strong who survived. Only those who had some purpose, some meaning in their lives found the moral strength to survive that hell on earth.

Man needs meaning in life. If we have no purpose in life, then why live? Suicide is the logical result of having nothing to live for. Catholic Archbishop Timothy Dolan of Milwaukee, Wisconsin highlights this profound reality of human life in his commencement address to students at Marquette University in June of 2003.

"Right after I was ordained a priest almost twenty-seven years ago, I received a telephone call from a grade-school classmate who wanted to visit me. I had not seen 'Eddie' in twelve years, but I had heard that life had not been very good to him, that his years of service in Vietnam had particularly scarred him, and that he had become a drug addict surviving on the back streets of St. Louis. How surprised I was when he showed up at the rectory looking happy, healthy, and confident, and even more shocked when he introduced me to the young woman he wanted to marry.

"He sensed my amazement and began to explain. "Tim, you know that I've been through tough times. I had lost everything – family, friends, faith, future. One day I almost lost my life. Another addict and I were in the basement of an abandoned warehouse shooting up heroin. I watched as he loaded up our two syringes with a triple, lethal dose and locked his glazed-over eyes onto mine. 'Let's cut to the chase,' the other addict whispered. 'Neither of us can find any purpose to life. Unless one of us can come up with a reason to live in the next thirty seconds, let's go out on a high with this triple dose of gold.'

"'I was desperate, sure,' recalled Eddie, 'but not ready to

end it all, so my scrambled brain went into overdrive to discover some purpose or meaning to life. And what came to
mind, Tim, was the third question and answer you and I
learned in second grade from our catechism: 'Why did God
make you? God made me to know him, love him, and serve
him in this world, and to be happy with him forever in the
next.'

"Eddie continued: 'That's what I blurted out just as the
other guy said, 'Time's up,' and began to look for his vein.
'Say that again,' he asked. 'God made me to know, love and
serve him in this world, and to be happy with him forever in
the next.' Eddie had tears in his eyes as he finished the story.
"The other guy shrugged and said, 'Sounds good to me,' and
we both dropped our syringes. That 'wisdom' I remembered
from second grade saved – and changed – my life.'"

Every human person seeks some meaning in their life and
religion is the natural expression of this search… and of joy
when it is discovered. Whether or not that religious discovery is true or not is another question, but the fact that man is
naturally religious cannot be denied. The life of Helen Keller
– deaf and blind from infancy – is eloquent witness to that.
At the age of nineteen-months she contracted a fever that left
her blind and deaf. When she was almost seven years old, her
tutor Anne Sullivan broke through the communication barrier by pumping cold water over her palms and tapping out
letters. Helen Keller quickly learned to read and write, and
by the age of ten began to speak. Though she had never heard
a word from the outside world about a Supreme Being, when
the local preacher spoke to her about God, Helen responded
joyfully, "I have been wishing for quite awhile that someone
would teach me about Him. For I have been thinking about

Him for a long time." Deep within our heart, we all thirst for the Eternal.

Man is naturally religious. He seeks profound answers to the meaning of life and instinctively reaches out to something greater than himself, something that is unchanging, something that answers the great question "Why?" Precisely because we cannot live without some purpose in life, religious freedom – the right to seek out ultimate meaning – is epitome of all other freedoms. It is inseparably tied to them all by reason of that very dignity which is the human person.[9]

The True Religion?

If religion is just the discovery of meaning, then there will be as many religions as there are reasons that people find for living. How can a religion be "true" if it depends on what one individual finds to be valuable?

Different people will find different things valuable, but that doesn't take away the fact that some things are more valuable in and of themselves. Some things are objectively better. My brother might be a Minnesota Vikings fan, while I root for the Denver Broncos, but to find out who is really better we look at their rankings.

No one religion exhausts the truth, but that doesn't make them all true either. Religions make contradictory claims, explain the world in different ways, and contain beliefs and practices that exclude the possibility of reconciliation with each other. The Aztec religion prescribed ritualistic torture and feasting on the dismembered bodies of their enemies, yet Christianity proclaims love of our enemies and doing good to those who hate us. Certain animist religions in Africa require family members to eat the brains of deceased relatives, yet for

Judaism it is sinful to eat the blood of any animal. Islam prescribes stoning to death for the adulteress, while Mormonism – according to its scriptures – lauds polygamy. Ancient rituals of the god Baal contained sacred prostitution, but Christianity teaches the sacredness of marriage and the evils of prostitution. To say that all religions are equally true is to reject not only common sense, but even rationality itself.

The elephant theory of religion has gained popularity in past years as peoples and societies recognized the need for peaceful coexistence and religious tolerance. According to this theory, if we blindfold five people, then tell them to go touch an elephant and explain what they feel, we will get five different explanations, all equally "true." Similarly, goes the argument, all the religions of the world just explain the "Divine" in different ways, and all are just as true as the next. No one religion exhausts the truth.

Though the elephant theory of religion is very catchy, it is oversimplistic. We might experience religion in different ways, but that does not change the object of religion or make all religions equally true. Truth is bigger than any one religion; that is why those who claim to *possess* the truth – fundamentalists of whatever stripe – will always fall short of their claim. Truth is owner and keeper of itself. The truest religion will not *possess* the truth, but rather *be possessed by the truth*. That is what the Catholic Church means when it claims to be custodian of the truth.[10] This is not blatant arrogance; on the contrary, it is a claim worth examining and verifying.

A "Universal Consensus" Religion?

Perhaps we cannot accept all religions as true, but what

about the possibility of taking the best from every religion and creating a "universal consensus" religion? Just like taking the best NBA players to make the Dream Team, right? Such a noble project could unite the great powers of religion into a single force for the good and advancement of humankind. What a noble goal! What a grandiose scheme!

What a dismal failure. The idea is not new. Various groups have attempted just such an ecumenical endeavor, drawing together various religions to seek the least common denominator and uniting around those core elements.

Unfortunately, religion is not just about the least common denominator, it is about ultimate truth and meaning in life. The various world religions are the footprints of mankind's search for ultimate meaning and when it comes to ultimate meanings, people hang on for dear life. We can lose everything else, but if we lose meaning in our life, then why live? Suicide is just a logical step away. It takes courage to seek out the truth, to examine one's own religious convictions in the light of reality and to see if my "truth" corresponds to the Truth.

Authentic religion cannot be arbitrarily choosing something to base our life on either, contrary to the New Age mentality. I cannot just capriciously give ultimate meaning to something – that would be a return to idol worship. Whether my idol is a golden calf or a Porsche 911 makes no difference. Just because I value something does not mean that that thing deserves value – I must search for and embrace that which has meaning in and of itself. A universal consensus – taking the lowest common denominator – can never work, because it fails to recognize what is true, good, and therefore the only worthy Ultimate Meaning of life.

Fundamentalists would agree... and *their* religion is the true one (whatever particular religion that might be). They rally around their system of explaining and giving meaning to life – their religion – and are often supported by a charismatic leader, an inspired text that is accepted absolutely, and belief in "salvation" from the evils of life.

There are many religions; there are many expressions of man's search for the ultimate meaning of life, but not all are equally legitimate or true. The pacifist Mahatma Gandhi recognized this also when he wrote, "Belief in one God is the cornerstone of all religions... In theory, since there is one God, there can be only one religion." Though the theory was clear for him, the practice was not. "I do not foresee a time when there would be only one religion on earth in practice," continued Gandhi. Different times, places, and cultures have given rise to varied expressions of man's search for God, and each of them contains kernels of the truth.[11] The task of each man and woman is to continue seeking the *fullness* of the truth. The fullness of our life – and our life after this life – depends upon it.

Back to the Religious Remedy

Our digression into an explanation of religion and man's search for meaning can help us to understand more fully why only authentic religion can fully counter the scourge of fundamentalism.

The religious remedy to fundamentalism mirrors the human cure. On the natural level we discovered the need for *mutual respect, dialogue,* and *honesty* to counter the fundamentalist phenomenon. This trio is the foundation for any society that wants to guide its members to authentic happiness. Respect, reason, and honesty are fully human, and only the society that guides itself by them can lead us to develop our human lives to the full.

Yet on their own they are not enough. They are still human, natural, limited. Human persons, on the contrary, are not merely natural: we are naturally *spiritual*. There is an inborn thirst for the infinite, for the eternal, for something beyond what we see and touch and feel. We have a natural intuition that there is a deeper meaning to life, that there is more to our existence than a few years of pains and pleasures before plunging into the abyss of death and the unknown. We are naturally spiritual, naturally religious, so when we are cut off from the spiritual or when religion is denied, part of our human existence is truncated. We are only fully human when we follow our spiritual nature.

The natural principles of *mutual respect*, *dialogue*, and *honesty* are elevated to this spiritual level when respect gives way to *charity*, when rational dialogue is unlocked to the richness of *faith*, and when we are free to discover the *truth* about God, man, and the meaning of life. In authentic religious expression alone do we find the religious remedy that unleashes us from the slavery of sin, superstition, and disbelief.

Mutual respect – from a purely natural point of view – is necessary to human life. We've all been thrown into the world, and that gives us some sense of solidarity with other human beings, but it's still a "dog-eat-dog" world ruled by the principle of survival of the fittest. It takes no expert in history to realize that man left to his passions and selfishness ends up repressing others and asserting his own power with total disregard for others. On his own, man becomes a monster.

Authentic religion transforms the man, supplying the support necessary to curb our selfish tendencies and darkest passions.

Authentic religion promotes mutual respect. In the ancient world, the rule of life was "An eye for an eye, a tooth for a tooth."[12] The teaching of Jesus Christ turned that rule upside down, revolutionizing the course of history. "You have heard that it was said 'Love your neighbor and hate your enemy,' but I tell you: Love your enemies and pray for those who persecute you."[13] This is incomprehensible without faith, without true religion. As the Indian philosopher Mahatma Gandhi wisely pointed out, "It is easy enough to be friendly to one's friends. But to befriend the one who regards himself as your enemy is the quintessence of true religion. The other is mere business."

For a Christian, the natural respect we should have for each other is taken a step further. We do not just respect others, we *reverence* them because we are more than just fellow travelers; we are children of God, brothers and sisters in Christ. Yes, we've all been thrown into the world together, but not randomly. God created us, he sent his only Son to die for us and save us from the clutches of eternal suffering, and his Spirit stays with us. We are not alone. Our life has meaning. The life of my brothers and sisters is valuable because God loves them.

And if that weren't enough, Jesus *commanded* us to "love one another as I have loved you." That is charity: total, unmeasured, uncalculated love. In the Gospel accounts that have come down to us, Christ didn't often command, but when he did, it was something serious. "Love one another as I have loved you." Charity is a vital matter for a Christian.

A Christian who does not forgive, who holds grudges, who remains indifferent when confronted with the pain of others or who ignores injustice in society is not an authentic Christian. Charity is the essence of the Gospel message and the spiritual epitome of natural respect.

Authentic religion elevates respect to the realm of charity, but not only that. It also gives us a new tool for *dialogue*. Rational discussion of the issues is human, while irrational argumentation and blind affirmations are inhuman. This is clear. Yet there is a whole new dimension that needs to be added to our discussions if they are to be fully rational: the spiritual. We are naturally spiritual. The gift of *faith* in God and his revelation complete our natural religious aspiration, making our discussions fully human, that is, fully natural and fully spiritual.

"Faith is the assurance of things hoped for, the conviction of things not seen."[14] Faith is not merely a rational calculation, nor is it the "wager" of Blaise Pascal. It is not the same as belief. I can *believe* in a person or a fact, trusting and confiding in them on a human level as trustworthy, but *faith* rises to a new level; it is not merely trust in a person, it is a response to God "who reveals himself and gives himself to man, at the same time bringing man a superabundant light as he searches for the ultimate meaning of his life."[15] As personal adherence to God and assent to his truth, Christian faith differs from our faith in any human person. It is right and just to entrust oneself wholly to God and to believe absolutely what he says. It would be futile and false to place such faith in a creature.[16]

Faith is certain. It is more certain than all human knowledge and more solid than any rational calculations because it is based on God – and he doesn't lie nor manipulate. To be sure, revealed truths can seem obscure to human reason and experience, but "the certainty that the divine light gives is greater than that which the light of natural reason gives."[17]

Reason and faith together free us from ideology. Reason alone leaves us with cold rationalizations and a truncated outlook on life; faith alone without the support of reason quickly falls into error and superstition. We need both faith and reason. "Faith and reason are like two wings on which the human spirit rises to the contemplation of truth; and God has placed in the human heart a desire to know the truth – in a word, to know himself – so that, by knowing and loving God, men and women may also come to the fullness of truth."[18]

Our dialogue isn't fully human until both faith and reason work together. No plane will fly with just one wing. Just ask any pilot and he'll confirm that. In the same way, the flight of our conversations can stay on track only when carried out in faith and reason. This duo has had a bumpy road since Galileo and the Enlightenment. It is only natural that difficulties and questions should arise as we attempt to resolve the seeming contradictions. But that is all they are, because "there can never be any real discrepancy between faith and reason. Since the same God who reveals mysteries and infuses faith has bestowed the light of reason on the human mind, God cannot deny himself, nor can truth ever contradict truth."[19]

The questions that arise from this dialogue between faith and reason naturally lead us to the *search for truth*, the spiritual remedy to ideology. Our natural desire to know the truth finds its fullest expression in the religious search for ultimate truth, for the meaning of our existence.

Every authentic religion is a search for meaning and incarnates in some form this *search for truth*. The definition of Buddhism is "noble truth" and this religion began "with the Truth embodied over 2500 years ago in the person of Gautama, the Buddha."[20] The Hindu religion also has the highest regard for truth, calling it "an eternal duty" and assuring us that "everything rests upon Truth."[21] According to the Bahá'í faith, there is only one reality; their spiritual leader Abdu'l-Bahá said, "Being one, truth cannot be divided, and the differences that appear to exist among the many nations only result from their attachment to prejudice. If only men would search out truth, they would find themselves united."[22] While Islam, too, places great stock in truth in itself, the emphasis is on the truth of Islam. It claims to be the one truth, the one true religion, as is argued in numerous publications and Web sites, to the exclusion of every other religion.[23] Mormonism makes similar claims.[24] Above and beyond these common religious expressions of search for truth, Jesus Christ claimed to be "the way, the truth, and the life."[25]

Who then is telling the truth? Can everyone be right? Are all religions true?

The answer exists, but it is an answer that each individual person must discover for himself. The question can be put off, but not eliminated, because it is tied to our ultimate purpose and destiny. Mahatma Gandhi expressed this personal search well when he wrote, "The Absolute Truth, the Eternal Principle, that is God. There are innumerable definitions of God, because His manifestations are innumerable. They overwhelm me with wonder and awe and for a moment stun me. But I worship God as Truth only. I have not yet found

Him. But I am seeking after Him.... I have had faint glimpses of the Absolute Truth, God, and daily the conviction is growing upon me that He alone is real and all else unreal."[26]

St Augustine of Hippo expressed the same yearnings for Truth when he wrote, "You have made us for yourself, and our hearts are restless until they rest in you."[27] No one can elude the search for God, for Absolute Truth. We need the religion that most fully corresponds to the Truth that each man and woman seeks because Truth is the internal force that makes external enforcement unnecessary. Truth is our protection from tyranny. When truth is ignored, only power and brute force get their way, and although that power might be masked with flowery language, academic jargon, or legal imposition, it is still just plain, raw power. "Truth... is the best antidote to ideological fanaticism, in the scientific, political and also the religious realm."[28]

Truth is both a *personal* and a *public* matter. The beauty and goodness of Truth attract us, or rather, they attract *me*. Truth is first a personal matter because I need the truth, I want to know what is true, and I want to build my life on that. We humans come with a built-in thirst for transcendence, an innate desire to seek and embrace an ultimate truth that lies far beyond the horizon of ourselves.

This personal search for truth strengthens the life of society. Governments at all levels should acknowledge this fundamental human desire, avoid interference with its full expression of this religious tendency, and actively promote its voluntary cultivation. Both the personal and the political sphere need a revolution of truth, because only a return to the truth about what and who we are can save us from the sickness of fundamentalism.

Christianity has steered a clear course through the cults, totalitarian regimes, and ideological fundamentalisms of the 20th century, often paying for its resistance to the powers that be with the blood of martyrs. As Pope John Paul II wrote in his 1991 letter *Centessimus Annus,* "the Church [does not] close her eyes to the danger of fanaticism or fundamentalism among those who, in the name of an ideology which purports to be scientific or religious, claim the right to impose on others their own concept of what is true and good. Christian truth is not of that kind. Since it is not an ideology, the Christian faith does not presume to imprison changing sociopolitical realities in a rigid schema, and it recognizes that human life is realized in history in conditions that are diverse and imperfect. Furthermore, in constantly reaffirming the dignity of the person, the Church's method is always that of respect for freedom."[29]

The only real protection against ideology – contrary to the prevailing wisdom of the age – is not secularism and the extirpation of religion from any influence in public life; the best protection against religious or irreligious fundamentalism is *authentic* religion. The future of society depends on religion and on a correct understanding of our relation to God.

True Open-Mindedness

True open-mindedness can never be attained through mere "tolerance." While tolerance – in the true sense of the word as *mutual respect* – is a great good, it is always subject to truth. When truth is forgotten, tolerance is worshipped to the point of forbidding any judgments at all. That is a clear sign that "open-mindedness" has resulted in brain loss.

If you are truly tolerant, you will respect other people's opinions. This does not mean agreeing with them, but rather giving them the right to profess their opinions. But, when tolerance is understood as a justification for license in a relativistic, no-holds-barred way, we falsify the meaning of reality. If our democratic experience is to endure we must urgently foster *mutual respect*, *dialogue*, and *honesty* on the human and spiritual levels, not the confusion of a naïve relativism that blurs the lines between good and evil.

Man's "natural and fundamental right [is] to know the truth and live according to that truth."[30] There is a reality that judges our systems to be right or wrong, good or bad; there is a human nature that can be corresponded to or rejected, but not without consequences; there is a God who ultimately judges our actions. Reality is relational, not relative.

Do not be afraid to call black, black or white, white. If we fail in this duty of conscience, we are doing an injustice to the true meaning of tolerance and cutting short authentic democratic debate. This is the problem of the ideological fundamentalism when it begins sticking on labels and cutting short truly open-minded debate of the issues. Like other varieties of fundamentalism, this new strain of political correctness contains elements of truth that should be welcomed: we should strive for peace, equality, and justice for all. We should love and accept every person as they are… and in that love we should seek what is best for them. Loving the person doesn't mean accepting the sin; open-mindedness doesn't mean letting your brains fall out; finding the truth in what others say doesn't mean denying the truth that we know and have a duty to proclaim.

In the confusion and darkness of our troubled times, we

can never forget that there is a Light of the world. We should not be afraid to proclaim our faith nor to be who we ought to be. That is what makes us "the salt of the earth, the light of the world." When we proclaim him fearlessly, backed up with the support of reason and the power of faith, he will enlighten the darkness, not only of society, but of each individual open to his grace.

We need to "live out the truth in charity, as the fundamental formula of Christian existence. In Christ, truth and charity coincide. Charity without truth would be blind; truth without charity would be like 'a cymbal crashing.'"[31] We *do* need greater mutual respect, open-mindedness, and honest debate just as multiculturalism advocates – yet all in pursuit of truth, not an ideological agenda.

This Truth shall make us free.

Endnotes

THE OPERATING SYSTEM

1   See for example the work by Episcopalian scholar Phillip Jenkins, *The New Anti-Catholicism: the Last Acceptable Prejudice,* Oxford University Press, May 2003 or *Anti-Catholicism in American Culture* by Robert P. Lockwood, Center for Media and Public Affairs, Our Sunday Visitor, January, 2000 or *Anti-Catholicism in America: The Last Acceptable Prejudice* by Mark Stephen Massa, Crossroad/Herder & Herder, September, 2003.

2   ALEXIS DE TOCQUEVILLE, *Democracy in America,* Bantam, New York, 2000, p216.

3   Metaphysics is the science that studies the ultimate explanations of reality. Aristotle, who realized that physical reality is not sufficient to explain all of human life, sought out the causes and principles of reality beyond and above (meta) the physical world.

4   The Lambeth Conference in 1930 removed the moral prohibition of birth control from the moral theology of the Anglicans. Following suit, virtually all Protestant denominations cast off their moral prohibitions against the use of birth control in the 1930's, leaving the Catholic Church as the only major Christian denomination that objected and continues to object to the use of birth control. Thirty-five years after the Anglican Lambeth Conference, the U.S. Supreme Court removed all legal prohibitions against birth control in *Griswold.* The widespread acceptance of the birth control pill has led to sexual promiscuity and increased the number of unintended pregnancies. Dr. Robert Kirstner of Harvard Medical School affirmed that "For years I thought the pill would not lead to promiscuity, but I've changed my mind. I think it probably has." Cf. ALL About Issues 5, June, 1981.

5   JOHN PAUL II, Message for the 34th World Day of Peace on January 1, 2002.

6   THOMAS SOWELL, *Random Thoughts,* February 14, 2003.

7   Pornography is generally a "man" problem. Males tend to be more aggressive, visually oriented, and easily aroused. Though pornography designed for women does exist, it has never had the wild success of the male pornography market.

8   BERNARD LEWIS, "I'm Right, You're Wrong, Go To Hell," *The Atlantic Monthly*, May 2003.

9   ALEXIS DE TOCQUEVILLE, *Democracy in America*, Bantam, 2000, New York, p. 305. "Fetters and headsmen were the coarse instruments which tyranny formerly employed; but the civilization of our age has refined the arts of despotism which seemed, however, to have been sufficiently perfected before. The excesses of monarchical power had devised a variety of physical means of oppression: the democratic republics of the present day have rendered it as entirely an affair of the mind as the will which it is intended to coerce. Under the absolute sway of one man the body was attacked in order to subdue the soul; but the soul escaped the blows which were directed against it and rose proudly superior... The master no longer says: 'You shall think as I do or you shall die'; but he says: 'You are free to think differently from me and to retain your life, your property, and all that you possess; but you are henceforth a stranger among your people. You may retain your civil rights, but they will be useless to you, for you will never be chosen by your fellow citizens if you solicit their votes; and they will affect to scorn you if you ask for their esteem. You will remain among men, but you will be deprived of the rights of mankind. Your fellow creatures will shun you like an impure being; and even those who believe in your innocence will abandon you, lest they should be shunned in their turn. Go in peace! I have given you your life, but it is an existence worse than death."

10   Cf. JOSEPH CARDINAL RATZINGER, Homily of April 18, 2005, in St. Peter's Basilica in Rome, the day before he was elected Pope Benedict XVI. "How many doctrinal winds we have known in these last decades, how many ideological currents, how many styles of thought... The thought of many Christians has often been tossed about by these waves, tossed from one end to the other: from Marxism to liberalism, to libertinism; from collectivism to radical individualism; from atheism to a vague religious mysticism; from agnosticism to syncretism and so on. Every day new sects are born and we see carried out what St. Paul says about the deception of men, about the cunning that leads into error.

"To have a clear faith, according to the Church's creed, is often labeled as fundamentalism. Meanwhile, relativism – that is, letting oneself be swung 'back and forth by any wind of doctrine' – is seen as the only attitude suited to modern times. A dictatorship of relativism is growing, that doesn't recognize anything as absolute, leaving our own ego and its whims as the only standard.

"We, on the contrary, have another standard: the Son of God, true man. He is the measure of true humanism. 'Adult' faith doesn't follow the waves of fashion and the latest novelties; adult and mature is that faith which is profoundly rooted in friendship with Christ. This friendship opens to us all that is good and gives us the criterion for discerning between true and false, between deception and truth.

"We must mature this adult faith, and towards this faith we must guide the flock of Christ. And it is this faith – only the faith – that creates unity and is fulfilled in charity. In this respect, St. Paul offers us – in contrast with the difficulties of those who are tossed about by the waves like little children – a new word: live out the truth in charity, as the fundamental formula of Christian existence. In Christ, truth and charity coincide. Charity without truth would be blind; truth without charity would be like 'a cymbal crashing.'"

11   KARL KEATING, *Catholicism and Fundamentalism*, Ignatius Press, San Francisco, 1988.

12   ROBIN MCKIE, "'Prophet' Opens Theme Park for Our Alien Heritage," *The Observer*, March 16, 2003.

13   Dispensationalism is a branch of Protestant theology dividing world history into various segments – dispensations. It is the precursor to modern "rapture" theories under the form that is so popular in North America. It originated in the 1830s in England with an ex-Anglican priest, John Nelson Darby [1800-1882], who created an entire system of theology called pre-millennial dispensationalism, based on a radical separation between Old Testament Israel, described as God's "earthly" people, and the New Testament Church, his "heavenly" people. The Rapture is the means by which God will remove the heavenly people from the world so that he can finish the work begun with his earthly people.

14   See for example the contrived dialogue between two Soviet citizens confined to the Gulag, the first one prodding the convinced communist who has an explanation for everything. *The Gulag Archipelago 2*, ALEXANDER SOLZHENITSYN, pp.324-327, Collins/Fontana 1976.

"Look over there: how poverty-stricken our villages are – straw thatch, crooked huts."

"An inheritance from the Tsarist regime."

"Well, but we've already had thirty Soviet years."

"That's an insignificant period historically."

"It's terrible that the collective farmers are starving."

"But have you looked in *all* their ovens?"

"Just ask any collective farmer in our compartment."

"Everyone in jail is embittered and prejudiced."

"But I've seen collective farms myself."

"That means they were uncharacteristic."

15 JULIUS STRAUSS, "Crusade to make Rasputin a Saint Splits Church," *The Telegraph*, February 6, 2003.

16 Ibid.

17 Ibid.

18 JIM CARLTON, "Mormon Author Faces Expulsion for Skepticism," *Wall Street Journal*, December 9, 2002.

19 Dennis & Rauni Higley, A Mormon Church Translator for 15 Years and Her High Councilman Husband, http://www.exmormon.org/stories.htm.

20 Ibid.

21 COLIN JOYCE, "Men in White Sheets Postpone End of the World to Next Thursday," *The Telegraph*, May 16, 2003

22 Cf. http://www.fountain.btinternet.co.uk/koresh/outline.html.

23 IBN ISHAQ, *The Life of Mohammed*, translated by A. Guillaume and published by Oxford University Press in 1955, p. 515.

24 "Imam Ousted From Rome Mosque After Calling for a 'Holy War,'" Zenit.org, Rome, June 16, 2003.

25 "Islam and Violence," http://www.answering-islam.org.uk/Terrorism/islam_and_violence.html.

26 *Islam,* Encarta Encyclopedia, 1999.

27 See the Muslim website www.islam-qa.com - question #5441.

28 ROBERT SPENCER, interview in the *National Catholic Register,* November 30-December 6, 2003, p. 6.

29 JOSH DEVON, "Yemeni Sheikh of Hate: Cultivating Jihad," *National Review Online*, January 7, 2003.

30 JOHN PAUL II, Encyclical letter *Fides et Ratio*, September 14, 1998.

31 Ibid.

32 MALCOLM BARBER, *The Trial of the Templars*, Cambridge: Cambridge University Press, 1978, p. vii.

33 TASLIMA NASRIN, interview in *Free Inquiry* magazine, winter 1998/1999, Vol. 19 No. 1.

34 TASLIMA NASRIN, *Free Inquiry*, Fall, 1994, Vol 14, No. 4, p9.

35 ALEKSANDER SOLZHENITSYN, *The Gulag Archipelago,* Collins/Fontana, Australia, 1974, p. 147.

36 J. BUDZISZEWSKI, *True Tolerance: Liberalism and the Necessity of Judgment,* Transaction Publishers, New Brunswick, NJ 08903, 1992, pp. 227-228.

37 JOHN PAUL II, *Centessimus Annus*, n.25.

SYMPTOMS OF A NEW FUNDAMENTALISM

1   Symptoms of a New Fundamentalism, JOHN PAUL II, address of Wednesday audience, February 19, 2003.

2   KENNETH R. SAMPLES, ERWIN M. DE CASTRO, RICHARD ABANES, & ROBERT J. LYLE. *Prophets of the Apocalypse: David Koresh and Other American Messiahs,* Baker Books, Grand Rapids, MI, 1994.

3   JOSEF PIEPER, *Abuse of Language, Abuse of Power,* Ignatius Press, San Francisco, 1992, p19.

4   GEORGE ORWELL, *1984.* Middlesex, England: Penguin Books, 1954. Page 171.

5   JOSEF PIEPER, *Abuse of Language, Abuse of Power,* p.31.

6   JEFF JACOBY, *Hate Speech from the Left,* December 29, 2003.

7   CONGREGATION FOR THE DOCTRINE OF THE FAITH, *Considerations Regarding Proposals to Give Legal Recognition to Unions between Homosexual Persons,* June 3, 2003.

8   WALTER E. WILLIAMS, *Racial Censorship,* October 15, 2003.

9   Andrew Johnson was impeached but acquitted by one vote and did finish his term, albeit with little effectiveness. He then ran for the Senate from Tennessee and lost.

10   LEWIS CARROLL, *Alice Through the Looking Glass.*

11   W. SHAKESPEARE, *Othello,* III, iii.

12   ALEXIS DE TOCQUEVILLE, *Democracy in America,* p. 257.

13   MORGAN KNULL, PH.D., "Slanted Polls Yield Biased News," *The World & I,* October 2002.

14   DAVID MURRAY, JOEL SCHWARTZ, AND S. ROBERT LICHTER, *It Ain't Necessarily So: How the Media Make and Unmake the Scientific Picture of Reality,* Rowman & Littlefield, Washington, D.C., Statistical Assessment Service (STATS), 2001.

15   MARTIN GARDNER, *Fads and Fallacies in the Name of Science,* New York, Dover, 1957.

16   FRANK J. TIPLER, *The Physics of Immortality: Modern Cosmology, God and the Resurrection of the Dead,* London, Macmillan, 1995.

17   ROBERT L. PARK, PH.D., *Seven Warning Signs of Bogus Science.*

18   PETER L. BERGER, "Whatever Happened to Sociology?" *First Things* 126 (October 2002): 27-29.

19   Ibid.

THE PATHOLOGY EXPOSED

1   PETER KREEFT, *A Defense of "Culture Wars:" A Call for Counterrevolution*

2   LESTER A. KIRKENDALL AND MICHAEL E. PERRY, *The Transition from Sex to Sensuality and Intimacy*, New York, Prometheus Books, 1984, p. 161.

3   See   http://www.cdc.gov/nchstp/dstd/Stats_Trends/Trends2000.pdf visited December 30, 2003.

4   See   http://www.cdc.gov/nchstp/dstd/Stats_Trends/Trends2000.pdf visited December 30, 2003.

5   MISH Sexual Health Update, Dec. 1993, Vol. 2, No.1.

6   PIA DE SOLENNI, "Against AIDS: Abstinence," *The Wall Street Journal*, October 14, 2003.

7   Ibid.

8   *California Medicine*, September, 1970; Vol 113, No. 3.

9   Ibid.

10 "Dictionary on the Family Helps Define Battle Against Doublespeak," Zenit.org, January 28, 2003.

11 http://www.christianitytoday.com/ct/2003/003/10.21.html, online article *"Saved by Sonogram:* "Ultrasounds Help Crisis Pregnancy Centers Reduce Abortion" by MARK STRICHERZ in *Christianity Today,* March, 2003, posted 02/24/2003. See also "Bonding With Baby; Why Ultrasound is Turning Women Against Abortion" by MARK STRICHERZ, *Crisis Magazine,* December 2002.

12 www.lifesite.net visited September 25, 2003. "4-D Ultrasound Shows Babies Smile and Cry in Womb"
Wednesday September 17, 2003

13 MICHELLE MALKIN, *The Most Powerful Smiles in the World*, September 19, 2003.

14 Ibid.

15 It should be noted that ultrasounds are also being used against life in the womb in some countries. For example, in India prenatal screenings are used to determine the sex of the child and given the cultural preference for a male child, a higher percentage of females are aborted. Ultrasounds are a tool, and as such they can be used for good or evil.

16 http://ippfnet.ippf.org/pub/IPPF_News/News_Details.asp?ID=2919, *"3-D Ultrasound Images Showing Foetus Smiling,"* September 17, 2003, as reported by *Kaiser Daily Reproductive Health Report*, September 16, 2003.

17 Ibid.

18 FRED JACKSON AND BILL FANCHER, *Poll Shows Surprising Support for Pro-Life Issues: Groups Rally in Washington to Lobby 108th Congress on Behalf of Unborn*, Agape Press, January 16, 2003.

19 DR. JOEL BRIND, *Journal of Epidemiology and Community Health*, 1996.

20 THOMAS A. SZYSZKIEWICZ, "Cancer Institute is Denying Abortion Breast-Cancer Link, Critics Say," *National Catholic Register*, May 11-17, 2003.

21 See for example *The Chicago Tribune* article of February 27, 2003 entitled "Scientists Reject Abortion, Breast Cancer Link."

22 See PROF. JOEL BRIND, PHD's *Early Reproductive Events and Breast Cancer: A Minority Report,* March 10, 2002, http://www.abortionbreast-cancer.com/minorityreport.htm

23 http://www.lifesite.net/ldn/2003/mar/03030409.html visited October 22, 2003.

24 DR ANGELA LANFRANCHI, "Breast Cancer and Abortion: the Facts," The Age, February 17, 2003.

25 Ibid.

26 See the *Executive Summary of the Heritage Foundation*, "Why Congress Should Ignore Radical Feminist Opposition to Marriage," http://www.heritage.org/Research/Features/Marriage/bg1662.cfm   visited November 5, 2003.

27 FREDERICK ENGELS, *The Origin of the Family, Private Property, and the State*, Chapter II, The Family

28 *Homosexual Activists Step Up the Pressure for Marriage Rights*, Zenit.org, March 15, 2003.

29 *Statement of the Catholic Medical Association: Homosexuality and Hope,* of April 18, 2003 at www.cathmed.org/index.html.

30 Ibid.

31 *What Could Bring On Same-Sex Attraction in Boys*, Catholic Psychiatrists Look at Roots of U.S. Scandals, Zenit.org, June 27, 2002.

32 See *Homosexuality 101: A Primer,* a special report by the Traditional Values Coalition. www.traditionalvalues.org

33 Ibid.

34 ROY WALLER AND LINDA NICOLOSI, *Study Trumpeted by Health Writer as Evidence that Some Are "Born Gay,"* October 10, 2003.

35 *Statement of the Catholic Medical Association: Homosexuality and Hope,* of April 18, 2003 at www.cathmed.org/index.html.

36 See "The Overhauling of Straight America" in the November 1987 edition of *Guide* magazine in which homosexual activists MARSHALL

KIRK and ERASTES PILL delineated their marketing campaign for legitimizing homosexuality. They detailed how they will defeat opposition to the homosexual agenda by using the media, desensitization, guilt, and other tactics to gain political and cultural power in America. According to the authors, Americans who oppose homosexuality must be vilified in the media as homophobes and intolerant. Homosexuals must be portrayed as victims in order to gain sympathy. Kirk and Pill urge homosexuals to talk about homosexuality so much that people become desensitized to it. However, they warn homosexuals: *"In the early stages of any campaign to reach straight America, the masses should not be shocked and repelled by premature exposure to homosexual behavior itself. Instead, the imagery of sex should be downplayed and gay rights should be reduced to an abstract social question as much as possible. First let the camel get his nose inside the tent—only later his unsightly derriere!"*

37 *Archives of Sexual Behavior,* Vol. 32, No. 5, October 2003, pp. 403-417.

38 See the Centers for Disease Control and Prevention official report http://www.cdc.gov/nchstp/dstd/Stats_Trends/Trends2000.pdf

39 "Medical Downside of Homosexual Behavior: A Political Agenda Is Trumping Science, Says Rick Fitzgibbons," September 18, 2003, www.zenit.org.

40 ROY WALLER AND LINDA A. NICOLOSI, *Spitzer Study Just Published: Evidence Found for Effectiveness of Reorientation Therapy,* based on the results of a study conducted by Dr. Robert L. Spitzer in the *Archives of Sexual Behavior,* Vol. 32, No. 5, October 2003, pp. 403-417.

41 Ibid.

42 ROY WALLER, "New Study Indicates Gays and Lesbians Prone To Psychological Symptoms and Substance Abuse, But School Harassment Rates Not Higher for Gay Males" reporting on findings in the *British Journal of Psychiatry,* December, 2003, p. 556.

43 Ibid.

44 *Archives of General Psychiatry,* 1999, Vol. 56, 883-884

45 TIMOTHY J. DAILY, PH.D., *Homosexuality and Child Sexual Abuse,* http://www.frc.org/get/is02e3.cfm

46 MICHELE ELLIOTT, *Child Sexual Abuse Prevention: What Offenders Tell Us* in *Child Abuse and Neglect* 19, 1995, p. 582.

47 MARIE, E. TOMEO, ET AL., "Comparative Data of Childhood and Adolescence Molestation in Heterosexual and Homosexual Persons," *Archives of Sexual Behavior* 30 (2001): 539.

48 HARRY W. HAVERKOS, ET AL., "The Initiation of Male Homosexual Behav-

ior," *The Journal of the American Medical Association* 262 (July 28, 1989): 501.

49 BILL WATKINS & ARNON BENTOVIM, "The Sexual Abuse of Male Children and Adolescents: A Review of Current Research," *Journal of Child Psychiatry* 33 (1992); in Byrgen Finkelman, *Sexual Abuse* (New York: Garland Publishing, 1995), p. 316.

50 GARY A. SAWLE, JON KEAR-COLWELL, "Adult Attachment Style and Pedophilia: A Developmental Perspective," *International Journal of Offender Therapy and Comparative Criminology* 45 (February 2001): 6.

51 CATHY SPATZ WIDOM, "Victims of Childhood Sexual Abuse – Later Criminal Consequences," *Victims of Childhood Sexual Abuse Series: NIJ Research in Brief,* (March 1995): 1.

52 WATKINS, p. 319. Watkins mentions several studies confirming that between 19 percent and 61 percent of male sex abusers had previously been sexually abused themselves.

53 TIMOTHY J. DAILY, PH.D, *Homosexuality and Child Sexual Abuse,* http://www.frc.org/get/is02e3.cfm

54 The attorney misses the obvious. Homosexuals enjoy the same right as all other citizens to marry someone of the opposite sex. Marriage, by nature and definition, is between a man and a woman. This is precisely what homosexual activists aim to change.

55 *Homosexuality 101: A Primer.*

56 See also Part VII of ALEXANDER SOLZHENISTSYN's *The Gulag Archipelago,* in which he highlights the attitudes of Soviet officials whenever faced with incriminating evidence against the abuses of the prison system. They had a rational response for every argument: every abuse was an "exception," the system had changed, how did he know things were the same now, etc., etc. For those blinded by an ideology and who have forgotten reality for an ideal, there will always be self-justifications and a fundamentalist re-interpretation of every fact that contradicts their predisposed stance.

57 Cf. JOHN RAWLS, *A Theory of Justice,* Harvard University Press, 1971. Rawls highly influential book has been the basis for the philosophical and ethical formation of thousands of university students.

58 See the *Statement of the Catholic Medical Association: Homosexuality and Hope,* of April 18, 2003 at www.cathmed.org/index.html.

59 ROY WALLER, *Newswriters Represent New Study as Proof of Biological Basis of Homosexuality,* October 7, 2003.

60 WARREN THROCKMORTON, PHD, *Homosexuality and Genes: Déjà vu All Over Again?* October 30, 2003

61 See for example "The Innate-Immutable Argument Finds No Basis in

Science, In Their Own Words: Gay Activists Speak About Science, Morality, Philosophy," an article published by A. DEAN BYRD, PH.D. SHIRLEY E. COX, PH.D. and JEFFREY W. ROBINSON, PH.D. in the *Salt Lake City Tribune*, May 27, 2001.

62 ROY WALLER AND LINDA A. NICOLOSI, *Spitzer Study Just Published: Evidence Found for Effectiveness of Reorientation Therapy,* see http://www.narth.com/ visited January 14, 2004.

63 See for example the results of a study conducted by DR. ROBERT L. SPITZER published in the *Archives of Sexual Behavior,* Vol. 32, No. 5, October 2003, pp. 403-417.

64 "What the Data Show About Marriage and Families: Range of Evidence Lends Credence to Backers of Traditional Lifestyles," Zenit.org, New York, September 20, 2003.

65 The *religious* institution of marriage merely builds upon this natural foundation, confirming it and strengthening it to face the natural difficulties of married couples.

66 U.S. Senator RICK SANTORUM, April 7, 2003 interview with the Associated Press.

67 http://www.religioustolerance.org/hom_marp.htm According to at least one recent 2003 poll, 67 percent of Americans are against gay marriages, not 50 percent, and homosexuals do not include anywhere near 5 percent of the population. Current studies suggest anywhere from 1.5 percent to 3 percent of the population is gay. Such exaggeration in the use of numbers is typical in "homosexual rights" propaganda.

68 http://www.religioustolerance.org/hom_marp.htm, visited May 12, 2003.

69 LAWRENCE MORAHAN, "Psychiatric Association Debates Reclassifying Pedophilia," CNSNews.com, June 11, 2003.

70 See for example the pastoral letter of Bishop Victor Galeone to the Catholics of his diocese, *When Spouses Speak the Truth With Their Bodies*, www.zenit.org, November 8, 2003. "These latest developments are mere symptoms of a vastly more serious disorder. Until the taproot of that disorder is cut, I fear that we will continue to reap the fruit of failed marriages and worsening sexual behavior at every level of society. The disorder? Contraception. The practice is so widespread that it involves 90 percent of married couples at some point of their marriage, cutting across all denominational lines. Since one of the chief roles of the bishop is to teach, I invite you to revisit what the Church affirms in this area, and more importantly, why." He goes on to lay out clearly God's plan for marriage – according to the teach-

ings of the Catholic Church – and highlight the logical connections between contraception and homosexual marriages. A fascinating and well-written letter.

71 JOHN LEO, *Black, White and Red-faced*, May 18, 2003.

72 MARK GAUVREAU JUDGE, *The Tyranny of Political Correctness*, April 23, 2003 in his commentary on the book *The West and the Rest: Globalization and the Terrorist Threat* by Roger Scruton.

73 RICHARD BERNSTEIN, *Dictatorship of Virtue*, p. 230-231.

74 Ibid, p. 38.

SPREADING THE CONTAGION

1 Spreading the Contagion, CARDINAL GEORGE PELL , "Dictatorship of Relativism: A Recipe for Disenfranchisement and Passivity," Canberra, Australia, September 23, 2005, Zenit.org. This address of Cardinal George Pell of Sydney was delivered at the National Press Club in the Australian capital.

2 JOHN DEWEY, *Democracy and Education*. 1916, Chapter Two: Education as a Social Function.

3 PETER KREEFT, *The Liberal Arts and Sexual Morality*.

4 DAVID BROOKS, Working Hard at Being Shallow and Sycophantic," *The Times*, May 16, 2003.

5 BRUCE GOLDBERG, *Educational Theory,* January 15, 1997.

6 DOUGLAS CARNINE, *Why Education Experts Resist Effective Practices (And What It Would Take to Make Education More Like Medicine),* April 2000, Thomas B. Fordham Foundation, 1627 K Street, N.W., Suite 600, Washington, D.C. 20006. http://www.edexcellence.net/library/carnine.html

7 Ibid.

8 GENE GLASS AND G. CAMILLI, *FT Evaluation,* National Institution of Education, ERIC document ED244738, as cited in NINA H. SHOKRAII, *Why Congress Should Overhaul the Federal Regional Education Laboratories*, Heritage Foundation Backgrounder, no. 1200, 1998.

9 CAL THOMAS, *The School Choice Revolution*, May 8, 2003.

10 See the National Center for Educational Statistics 2002 report published in March of 2003 at http://nces.ed.gov/pubsearch/pubsinfo. asp?pubid=2003026.

11 THOMAS SOWELL, *A sign of the times*, May 16, 2003.

12 www.nces.ed.gov/nationsreportcard.

13 See   http://yya.oca.org/TheHub/TOC/General/FamilyIssues/Chris-tianTV.htm visited May 12, 2003.

14 See the study of the *Manhattan Institute*, drawing on U.S. Department of Education statistics as cited in *Throwing Money at the Schoolhouse Frauds* by SUZANNE FIELDS, September 22, 2003.

15 See the "Today's College Students and Yesteryear's High School Grads" report by Zogby International, commissioned by the National Association of Scholars.

16 FRED BAYLES, "In Mass., Those Who Can't (Spell or Write), Teach," *USA Today*, June 24, 1998.

17 See for example the government report comparing the two at http://www.nces.ed.gov/nationsreportcard/reading/results2002/schooltype.asp

18 DAVID LIMBAUGH, *Homeschoolers in the Trenches*, June 18, 2003.

19 WAYNE LAUGESEN, "Home School Groups Cry Foul After CBS News 'Hatchet Job,'" *National Catholic Register*, November 2-8, 2003.

20 See *The Scholastic Achievement and Demographic Characteristics of Home School Students in 1998*, an independent study by LAWRENCE M. RUDNER, PH.D., Director of the ERIC Clearinghouse on Assessment and Evaluation. Additional support for those conclusions can be found in the 2001 *Home Schooling Achievement* report at http://www.hslda.org/docs/study/comp2001/HomeSchoolAchievement.pdf.

21 See the study *Home Educated and Now Adults: Their Community and Civic Involvement, Views About Homeschooling, and Other Traits* conducted by DR. BRIAN D. RAY, president of the National Home Education Research Institute (NHERI), in 2003. www.nheri.org.

22 RICHARD BERNSTEIN, *Dictatorship of Virtue*, p. 311.

23 SUZANNE FIELDS, *Throwing money at the schoolhouse frauds,* September 22, 2003.

24 THOMAS SOWELL, *A sign of the times*, May 16, 2003.

25 Linda Brodkey is a professor of literature at the University of California, San Diego who attracted national attention in 1990 while teaching at the University of Texas in Austin. As a leading proponent of Critical theory applied to literature, she proposed a new writing course for incoming freshman. Yet for a writing class, there was precious little about writing in it. Instead of grammar, sentence construction, logical presentation, or contact with classic writers students were to use one-sided readings on civil rights cases pertaining to Titles VII (anti-discrimination) and IX (gender equity), a popular feminist sociology text

entitled *Sexism and Racism*, and other photocopied material chosen for their multicultural propaganda.

26 LINDA BRODKEY, *Writing Permitted in Designated Areas Only*, Minneapolis: University of Minnesota Press, 1996, p. 72.

27 RICHARD BERNSTEIN, *Dictatorship of Virtue*, p. 317.

28 Ibid, p. 315.

29 Ibid, p. 317.

30 GEORGE SANTAYANA, *Life of Reason*, 1905, vol. 1, Introduction.

31 RICHARD BERNSTEIN, *Dictatorship of Virtue*, p. 252

32 LYNN VINCENT, *BMOC: Big mandate on campus - College "diversity" activists grab freshmen at orientation-and won't let go until everyone holds the same view*, World, September 14, 2002.

33 DAVID LIMBAUGH, *NEA: Politicizing 'Education*, July 12, 2003.

34 WILLIAM RASPBERRY, *A Calling*, Dallas Morning News, June 3, 2000.

35 DIANE RAVITCH, *Education After the Culture Wars*, Daedalus, Summer 2002, p. 14.

36 TUVIA GROSSMAN, *Victim of the Media War*, Sunday, November 05, 2000.

37 JOHN PAUL II, Papal Message for World Communications Day 2003, *Media at the Service of Authentic Peace*, Vatican City, January 24, 2003.

38 See for example the trend of assasinations of media directors and reporters in post-Soviet Russia. From the beginning of Vladimir Putin's reign until the summer of 2004, 16 journalists were brutally murdered for exposing corrupt government deals, mafia operations, or other "disruptive" activities.

39 Cf. JOHN XXIII, "Pacem in Terris," n. 12.

40 DAVID MURRAY, JOEL SCHWARTZ, AND S. ROBERT LICHTER, *It Ain't Necessarily So: How the Media Make and Unmake the Scientific Picture of Reality.*

41 MATTHEW ROBINSON, *Mobocracy: How the Media's Obsession With Polling Twists the News*, Forum, 2002.

42 *The Media Elite*, Center for Media and Public Affairs, 1980.

43 BERNARD GOLDBERG, *Bias: A CBS Insider Exposes how the Media Distort the News*, Regnery, Washington, 2002.

44 L. BRENT BOZELL III AND BRENT BAKER, *And That's the Way It Isn't*, 1990.

45 See comment to note 89.

46 ERIC ALTERMAN, *What Liberal Media?*, Basic Books, February 2003, p. 3.

47 *The State of the News Media 2004*, www.journalism.org

48 ROD DREHER, *Hate is Hate is Hate*, Washington Times, 04.12.2002.

49 BERNARD GOLDBERG, *Networks Need a Reality Check*, Wall Street Journal, February 13, 1996.

50 http://www.fair.org/reports/journalist-survey.html#orientation

51 BERNARD GOLDBERG, *Bias: A CBS Insider Exposes how the Media Distort the News*, p. 24.

52 *Blind to the Spirit: How the Media Treat Religion*, Seattle, Washington, September 20, 2003, www.Zenit.org.

53 Ted Turner, as quoted in *Bias: A CBS Insider Exposes how the Media Distort the News*, p. 128.

54 See the New *York Times*, March 4, 2003.

55 ROD DREHER, *Hate is Hate is Hate*, Washington Times, December 4, 2002.

56 *Blind to the Spirit: How the Media Treat Religion*, Seattle, Washington, September 20, 2003, www.Zenit.org.

57 CONGREGATION FOR THE DOCTRINE OF THE FAITH, *Doctrinal Note on some questions regarding the participation of Catholics in political life*, November 24, 2002

58 *Cardinal Ratzinger Calls Relativism the New Face of Intolerance*, Zenit.org, December 1, 2002.

59 As quoted by Dietrich von Hildebrand in *The New Tower of Babel*, Sophia Institute Press, New Hampshire, 1994, p. 52.

60 LAMAR ALEXANDER, *Putting the Teaching of American History and Civics Back into Our Classrooms*, Heritage Lecture #784, delivered March 14, 2003.

61 BRADFORD WILSON, *The Culture Wars in Higher Education*, Phi Kappa Phi Journal, Winter 1999.

62 MONA CHAREN, *"Don't Know Much about History"*, July 15, 2003.

63 DENNIS PRAGER, *The Legal System is Now Our Enemy*, June 3, 2003.

64 *United States of America v. Alstötter et al.*, "The Justice Case", 3 T.W.C. 1 (1948), 6 L.R.T.W.C. 1 (1948), 14 Ann. Dig. 278 (1948).

65 See for instance http://www.law.umkc.edu/faculty/projects/ftrials/Simpson/simpson.htm or the book written by Dershowitz himself, *Reasonable Doubts : The Criminal Justice System and the O.J. Simpson Case,* in which he tacitly admits that O.J. was guilty, but that loopholes in the penal justice system allowed the 'Dream Team' of lawyers to help him to evade the murder charge.

66 C-SPAN broadcast on Saturday, August 25, 2001 at 8:01 PM. Organized Religion Debate, Franklin & Marshall College, Lancaster, Pennsylvania, ID: 159474 - 09/27/2000 - 2:03. Keyes, Alan, Founding Chair, Declaration Foundation (1998-) vs. Dershowitz, Alan, Professor, Harvard University, Law School (1988-) with Richard Kneedler,

President of Franklin & Marshall College and Stanley Michalak moderating.

67 ALEXIS DE TOQUEVILLE, *Democracy in America*, p. 171.

68 A well-documented study of the changes in the Supreme Court can be found in the book, *Behind the Lodge Door* by PAUL A. FISHER. The book analyzes the influence and agenda of Freemasonry in the U.S. in general, but especially relative to religious education, opposition to the Catholic Church, directing national social policy and Supreme Court activity.

69 1890 – *Harvard Law Review* publishes "The Right to Privacy." 4 *Harvard Law Review*, pp. 193-220. Authors Samuel Warren and Louis Brandeis (the future Supreme Court justice) state their case for invasion of privacy as a legal tort. More than 100 years later, privacy experts cite that article as the cornerstone for all privacy law. 1928 — Brandeis offers concept of "right to be let alone" to the U.S. Supreme Court in dissent in *Olmstead v. U.S.*, 277 U.S. 438, a case involving the wiretapping of a liquor dealer.

70 BRUCE FEIN, *Who creates privacy rights?*, The Washington Times, April 29, 2003.

71 THOMAS SOWELL, *Judging Judges*, November 20, 2002.

72 CNN March 3, 2003 broadcast. Anchor Wolf Blitzer posed the question on the use of torture on terrorists to noted author and Harvard University law professor Alan Dershowitz and to Ken Roth, the executive director of Human Rights Watch.

73 ALAN M. DERSHOWITZ, Editorial article in The Los Angeles Times, November 8, 2001.

74 Cf. CONGREGATION FOR THE DOCTRINE OF THE FAITH, *Doctrinal Note on some questions regarding the participation of Catholics in political life*, November 24, 2002

75 JOHN PAUL II, *Centesimus Annus,* 1991, n. 46.

76 An *end* is a goal toward which we tend. The *final end* is the overarching goal of our life, the prize we set our sites on. Every person has a natural *final end,* that happiness which they tend toward by their human nature; but we also have a chosen *final end,* that is, what we choose to aim for because we think it will lead to our happiness. The drama of human life depends on whether our chosen goal of life will really lead to happiness. This is the question that every person must face in their own life.

77 BENEDICT XVI, *Deus Caritas Est,* n.28.

78 CONGREGATION FOR THE DOCTRINE OF THE FAITH, *Doctrinal Note on some questions regarding the participation of Catholics in political life,* No-

vember 24, 2002, n.1.

79 Cf. BENEDICT XVI, *Deus Caritas Est,* n.1: "Being Christian is not the result of an ethical choice or a lofty idea, but the encounter with an event, a person, which gives life a new horizon and a decisive direction."

80 Ibid, n.28. The encyclical letter continues: "*This is where Catholic social doctrine has its place: it has no intention of giving the Church power over the State. Even less is it an attempt to impose on those who do not share the faith ways of thinking and modes of conduct proper to faith. Its aim is simply to help purify reason and to contribute, here and now, to the acknowledgment and attainment of what is just. The Church's social teaching argues on the basis of reason and natural law, namely, on the basis of what is in accord with the nature of every human being. It recognizes that it is not the Church's responsibility to make this teaching prevail in political life. Rather, the Church wishes to help form consciences in political life and to stimulate greater insight into the authentic requirements of justice as well as greater readiness to act accordingly, even when this might involve conflict with situations of personal interest. Building a just social and civil order, wherein each person receives what is his or her due, is an essential task which every generation must take up anew. As a political task, this cannot be the Church's immediate responsibility. Yet, since it is also a most important human responsibility, the Church is duty-bound to offer, through the purification of reason and through ethical formation, her own specific contribution towards understanding the requirements of justice and achieving them politically. The Church cannot and must not take upon herself the political battle to bring about the most just society possible. She cannot and must not replace the State. Yet at the same time she cannot and must not remain on the sidelines in the fight for justice. She has to play her part through rational argument and she has to reawaken the spiritual energy without which justice, which always demands sacrifice, cannot prevail and prosper. A just society must be the achievement of politics, not of the Church. Yet the promotion of justice through efforts to bring about openness of mind and will to the demands of the common good is something which concerns the Church deeply.*"

81 ALEXIS DE TOCQUEVILLE, *Democracy in America,* p.351.

82 CONGREGATION FOR THE DOCTRINE OF THE FAITH, *Doctrinal Note on some questions regarding the participation of Catholics in political life,* November 24, 2002, n.5.

83 *Ibid.,* n.1.

THE REMEDIES: BEYOND TOLERANCE

1 BENEDICT XVI, *Deus Caritas Est,* n.28.

2 JOHN PAUL II, *Centesimus Annus,* n.44.

3 See http://www.aneki.com/suicide.html. The nations in the top ten list of suicides are all former communist countries where God and man's authentic freedom were denied and religion stripped from societies. The top nations are Lithuania (42 suicides per 100,000 inhabitants per year), Russia, Belarus, Latvia, Estonia, Hungary, Slovenia, Ukraine, Kazakhstan, and Finland. Countries with strong religious influences show the lowest suicide rates. The United States factors in around 18.7, with about 30,000 suicides per year.

4 This is typical of the reductionist approach of various sciences to religion. Pyschology can tell us religion is simply certain rites and practices based on psychological induced tendencies, sociology can tell us religion is merely a system of social organization, physics can classify religion as mythology for those who don't know science, and economics can tell us religion is a money-making scheme, yet all of these approaches only touch on a few limited aspects of religion and give a limited insight into the subject. Only a global vision and a truly open mind can see religion for what it really is.

5 RICHARD JOHN NEUHAUS, *More Galluping,* First Things, March, 1993.

6 Idem.

7 According to the 2001 ARIS survey http://www.gc.cuny.edu/studies/aris.pdf.

8 IAN S. MARKHAM, *Plurality and Christian Ethics,* Cambridge University Press, 2002.

9 JOHN PAUL II, *Letter to Secretary General of the United Nations,* December, 1978.

10 For a Christian, Jesus Christ is Truth (John 14:6) and the Catholic Church claims to be the custodian of the mission and message of Jesus Christ. Declaration of the CONGREGATION OF THE DOCTRINE OF THE FAITH, *Dominus Iesus,* n. 16, August 6, 2000. "The Catholic faithful *are required to profess* that there is an historical continuity — rooted in the apostolic succession — between the Church founded by Christ and the Catholic Church: "This is the single Church of Christ... which our Saviour, after his resurrection, entrusted to Peter's pastoral care (cf. *Jn* 21:17), commissioning him and the other Apostles to extend and rule her (cf. *Mt* 28:18ff.), erected for all ages as 'the pillar and mainstay of the truth' (*1 Tim* 3:15). This Church, constituted and organized as a soci-

ety in the present world, subsists in [*subsistit in*] the Catholic Church, governed by the Successor of Peter and by the Bishops in communion with him". With the expression *subsistit in,* the Second Vatican Council sought to harmonize two doctrinal statements: on the one hand, that the Church of Christ, despite the divisions which exist among Christians, continues to exist fully only in the Catholic Church, and on the other hand, that "outside of her structure, many elements can be found of sanctification and truth", that is, in those Churches and ecclesial communities which are not yet in full communion with the Catholic Church. But with respect to these, it needs to be stated that "they derive their efficacy from the very fullness of grace and truth entrusted to the Catholic Church"."

11 SECOND VATICAN COUNCIL, Declaration *Nostra aetate,* 2 and Declaration of the CONGREGATION OF THE DOCTRINE OF THE FAITH, *Dominus Iesus,* 2, August 6, 2000. "The Catholic Church rejects nothing of what is true and holy in these religions. She has a high regard for the manner of life and conduct, the precepts and teachings, which, although differing in many ways from her own teaching, nonetheless often reflect a ray of that truth which enlightens all men".

12 From the Code of Hammurabi. Hammurabi was King of Babylon, 1792-1750BC. The code survives today in the Akkadian language. This ancient rule of law was nearly universal in the ancient world and the text is also taken up by Jewish teaching and can be found in Exodus 21:24.

13 MATTHEW 5:43-44

14 HEBREWS 11:1.

15 Catechism of the Catholic Church, n. 26. For a full explanation of the Christian understanding of faith, there is no better source than the first three chapters of the *Catechism of the Catholic Church,* published originally in 1992 with the authoritative version published in 1997. Though written specifically for Catholics, this section of the Catechism is recognized by most Christians as representative of what they also believe.

16 Ibid., n. 150.

17 Ibid., n. 157. This thought was also succinctly expressed by Mahatma Gandhi when he wrote, "The word *Satya* (Truth) is derived from *Sat* which means 'being '. And nothing is or exists in reality except Truth. That is why *Sat* or Truth is perhaps the most important name of God. In fact, it is more correct to say that Truth is God than to say that God is Truth. And where there is Truth, there is also Knowledge, pure Knowledge. Where there is no Truth, there can be no true Knowl-

edge. That is why the word *Chit* or Knowledge is associated with the name of God. And where there is true Knowledge, there is always Bliss (Anand). Sorrow has no place there. And even as Truth is Eternal, so is the Bliss derived from it. Hence we know God as *Sat-Chit-Anand* one who combines in Himself, Truth, Knowledge, and Bliss."

18 JOHN PAUL II, Encyclical Letter *Fides et Ratio,* 1998, Introduction.

19 VATICAN I, *Dei Filius* 4: DS 3017.

20 www.btsd.net/Buddhism2.html.

21 The Mahabharata, Santi Parva, Section CLXII, Translated by Sri Kisari Mohan Ganguli, as found on the website http://www.hinduism.co.za/truth.htm, visited June 2003. "That which is called Truth always exists in a pure and unmingled state in every one of those four orders. With those that are good, Truth is always a duty. Indeed, Truth is an eternal duty. One should reverentially bow unto Truth. Truth is the highest refuge (of all). Truth is duty; Truth is penance; Truth is Yoga; and Truth is the eternal Brahman. Truth has been said to be Sacrifice of a higher order. Everything rests upon Truth. I shall now tell thee the forms of Truths one after another, and its indications also in due order. It behoveth thee to hear also as to how Truth may be acquired. Truth, O Bharata, as it exists in all the world, is of thirteen kinds. The forms that Truth assumes are impartiality, self-control, forgiveness, modesty, endurance, goodness, renunciation, contemplation, dignity, fortitude, compassion, and abstention from injury. These, O great monarch, are the thirteen forms of Truth. Truth is immutable, eternal, and unchangeable. It may be acquired through practices which do not militate against any of the other virtues. It may also be acquired through Yoga. When desire and aversion, as also lust and wrath, are destroyed, that attribute in consequence of which one is able to look upon one's own self and one's foe, upon one's good and one's evil, with an unchanging eye, is called impartiality."

22 ABDU'L-BAHÁ, *Paris Talks,* London: Bahá'í Publishing Trust, 1969, p. 129.

23 See for example www.it-is-truth.org or http://www.iol.ie/~afifi/BIC-News/Sabeel/sabeel2.htm arguing for the logical proof of Islam's truth.

24 See Part Two of this book in the discussion on Mormonism. For Christianity, we have but to consider Jesus' own words: "I am the Way, the Truth, and the Life." Christian teaching is replete with references to truth. Consider for example this sermon of St. Augustine: Awake, mankind! For your sake God has become man. Awake, you who sleep, rise up from the dead, and Christ will enlighten you. I tell

you again: for your sake, God became man. You would have suffered eternal death, had he not been born in time. Never would you have been freed from sinful flesh, had he not taken on himself the likeness of sinful flesh. You would have suffered everlasting unhappiness, had it not been for this mercy. You would never have returned to life, had he not shared your death. You would have been lost if he had not hastened 'to your aid. You would have perished, had he not come. Let us then joyfully celebrate the coming of our salvation and redemption. Let us celebrate the festive day on which he who is the great and eternal day came from the great and endless day of eternity into our own short day of time. He has become our justice, our sanctification, our redemption, so that, as it is written: Let him who glories glory in the Lord. Truth, then, has arisen from the earth: Christ who said, I am the Truth, was born of the Virgin. And justice looked down from heaven: because believing in this new-born child, man is justified not by himself but by God. Truth has arisen from the earth: because the Word was made flesh. And justice looked down from heaven: because every good gift and every perfect gift is from above. Truth has arisen from the earth: flesh from Mary. And justice looked down from heaven: for man can receive nothing unless it has been given him from heaven.

25 JOHN 14:6.

26 MAHATMA GANDHI, *The Story of My Experiments with Truth - An Autobiography*, Part V, XLIV, Farewell. "The fleeting glimpses that I have been able to have of Truth can hardly convey an idea of the indescribable lustre of Truth, a million times more intense than that of the Sun, we daily see with our eyes. In fact, what I have caught is only the faintest glimmer of that mighty effulgence. I feel the warmth and sun-shine of His presence." See also John Paul II, Encyclical Letter *Veritatis Splendor,* August 6, 1993. "The splendor of truth shines forth in all the works of the Creator and, in a special way, in man, created in the image and likeness of God (cf. Gen 1:26). Truth enlightens man's intelligence and shapes his freedom, leading him to know and love the Lord. Hence the Psalmist prays: "Let the light of your face shine on us, O Lord" (Ps 4:6)."

27 AUGUSTINE OF HIPPO, *Confessions*, I,1.

28 JOHN PAUL II, *Relativism Threatening Democracy*, www.zenit.org, October 19, 2004.

29 JOHN PAUL II, *Centesimus Annus,* 1991, n.46.

30 Ibid, n. 29.

31 JOSEPH CARDINAL RATZINGER, *Homily*, April 18, 2005.